AF652239

Gender and Human Rights

Gender and Human Rights

Status of Women Worker in India

Anu Saxena

SHIPRA

All rights reserved. No part of this work may be reproduced, stored in a retrieval system or transmitted in any form or by any means, electronic, mechanical, photocopying, recording or otherwise without the prior written permission of the copyright owner and the publishers.

(2021& 2017 PoD; First Published in 2004)

Rs. 1250, US$ 50

ISBN: 978-81-7541-153-1

2023 Impression, PoD

Gender and Human Rights

© Anu Saxena, 2004

Published by:
SHIPRA PUBLICATIONS
LG 18-19, Pankaj Central Market,
IP Ext., Patparganj, Delhi 110092, India
+91 11 22235152/6152, 9650028065
info@shiprapublication.com
www.shiprapublication.com

Acknowledgements

I wish to express my sincere thanks to Prof. N.B. Mody, Head, Department of Civics and Politics, University of Mumbai for extending full cooperation and support at every stage of this work, conducted under University Grants Commission/Department of Special Assistance Programme in 2002-03.

My thanks are also due to the management and staff of National Textile Corporation (South Maharashtra) for extending full cooperation in conducting this study.

I gratefully acknowledge the assistance given to me by the library staff of Jawaharlal Nehru Library, Kalina Campus, University of Mumbai, Rajabhai Tower Library, Fort Campus, University of Mumbai, S.N.D.T. University Library, Mumbai, Maharashtra Institute of Labour Studies Library, Mumbai, Ambedker Institute for Labour Studies Library, Mumbai, National Labour Institute Library, Noida, Ministry of Labour Library, New Delhi, Central Secretariat Library, New Delhi, Planning Commission Library, New Delhi and United Nations Information Centre, New Delhi.

I also wish to express my thanks to my family, particularly my father-in-law, Mr. K.D. Saksena, for his valuable inputs and my husband, Rishabh, whose encouragement and support made this work possible

Contents

Chapter 1

Introduction

All human beings possess certain intrinsic rights that need to be respected by society to enable them to lead a life with dignity. But human dignity is frequently violated on grounds of gender. Women belong to those marginalised sections of society that are subjugated in every sphere of their life.

International concern with the status of women and the reflection of that concern in treaties regulating particular fields of social activity is not a new phenomenon. The first half of the 20th century saw the adoption of treaties that addressed particular social problems such as trafficking in persons or regulation of participation of women in the workforce.

The principle of equal protection and non-discrimination on the basis of sex is clearly enshrined in the United Nations Charter. The UN Charter calls for promoting respect for human rights for all without distinction on the basis of race, sex, language or religion. The principle of equal rights and non discrimination also found its way into the two main international covenants – the International Covenant on Civil and Political Rights and the International Covenant on Economic, Social and Cultural Rights.

Despite the existence of numerous international conventions and declarations devoted to women's rights, violations of women's rights is a global phenomenon. Women's issues have been marginalised in the human rights agenda. The problem of gender discrimination does not appear to be very high on the hierarchical list of human rights.

The Convention on the Elimination of Discrimination Against Women (CEDAW) was adopted in 1981 to give visibility to the rights of women and bring them on the forefront of the human rights agenda. CEDAW was one of the most notable tools for promoting women's rights that emerged out of the 1975-85 'Decade for Women'. CEDAW was adopted with the intention of bringing the international law of human rights into the private realm, where most gendered violations of women's rights take place. The home, family and workplace had been hitherto left outside the scope of human rights law. CEDAW can be described as a comprehensive bill of human rights law concerning women.

CEDAW contains a detailed exposition of the women's right to work (Article 11 and 13). The task of ensuring human rights for women is incomprehensible without taking into account the economic conditions that characterise women's lives around the world. Rights abuses are strongly correlated to the victim's economic power. The study of women as a category of workers is of crucial importance because the economic role that women play cannot be isolated from their total well being.

Gender-based discrimination at work is perhaps the most enduring and universal phenomenon in the world today. Women constitute half of the world's population and perform two thirds of the world's work but earn only a third of the total income and own less than a tenth of the world's resources.

This study addresses the following issues:

- Role of the CEDAW in the protection and promotion of women's rights.
- Invisibility and under-enumeration of the work performed by women in India in the data collection systems.
- Trends in the work participation rates of women across various parameters.
- Gender-based wage differentials.
- Gender-based division of labour.
- Concentration of women in 'female-dominated' occupations.
- Study of women's participation in the textile industry of Mumbai and Bhiwandi.
- State action for the protection and advancement of rights of women workers in India.

Owing to the nature of the subject matter, both quantitative and qualitative methods are used to analyse the status of women workers in India. In order to arrive at a macro picture of women at work in India, the two main sources of data are the decennial population Censuses of India and the National Sample Surveys conducted by the National Sample Survey Organisation.

In order to arrive at an understanding of women's participation in the textile industry of Mumbai and Bhiwandi, the research methodology included an open-ended questionnaire designed to elicit the required information from the women workers. Unstructured interviews of supervisors/managers/ trade union officials were also conducted to collect data. In order to have a historical perspective on the change in work participation rates over time, data in a specific format was also obtained from the management of the mill sector in this industry.

The first chapter is introductory in nature and deals with the importance and objectives of the study.

The second chapter seeks to evaluate the contribution of CEDAW in protecting the rights of women. A detailed examination of the provisions of CEDAW, Optional Protocol to CEDAW, reservations entered into by State Parties are undertaken in this chapter. The role of the CEDAW Committee in the implementation of the Convention and the contribution of the Convention in advancement of women's rights is also undertaken.

The third chapter attempts to provide a macro picture of women workers in India. It discusses the problem of underestimation of women's work in the existing data systems. The trends in work participation rates of women workers across various parameters—employment status, geographical distribution, age composition, literacy levels, broad industry groups, sectors of employment – is also undertaken. This chapter also examines the phenomenon of gender-based discrimination in wages.

The fourth chapter discusses the trends and nature of women's employment in the textile mills of Mumbai and powerlooms of Bhiwandi. It examines the trends in women's employment in the mill sector, the nature of production organisation, division of labour on the basis of gender and working condition. Two National Textile Corporation (South Maharashtra) Mills—Apollo Textile Mills and New City of Bombay Manufacturing Mills—providing employment to 51 women workers, were selected for conducting the study. Five powerloom units in Bhiwandi, which provide employment to 18 women were also a part of the study. By selecting NTC mills in Mumbai and powerloom units in Bhiwandi, this study attempts to analyse the situation of women workers in both the organised and unorganised sectors of the textile industry.

The fifth chapter discusses the action taken by the state since independence in protecting and advancing the rights of women workers. It reviews the constitutional, statutory and developmental measures adopted by the Indian government for promotion of rights of women at work. The role of the judiciary in protecting and promoting the rights of women workers is also discussed.

In the last chapter concluding observations are made.

Chapter 2

Convention on Elimination of Discrimination Against Women

An Analysis

International concern with the elimination of discrimination against women is not a new phenomenon. Despite the existence of numerous declarations and conventions, discrimination against women is endemic. Violations of women's rights did not receive the required attention in the human rights movement. Human rights law tended to exclude much of women's experiences. International human rights standards are perceived to be gender neutral. However, this neutrality often amounted in practice to a disregard of women's rights.

The achievement of equal rights guarantees in the public sphere was the first and easier task of the women's rights movement. But most gendered violations of women's rights take place in the private sphere, which was regarded as outside the scope of both national and international human rights laws. The home, family and workplace were left outside the scope of human rights law. Discrimination against women was viewed as natural or inevitable and often justified in the name of cultural traditions. The state was not willing to accept responsibility for abuses that took place in the private sphere. However, through inadequate action, abuses of women's rights are often condoned and sometimes even sanctioned by the state. Moreover, the denial of women's rights in the private sphere limited their ability to exercise their rights in the public sphere.

The concept of human rights, however, is a vibrant one and is not the property of any one group. While these concepts began in a particular historical movement and were defined in terms of the needs of a limited sector of the population, their dynamism stems from the fact that more people are claiming them and, in the process, expanding the meaning of 'rights' to incorporate their own hopes and needs. Much of the creativity of the human rights movement over the past fifty years has come from expanding the concept to address areas such as racial discrimination, disappearances, socio-economic rights, and the collective right to sustainable environment. So, too, women are transforming the concept of human rights to address the degradations and violations that are a fundamental threat to their human dignity, right to life, liberty and security of person [1]

The principle of non-discrimination on the basis of sex and assurance of equal protection has been emphasised in both national and international law. The United Nations Charter contains the equal protection norm. The charter's preamble states the determination of the peoples of the United Nations to reaffirm faith in the"equal rights of men and women."

Article 1(3) calls for promoting "fundamental freedoms for all without distinction as to race, sex, language or religion."

Article 55(c) reiterates promoting "respect for observance of human rights and fundamental freedoms for all without distinction as to race, sex, language or religion."

The Universal Declaration of Human Rights (UDHR), the International Covenant on Civil and Political Rights (ICCPR) and the International Covenant on Economic, Social and Cultural and Rights (ICESCR) also underlined the principle of non-discrimination and equal protection. Article 2 of the UDHR states that "everyone is entitled to all the rights and freedoms set forth in the Declaration, without distinction of any kind such as race, colour, sex, language, religion, political or other opinion, property, birth or other status." Article 2 of the ICCPR undertakes to "respect and to ensure to all individuals within its territory and subject to its jurisdiction the rights recognized in the present Covenant, without distinction of any kind, such as race, colour, sex, language, religion, political or other opinion, national or social origin, property, birth or other status. "Article 2 of the ICESCR also prohibits discrimination on the basis of sex.

In addition to the principle of non-discrimination, these instruments also contained provisions relating to marriage, family and motherhood. Under Article 16(2) of the UDHR, "men and women are entitled to equal rights as to marriage, during marriage and at its dissolution. "It provided that "marriage shall be entered into only with the full consent of the intending spouses. "Article 23(2) called for equal pay for equal work and Article 25(2) stated that "motherhood and childhood are entitled to special care and assistance."

Article 23(4) of the ICCPR provided for equality between men and women during marriage and its dissolution. Article 6(5) prohibited the use of death penalty on pregnant women.

The ICESCR [Article 7(1)] states the right of workers to "fair wages and equal remuneration for work of equal value without distinction of any kind, in particular women being guaranteed conditions of work not inferior to those enjoyed by men, with equal pay for equal work." Under Article 10(2), state parties to the Covenant recognize that "special protection should be accorded to mothers during a reasonable period before and after childbirth. During such period working mothers should be accorded paid leave or leave with adequate social security benefits."

The text of these instruments has been sharply criticised. While they emphasise the prohibition of discrimination on the basis of sex, they contribute little to the articulation of specific issues affecting women. The approach followed was generic rather than gender specific, hence gender discrimination did not have prominence, and women were not addressed as women, but only as child-bearers and child-rearers. Indeed, much of the United Nations work at this time tended to deal with 'women and children,' thus reducing women's concerns to motherhood [2].

The record of the treaty bodies, established to monitor the implementation of the ICCPR and ICESCR, in integrating the gender perspective in their work, is also far from satisfactory. The Human Rights Committee, which oversees the ICCPR, has a mixed record when it comes to consideration of gender issues. On the positive side, the Human Rights Committee stands above several of the other treaty bodies in its willingness to deal with the concept of discrimination, and to extend the prohibition on discrimination to other rights protected in the ICCPR. This willingness is evident in several of its general comments, as well as in relation to the individual complaint procedure. The Human Rights Committee regularly questions states about the position of women *de facto, as* well *de jure,* and generally addresses at least one or two aspects of the human rights of women in its concluding observations. In 1995, the Committee amended its reporting guidelines to request that state parties provide gender specific information in their reports. While these developments must be lauded and encouraged, a certain lack of consistency in the Human Rights Committee's approach to the human rights of women, and to the incorporation of a gender perspective into its work can still be detected. Guidelines for reporting do not seek to elicit from states sufficient information on the position of women, and do not uniformly explain the ways in which individual articles must apply to women. State reports generally stress on laws rather than discriminatory practices. Concluding observations on the reports of state parties indicate that the attention given by the Human Rights Committee to issues directly affecting women during the reporting process is uneven and often perfunctory in terms of both breadth and depth. A very high number of general comments – including those relating to torture, bodily integrity, the right to life, and freedom of thought, conscience, and religion – are totally gender neutral.[3] The Committee rarely raises practices such as genital mutilation, polygamy, bride price, dowry system and genital mutilation. The Human Rights Committee's comments on privacy omit any reference to women's control over their bodies and its comments on the right to life do not consider the issues related to right to access to abortion. Issues like forced prostitution are rarely considered under the Covenant's provision on prohibition of slavery. While none of these institutions and practices are specifically mentioned in the ICCPR, it is hard to see how women can be guaranteed the full enjoyment of the human rights and fundamental freedoms to which they are entitled under the Covenant so long as these and other forms of oppression continue. It would appear that the Covenant does not apply to these violations of the human rights of women [4].

The Economic, Social and Cultural Rights Committee requires state parties to provide information on the situation of women, both *de facto* and *de jure*, with respect to a number of articles, including the right to work, right to just and favourable conditions of work, right to social security, right to an adequate standard of living, right to health and right to education. In it general comments on specific articles of the ICESCR, the ESCR Committee has tried to introduce some kind of gender perspective. With regard to the examination of state parties reports, the ESCR

Committee has pointed to its formulation of list of issues and the oral questions raised during consideration of reports as evidence of its "long-standing concern for the enjoyment and protection of the economic, social and cultural rights of women." Despite these achievements, the ESCR Committee has missed a number of important opportunities. While the guidelines for reporting do indeed make an effort to address gender issues, not all articles are covered equally well. Guidelines for reporting on implementation of Article 2 (prohibition on discrimination), Article 3 (equality between men and women in respect of all rights contained in the ICESCR), and Article 15 (the right to participate in the cultural life and to benefit from scientific progress) do not refer to gender. The ESCR Committee has recognized that in relation to the human rights of women and its own methods and procedures, much remains to be done [5].

The Convention against Torture and other Cruel, Inhuman or Degrading Treatment or Punishment and the International Convention on the Elimination of all Forms of Racial Discrimination do not contain any reference to the principle of non-discrimination on the basis of sex. The Committee on the Elimination of Racial Discrimination and the Committee against Torture have not addressed the gendered aspects of racial discrimination and torture.

Women's issues are not commonly dealt with in the mainstream international human rights debates or bodies of the United Nations. The problem of gender discrimination does not appear to be very high on the hierarchical list of human rights. Other treaty bodies of the United Nations have failed to take full cognizance of women's rights.

The United Nations has also adopted conventions that focus on specific aspects of women's lives. These are:

- Convention on the Political Rights of Women, 1952
- Convention on the Nationality of Married Women, 1957
- Convention on Recovery Abroad of Maintenance, 1956
- Convention on the Consent to Marriage, 1962

The United Nations in 1967 adopted the Declaration on the Elimination of Discrimination against Women. It was a broad statement, in non-binding form, of women's rights to equality and non-discrimination in many areas of life.

Within the United Nations system, questions concerning women's rights and gender-based discrimination were for many decades subsumed under the terms 'status of women' and 'advancement of women.' In 1947, a Commission on Human Rights and a Commission on the Status of Women were established as separate functional commissions of the Economic and Social Council (ECOSOC).

Attempts to eliminate racial discrimination served as useful precedent in subsequent international attempts to outlaw discrimination based on sex. Following the adoption of the Convention on the Elimination of All Forms of Racial Discrimination, it was felt that a similar instrument could be established to eliminate discrimination against women.

The campaign for giving greater priority to women's rights gathered momentum in the 1970s with the proclaiming of 1975 as the International Women's Year, followed by a Women's Decade and the holding of world conferences on women. The most important thing that came out of the decade was the Convention on the Elimination of Discrimination Against Women (CEDAW).

In 1974 the ECOSOC appointed a 15-member Working Group to consider drafting a women's convention. In 1976, the Commission on the Status of Women (CSW) took up the draft convention prepared by the Working Group with the objective of having a convention ready for the 1980 World Conference on Women in Copenhagen.

In 1979, the General Assembly adopted the Convention and opened it for signature and ratification. The Convention came into force on 3rd September 1979, having received 20 ratifications. Often described as the international bill of rights for women, CEDAW has been ratified by 171 states as of March 2003. Annexure I contains the text of the Convention. A list of State Parties that have signed and ratified the Convention is provided in Annexure II.

Provisions of CEDAW

Consisting of a preamble and 30 articles, CEDAW defines what constitutes discrimination against women and sets up an agenda for national action to end such discrimination.

The preamble to the Convention states that despite the affirmation of equal rights of men and women in the UN Charter, the UDHR and the International Covenants, extensive discrimination against women continues to exist. Critics have highlighted that it is ironical that the international community decided that the solution to the problem of violation of women's rights protected by human rights instruments lay in creating another international instrument. However, despite these criticisms, CEDAW was definitely a step forward in protection of women's rights.

The Convention is divided into six parts. The first part (Article 1-6) defines discrimination and broadly outlines the nature of state obligations, in terms of law, policy and programmes that the state needs to undertake in order to eliminate discrimination. Article 1 defines discrimination as ".... any distinction, exclusion or restriction made on the basis of sex which has the effect or purpose of impairing or nullifying the recognition, enjoyment or exercise by women, irrespective of their marital status, on a basis of equality of men and women, of human rights and fundamental freedoms in the political, economic, social cultural, civil or any other field. "By formulating such a comprehensive definition of 'discrimination,' the convention provides a fundamental basis for eliminating discrimination.

By ratifying the Convention, State Parties agree to pursue by all appropriate means and without delay a policy of eliminating discrimination against women (Article 2). State parties commit themselves to adopting appropriate legislative and other measures, including sanctions where appropriate, prohibiting discrimination against women. [Article 2(b)]. State Parties to the convention also commit themselves to adopting temporary special measures aimed at accelerating *de facto* equality between men and women. Such special measures shall not be deemed discriminatory. (Article 4). Article 5(a) provides that state parties should modify the "social and cultural patterns of conduct of men and women, with a view to achieving the elimination of prejudices and customary and all other practices which are based on the idea of the inferiority or the superiority of either of the sexes or on stereotyped roles for men and women."

CEDAW is based on the principle of state obligation. It recognizes that despite legal rights being granted to women in many countries, discrimination persists, and women's access to legal rights are curtailed by denial of women's rights to economic and social development. Hence, it bridges the traditional divisions between civil and political rights and socio-economic rights and it mandates both legal and development policy measures to guarantee the rights of women. The Convention draws a distinction between *de facto* and *de jure* rights. It emphasises that there must be the practical realisation of rights. While most state constitutions prohibit discrimination on the basis of sex, CEDAW goes a step further. The Convention, by defining discrimination as any restriction, exclusion or distinction which has the effect of denying women the enjoyment of rights and by obligating the state to ensure the practical realisation of rights through positive action, takes women's disadvantaged position into consideration and expects the state parties to cater for the difference, thus requiring a concept of substantive equality to underpin all initiatives for women's advancement [6].

Part II of the Convention deals with rights of women in the political and public arena. It also grants to women equal rights to their nationality and the nationality of their children [Article 9(1)(2)].

Part III of Convention contains the rights to education (Article 10), employment (Article 11), health care and family planning (Article 12), economic and social benefits (Article 13). It also focuses on the problems faced by rural women and calls on state parties to eliminate discrimination against women in rural areas. (Article 14).

Part IV of the Convention deals with legal and civil rights. Article 15 grants women equality before law. Article 16(1) calls upon state parties to eliminate discrimination against women in all matters relating to marriage and family relations. Article 16(2) prohibits child marriage.

Part V of the Convention establishes a Committee on the Elimination of Discrimination Against Women (CEDAW Committee) to monitor the progress made in the implementation of the Convention. Article 17-22 detail the establishment and functions of the CEDAW Committee.

Part VI (Articles 23-30) deals largely with administrative and other procedural aspects of the Convention.

CEDAW can be described as a comprehensive sex discrimination instrument. It calls on State Parties to eliminate discrimination against women across a broad range of areas, including civil and political rights and economic, social and cultural rights. It has incorporated many of the standards contained in the earlier specific conventions on women. To a large extent it codified the existing gender-specific conventions on women and general human rights instruments containing guarantees of freedom from discrimination on the grounds of sex, though it adds some significant new provisions.

CEDAW made a significant attempt to bring international law of human rights into the private realm. The Convention requires State Parties to address social, cultural and traditional patterns, which perpetuate stereotyped roles of women. State Parties are required to take all appropriate measures to eliminate discrimination against women [7].

CEDAW is dominated, albeit with some important exceptions, by gender-neutral language. The provisions are based on the principle that men and women are to be treated equally in order to ensure that gender will no longer operate as basis for allocation of benefits and burdens in society. Indeed, the title of the Convention itself arguably presupposes a male standard to the extent that it calls for the elimination of discrimination against women in the male world. In both the domestic and international arenas, rights discourse has come under considerable criticism in recent years by feminists and others who challenge the 'myth of rights,' both in the women's movement and in politics at large. The critique has focussed on the inability of legal rights to alter the underlying structure of domination within society. The acquisition of rights, of course, is of considerable value in certain circumstances. Anyone who witnessed the battle over the Equal Rights Amendment in the United States can attest to "the substantial symbolic freight" of rights for women. Many of the provisions that use gender-neutral language play this symbolic role, which is an essential first step to beginning the difficult work of changing the distribution of burdens and benefits of society [8].

Nevertheless, a strategy based solely on the acquisition of legal rights using 'male' rights as a standard may provide benefits for women that are more symbolic than actual. To its credit, CEDAW uses the language of correction rather than equality to address several issues. The Convention allows for a full range of corrective strategies that would safeguard measures that might otherwise be eliminated in a "purely equal rights approach.' Article 4 (1), for example, calls on State Parties to adopt temporary special measures that deviate from equal treatment in order to achieve *de facto* equality. Corrective language is used to address issues like maternity. Article 11 requires State Parties to prevent discrimination against women on the grounds of marriage or maternity, to provide maternity leave with benefits, including the protection of job seniority and to provide special protection to women during pregnancy in types of work proved to be harmful to them. Another example of corrective language is found in Article 10, whereby states are required to act affirmatively to ameliorate female dropout rates and to organise programmes to assist girls and women who have left school prematurely[9].

The Convention desegregates women's problems in regional and functional terms. Article 14 calls upon States Parties to take into account the particular problems faced by rural women. It underscores strategies for realising goals that permeate the entire Convention, such as mobilisation through functional grass root groups and participation in local decision making. CEDAW is not a convention in which solutions are to be provided only by the central authority of the state[10].

However, in certain areas the Convention relies heavily on the equal rights language to achieve justice for women. Article (1) of the CEDAW, for example, provides for a blanket call for the equality of men and women in all matters relating to "marriage and family relations." The long, culturally diverse list of practices that effectively treat women as objects or property of men cannot be adequately addressed by such a vague invocation to equal treatment. Many of these practices are considered so 'normal,' 'natural,' or 'inevitable' that only a clear rejection of specific practices will help[11].

CEDAW has no provision specifically addressing issues like bodily security, arbitrary deprivation of life, torture and arbitrary detention because these issues were dealt with in the ICCPR and Convention against Torture.

The Women's Convention also does not directly address the issue of violence against women. However, in its consideration of state reports and in three of its General Recommendations (12, 14 and 19), the CEDAW Committee has stated that violence constitutes a form of discrimination. General Recommendation No. 12 (1989) on Violence Against Women describes how this issue is covered by the Convention. The emphasis in the Recommendation is upon utilising the existing anti-discrimination provisions of CEDAW to address the problem of violence against women[12]. It requires State Parties "to act to protect women against violence of any kind occurring within the family, at the workplace or in any other area of social life." State Parties are, therefore, required to include in their periodic reports to the CEDAW Committee details of action taken to eliminate violence against women, including sexual violence, abuses in the family, sexual harassment at the workplace etc[13].

Recommendation No. 14 called on State Parties to take appropriate and effective measures to end the practice of female circumcision, including the support of women's organisations at the national and local levels and the encouragement of politicians, professionals, religious and community leaders and the media to cooperate in influencing attitudes in the eradication of female circumcision[14].

The approach of interpreting violence against women as a violation of the anti-discriminatory provisions finds detailed expression in General Recommendation No. 19. It defines gender-based violence as a form of discrimination that "seriously inhibits women's ability to enjoy rights and freedoms on a basis of equality with men." It reaffirms the principle laid down in Article 2 (e) and 2(f) and Article 5 of the Convention that discrimination is not restricted to action by or on behalf of governments and calls on State Parties to take all appropriate measures to eliminate discrimination by any person, organisation or enterprise. The CEDAW Committee called upon State Parties to take appropriate protective and support services for victims and gender-sensitive training of judicial and law enforcement officials for the effective implementation of the Convention[15].

In December 1993, the General Assembly adopted the Declaration on the Elimination of Violence Against Women (DEVAW). The CEDAW Committee monitors compliance with DEVAW.

While the Convention includes provisions about the reproductive rights of women and underlines the equal rights of men and women to decide freely on the number and spacing of their children, it is silent on the issue of abortion. The controversial nature of the issue was responsible for its omission from the convention. A brief reference to abortion is made in General Recommendation No. 19, which calls upon State Parties to ensure that "measures are taken to prevent coercion in regard to fertility and reproduction and to ensure that women are not forced to seek unsafe medical procedures such as illegal abortion because of lack of appropriate services in regard to fertility control."[16] The CEDAW Committee has also criticised states which have restrictive abortion laws or which do not provide women access to safe abortion. Restriction on abortion has been condemned by the CEDAW Committee as a violation of women's right to life and health.

Though the Convention is criticised for not including a number of other key issues like caste-based discrimination, new economic policies, its strength lies in its interpretation. Like other human rights instruments, it is worded in an abstract manner so that it can apply to diverse societies and situations and so that its interpretation can evolve to meet changing circumstances. Although particular issues are not mentioned explicitly, that does not preclude that they are covered implicitly.

Reservations to CEDAW

In order to encourage the process of undertaking human rights obligations, governments are allowed to identify and reserve the right not to apply specific provisions of a convention. However, reservations cannot be incompatible with objective of the concerned convention. Article 28(1) of CEDAW adopts the impermissibility principle contained in the Vienna Convention on the Law of Treaties. It states that a reservation incompatible with the object and purpose of the present Convention shall not be permitted.

The procedure of entering into reservations was designed to secure greater participation of countries in human rights treaties. Another reason for allowing states to adopt treaties with reservations is that most states are apprehensive about the possible consequences of accepting a human rights treaty, not least because such treaties may have a dynamic force, and interpretation of their scope and impact is less certain than commercial treaties. Reservations are seen to offer an assurance that the state can protect its interest to the fullest extent possible[17].

State Parties to CEDAW have filed many formal reservations to the Convention. In fact, CEDAW is the most heavily reserved treaty in the United Nations human rights system, thereby undermining its efficacy. As of May 2001, 56 State Parties had entered into 157 reservations to the Convention. Table 1 summarises the reservations by articles.

Table 1: CEDAW Reservations by Articles

Country (1)	*Abridged Reservations and Interpretations to Articles* (2)
1. Algeria	2, 9(2), 15(4), 16, 29
2. Argentina	29
3. Australia	11(2), 7(b)
4. Austria	11
5. Bahamas	2(a), 9(2), 16(h), 29
6. Bangladesh	2, 16(1c)
7. Belgium	15(2), 15(3)
8. Brazil	29
9. Chile	Generally worded reservation
10. China	29
11. Cuba	29
12. Democratic People's Republic of Korea	2(f), 9(2), 29
13. Egypt	2, 9(2), 16, 29
14. El Salvador	29
15. Ethiopia	29
16. France	9, 5b, 14(2c), 14(2h), 16(1g), 29
17. Germany	Preambular Paragraph11, 7b
18. India	5a, 16(1), 16(2), 29
19. Indonesia	29
20. Iraq	2(f), 2(g), 9(1), 9(2), 29
21. Ireland	13(b), 13(c), 11(1), 13(a), 16(1d), 16(1f)
22. Israel	7(b), 16, 29
23. Italy	Reservation the right to exercise the Article 19 Vienna Convention on the Law of Treaties
24. Jamaica	29

(1)	(2)
25. Jordan	9(2), 15(4), 16(1c), 16(1d), 16(1g)
26. Kuwait	7(a), 9(2), 16(f), 29
27. Lebanon	9(2), 16(1c), 16(1d), 16(1f), 16(1g), 29
28. Lesotho	2 (with a special reference to 2e)
29. Libyan Arab Jamahiriya	2, 16(c),16(d)
30. Liechtenstein	1
31. Luxembourg	7, 16(1g) 5(a), 7(b), 9(2), 11,
32. Malaysia	16 (1a), 16 (1c), 16(1f), 16(1g) 16(2)
33. Maldives	7(a), 16
34. Malta	11, 13, 15, 16(1e)
35. Mauritania	Subject to Shariah Law and the Constitution of the State
36. Mauritius	11(1b), 11(1d) 16(1g), 29
37. Mexico	Generally worded reservation
38. Morocco	2, 9(2), 15(4), 16, 29
39. Myanmar [Burma]	29
40. Netherlands	Preambular Paragraph 11
41. New Zealand and Niue	11(2b)
New Zealand – Cook Islands	11(2b), 2(f), 5(a)
42. Niger	2(d), 2(f), 5(a), 5(b), 15(4), 16(1c), 16(1e), 16(1g), 29
43. Pakistan	29
44. Republic of Korea	16(1g)
45. Saudi Arabia	9(2), 29
46. Singapore	2, 11(1), 16, 29
47. Spain	The ratification of the Convention by Spain shall not affect the constitutional provisions concerning succession to the Spanish crown.
48. Switzerland	7(b), 16(1g), 15(2), 16(1h)
49. Thailand	16, 29
50. Trinidad and Tobago	29
51. Tunisia	9(2), 15(4), 16 (1c), 16(1d), 16(1f), 16(1g), 16(1h), 29
52. Turkey	9(1), 29

(1)	(2)
53. UK of GB and Northern Ireland	4(1), 9, 11, 15(3), 16(1f)
54. Venezuela	29
55. Viet Nam	29
56. Yemen	29

Source: IWRAW Asia Pacific training manual (2002) on the CEDAW Convention.

Many of the reservations are incompatible with object and purpose of the convention. As can be seen from Table I, most reservations refer to specific provisions of the Convention. Many of the reservations address key elements of the Convention; particularly Article 2 (which identifies measures to be taken by State Parties to eliminate discrimination), Article 16 (which calls on State Parties to eliminate discrimination in matters relating to marriage and family relations) and Article 29 (resolution of disputes between State Parties on the interpretation and application of CEDAW by the International Court of Justice).

Many State Parties justify reservation to CEDAW on traditional, religious or cultural grounds. Representatives of these states often claim that CEDAW and other women's rights instruments represent 'western' conceptions of women's rights that are ethnocentric and inapplicable to their cultures. In this view, 'western' conceptions of human rights (including women's rights) constitute a hegemonic or neo colonist discourse. It is colonist, say such theorists, to treat non-western women as undifferentiated victims of their own cultural practices or beliefs such as foot-binding, genital mutilation, wearing of the veil or overarching subservience of women. That ethnocentric philosophic beliefs are at the root of CEDAW and other human rights instruments cannot be denied. Nonetheless, CEDAW and other human rights instruments have contributed greatly to a universal philosophy of human dignity worthy of legal protection on an international scale. Non-deontological perceptions of particular practices are largely irrelevant – virtually everyone, Western and otherwise, now accepts that slavery is an evil and a human rights violation even though it was deeply rooted in the cultures of slaveholders. The same can be said of genital mutilation and other harmful practices. Cultural change is inevitable if states agree to protect minimum standards of human rights, as the preamble of CEDAW implies. In fact, CEDAW explicitly elevates its conception of women's human rights above cultural values; affirmatively requiring that signatories take appropriate measures to modify the social and cultural patterns of conduct to eliminate prejudices and customary practices that perpetuate gender-based stereotypes[18].

The potential for conflict between the objectives of the Convention and State Parties' reservations on grounds of religious and customary laws and practices have become a matter of concern. The concern about serious conflict has grown in recent years with the increasing power and prominence of fundamentalist religious groups, many of which actively oppose the transformative impetus of the human rights movement for women. A common feature of such groups is their commitment to the maintenance of traditional gender roles[19].

While reservations made possible the ratification of CEDAW by virtually all countries because they can opt out of some of its requirements, they also jeopardised the integral and effective application of the Convention as a whole. In other words, the problem is that the formal adherence to CEDAW is not accompanied by full commitment to the Convention[20]. The net result has been the widespread view that international obligations assumed through the ratification of CEDAW are somehow 'separate' and 'distinct' from and less binding than those of other human rights treaties[21].

At present there is no mechanism within the UN to regulate the practice of reservations or to bar reservations that undermine the basic principles of CEDAW. As a result of the many reservations entered to the Convention, the CEDAW Committee was concerned with the issue of reservations since its inception. At its third session, the Treaty Section of the Office of Legal Affairs of the United Nations Secretariat provided a legal opinion, stating that "the functions of the CEDAW Committee do not appear to include a determination of the incompatibility of reservations"[22].

However, the CEDAW Committee has formulated two General Recommendations on reservations (General Recommendation No. 4 and General Recommendation No. 20). General Recommendation No. 4 suggested that all State Parties should reconsider reservations with a view to withdrawing them.[23] In its General Recommendation No. 21, the CEDAW Committee addressed reservations to Article 16 of the Convention[24]. The Committee also adopted a statement on reservations to the Convention as its contribution to the commemoration of the fiftieth anniversary of the UDHR. In addition, its guidelines for the preparation of reports by State Parties set out specific requirements for states, which have ratified the Convention with reservations[25].

However, the CEDAW Committee does not have the power of assessing the compatibility of reservations with the Convention. In comparison, the Convention on the Elimination of All Forms of Racial Discrimination includes a process for rejecting reservations by State Parties if they are deemed incompatible with the purpose of the Convention, provided that at least two-thirds of the State Parties object to the reservation. While CEDAW could include in its rules of procedure for some system of assessing the compatibility of reservations, it has not yet been done. The absence of any such applicable procedure has given rise to serious problem[26].

As a result of initiative of some State Parties, Canada placed the issue of reservations on the agenda of meeting of parties to the Convention, which took place in 1986. At this meeting the UN Secretary-General was asked to solicit all parties views on reservations. However, very few governments submitted their views; only seventeen out of more than hundred State Parties at that time. Moreover, these reiterated the disagreements among governments, evidenced before and continued thereafter[27].

The issue of reservations to CEDAW has entered the political arena and debates have been held at the ECOSOC and General Assembly. Since the most explicit and all-encompassing reservations were entered into by those governments which invoked the Shari'a, objections have been raised that the movement against reservations was anti-Islamic. The attitude of governments was that it is preferable to have the maximum number of countries formally participating in the Convention than to uphold a commitment to the primary requirements of the Convention.

The issue was placed on the agenda of the Sub-Commission on the Prevention of Discrimination and Protection of Minorities. The Sub-Commission adopted a resolution in August 1992. The sub-commission expressed concern that reservations to the

Convention, in particular those in relation to Article 2, Article 7, Article 11, Article 15 and Article 16, might diminish the international legal norm and legitimise its violation. It held that such reservations contribute to the phenomenon of exploitation of women[28].

While some countries like France, Ireland, Malawi, New Zealand, Republic of Korea and Thailand have withdrawn substantive reservations, few reservations to Article 2 have been withdrawn or modified and reservations to Article 16 are rarely withdrawn.

Reservations to the substantive provisions of CEDAW pose a challenge to the effectiveness of the Convention and there is an urgent need to introduce a procedure of reservations comparable to that of other human rights instruments.

Optional Protocol to CEDAW

One of the main weaknesses of the enforcement procedure of the Convention was the absence of a right of individual petition. Little attention was paid to the possibility of an individual complaint procedure during the drafting of CEDAW for a number of reasons. The subject matter of the Convention was considered by some states to be insufficiently serious to merit a right to individual petition, while others were concerned about proliferation and the lack of evidence of the success of other individual petition procedures.

The conceptual challenge to traditional human rights theory posed by the issue of violence helped shape the debate on how women's rights could be realised. In 1991, the Expert Group on Violence Against Women recommended that consideration be given to an Optional Protocol containing the right of individual petition. At the same time, the CSW began to reconsider its own procedures for responding to violations of women's human rights. The CSW supported the introduction of a special rapporteur on violence but did not at that time formally commit itself to an optional protocol on individual petition. At its 1992 session, in the context of its consideration of the questions, members of the CEDAW Committee began to press for the introduction of an Optional Protocol that would establish a right of individual petition to the committee. The issue gained momentum following the Vienna World Conference, and in 1994, an expert group meeting in Maastricht produced a draft Optional Protocol. The Beijing Platform of Action gave firm endorsement for an Optional Protocol and at its fourteenth session, the CEDAW Committee broadly adopted the Maastricht draft. In response to request from the CSW, the Secretary General issued an invitation to governments, non-governmental organisations and inter-governmental groups such as the Council of Europe to submit their comments on the desirability and feasibility of an Optional Protocol[29]. In 1997, the Chairperson of the Working Group submitted a draft of the Optional Protocol that served as a basis for the next three years of negotiations[30].

On 12th March 1999, the forty-third session of the CSW adopted by consensus the Optional Protocol to the CEDAW. On 6th October 1999, the UN General Assembly, acting without a vote, adopted the 21-article Optional Protocol to the Convention and called on State Parties to become a party to the new instrument as soon as possible. The Optional Protocol came into force on 22nd December 2000 following 10 ratifications. As of 12th Jan 2003, it has been signed by 75 states and ratified by 49. Annexure III contains the text of the Optional Protocol. Annexure IV contains a list of State Parties.

Angela King, Assistant Secretary General and Special Adviser to the Secretary.General on Gender Issues and Advancement of Women, said that the new Optional Protocol would be a useful and effective addition for the protection and promotion of women's human rights. "The Optional Protocol," she said, "provides an international remedy for violations of women's rights. It will act as an incentive for governments to take a fresh look at the means currently available to women at the domestic level to enforce their rights. This is perhaps the most important contribution of the Optional Protocol." She added that such action at the national level would create an environment for women and girls to fully enjoy all their human rights, and it would also allow their grievances to be addressed with "the efficiency and speed they deserved"[31].

The Optional Protocol to the CEDAW broadly follows the model of other individual complaints procedures available under other international human rights treaties, such as the First Optional Protocol to the ICCPR, the Convention on the Elimination of Racial

Discrimination and the Convention against Torture and Other Forms of Cruel, Inhuman or Degrading Treatment or Punishment.

States, which ratify the Optional Protocol, recognize the competence of the CEDAW Committee to receive and consider communications under the protocol. (Article 1). The Division for the Advancement of Women in the Department of Economic and Social Affairs provides the technical assistance and substantive servicing for the Convention and its Optional Protocol.

Key Elements of the Optional Protocol

Admissibility

The Optional Protocol of the CEDAW offers a wider formulation of standing than that available before other treaty-based bodies. Article 2 of the CEDAW Optional Protocol provides that "communications may be submitted by or on behalf of individuals or groups of individuals, under the jurisdiction of a State Party, claiming to be victims of a violation of any of the rights set forth in the Convention by that State Party". This is a significantly wider grant of standing than that under ICCPR and although it most closely mirrors the approach to standing under Article 14(1) of the Convention on Elimination of Racial Discrimination, it goes wider than both. Under the Torture Convention [Article 22 (1)], and the Optional Protocol of the ICCPR (Article 1 and 2), only individuals can submit communications to the respective bodies. The Human Rights Committee has been cautious in its approach to standing, granting standing to submit a communication to the family of victims where the victim is unable to do so, but has refused standing to NGOs to take a group action or submit communications on behalf of individuals. The admissibility of group action in the Optional Protocol to the CEDAW is particularly significant given the structural nature of inequalities that often escape resolution by way of individual litigation. By permitting groups to lodge an application before the CEDAW, the Optional Protocol would encourage challenging domestic practices at an international level without exposing individuals to the risks often associated with litigation[32].

The Optional Protocol to the CEDAW has incorporated the existing jurisprudence of the Human Rights Committee on the exhaustion of domestic remedies. Article 4 (1) of the CEDAW Optional Protocol provides that the "committee shall not consider a communication unless it has ascertained that all available domestic remedies have been exhausted unless the application of such remedies is unduly prolonged or unlikely to bring relief." This is a climb down from the original draft of the Optional Protocol, which contained no requirement that all available domestic remedies be exhausted. The inclusion of this clause on exhaustion of domestic remedies is unfortunate given the lack of awareness among women of their legal rights because of low levels of female literacy across the world and the victimisation suffered by many women seeking to use the law.

Inquiry Procedure

Article 8(1) and (2) gives the CEDAW Committee the right to launch an inquiry on its own initiative into grave or systemic violations by a State Party. The Committee may designate one of its members to conduct an inquiry where warranted and with the consent of the State Party, the inquiry may include a visit to its territory. Only the Committee Against Torture has a similar power of inquiry. Through this procedure the CEDAW Committee has the power of addressing a broad range of issues that are not amenable to the individual complaints procedure. The Committee can address issues relating to the causes that maintain women's inequality. However State Parties have the freedom to opt out of this clause. Article 10 of the Optional Protocol provides that a State Party has the option of refusing to recognize the competence of the Committee to initiate and conduct an inquiry, as established under Article 8 and 9.

Remedies and Follow-up Measures

The CEDAW Committee also has the power to recommend interim measures to a State Party after receipt of a communication and prior to its final decision in order to protect the alleged victims from irreparable harm (Article 5). The Committee is authorised to recommend remedial measures to give effect to the obligations under the Convention. State Parties have six months to consider the communication and provide a written response, including remedial steps taken. The Committee may request further information from the State Party, including in subsequent reports (Article 7). However, like the First Optional Protocol of the ICCPR, there is no formal requirement that the State Parties comply with Committee's final views.

No reservations are permitted to the Optional Protocol, though State Parties may opt out of the inquiry procedure.

The Optional Protocol has put the rights of women on a similar footing to the enjoyment of civil and political rights, the protection of right to freedom against racial discrimination and torture. Despite the low rate of ratification so far, the importance of the Optional Protocol cannot be undermined. By bringing the CEDAW in line with other treaty-based bodies, the seriousness of responding to women's issues at the international level will be emphasised. In addition to improving the understanding of rights and obligations in the CEDAW, the jurisprudence emerging as a result of the Optional Protocol will help in developing progressive interpretation of women's rights at both national and international level. How the CEDAW Committee will interpret its powers under the Optional Protocol and whether it will address the complexly interwoven strands – economic, social, cultural, political, legal – of the problem of women's subordination remains to be seen.

Committee on the Elimination of Discrimination against Women (CEDAW Committee)

Part V of the Convention (Articles 17-22) outlines the structure and functions of the CEDAW Committee. The Committee consists of twenty-three members who serve in their personal capacity, though they are nominated and elected by State Parties with due consideration to equitable geographical distribution and representation of different forms of civilizations and legal systems. The CEDAW Committee has the largest number of members amongst all UN human rights treaty bodies. Their term lasts four years, with only half of the Committee members replaced each time elections take place. A total of sixty-nine members have served as members of the Committee since 1982. All its members have been women, with a single exception. The office of the Committee consists of a Chairperson, three Vice-Chairpersons and a Rapporteur. The Convention also stipulates that the Secretary-

General will provide the necessary facilities and staff to service the meetings of the Committee.

Functions of the CEDAW Committee

The CEDAW Committee monitors the implementation of the Convention. In addition to considering reports submitted by State Parties and evaluating progress made in its concluding comments, the Committee also formulates general recommendations on eliminating discrimination against women. It also receives information from specialized agencies and NGOs.

Consideration of Reports

Article 18 of CEDAW requires State Parties to submit reports to the Committee, for its consideration, on the measures they have taken to comply with their treaty obligations one year after becoming a state party, and subsequently at least four years thereafter.

Article 20 of the Convention provides that it shall normally meet for a period of not more than four weeks annually in order to consider the reports submitted by State Parties. No other human rights treaty contains an explicit limitation on its meeting time. Given the large number of ratifications of the Convention, it was clear from the outset that the sessions specified in Article 20 would not be sufficient to discharge its functions. The committee has tried to devise various alternatives to deal with the shortage of time. Since 1990, a pre-sessional working group of the Committee is convened before each session to prepare a list of issues and questions relating to periodic reports for transmission to the representatives of State Parties before the meetings at which their reports are to be considered. The report of the pre-sessional working group and responses of State Parties to the list of issues and questions are placed before the CEDAW Committee.

In 1990, the General Assembly started to allow the Committee to meet on an exceptional basis for an extra week every year. In order to arrive at a permanent solution, the State Parties to the Convention adopted an amendment to Article 20(1) in May 1995. The amendment provides that the CEDAW Committee will normally meet annually but the duration of its meeting will be determined by State Parties, subject to the approval of the General Assembly.[33] The amendment will enter into force after it is approved by two-third of the State Parties. Thirty-five State Parties have accepted the amendment, the most recent being Cyprus on 31st July 2002[34] . In 1996, the General Assembly approved another increase in additional meeting time for the Committee for an interim period, allowing it to meet for two three-week sessions annually[35].

The latest session of the Committee (27th session) was held from 3rd to 21st June 2002 and an exceptional session was held from 5th to 23rd August 2002.

Prior to the beginning of its 27th session on 31st June 2002, the Committee had considered 116 initial reports, 84 second, 63 third, 28th fourth and 7 fifth periodic reports[36].

According to practice, the CEDAW Committee comes out with a tentative list of State Parties due to report for the succeeding session. This is tentative because a government may decline or may not be ready to submit its report.

The Committee has provided broad guidelines for writing of the report, both initial and periodic. The Country Rapporteur (a member of CEDAW with primary responsibility for one country) prepares an analysis of the State Parties' report. She sends this to a pre-session working group. This working group also receives questions from other members of the Committee and compiles a list of questions, which is then sent to the State Party. The reports, which are expected to cover legislative, judicial, administrative or other measures taken to improve the situation of women, are presented to the Committee by governmental representatives The state representative makes an oral presentation. The Committee raises questions and seeks clarifications. The government is then given a few days to prepare their replies. They then return for a second round of review. Subsequent reports of State Parties, called periodic reports, are submitted every four years thereafter. At this stage, the pre-sessional working group prepares a set of questions at its previous session in order to elicit clarifications or to ask for more information if the report is not comprehensive enough. These are then sent to the government and they have to submit written replies.

Apart from these reports, the Committee can also request a State Party to submit a report on an exceptional basis. Generally, countries whose governments are asked to give such reports are often in the midst of internal political or armed strife, which raises concern over the situation of women in the said country. The Committee began this practice in 1994 when it asked Yugoslavia to submit a report on an exceptional basis. Since 1994, the Committee has been committed to investigating similar grave violations of rights being experienced by women in any part of the world. In 1996 (15th session), Rwanda and in 1997 (16th and 17th session), Democratic Republic of Congo submitted reports on an exceptional basis[37].

The CEDAW Committee, like other human rights treaty bodies, is faced with the problem of non-reporting. As of June 2002, 241 reports were overdue. Out of these, 114 reports were more than five years overdue, of which 37 were initial reports. While on the one hand, the Committee is faced with the problem of non-reporting by State Parties, on the other hand it is also faced with the problem of growing backlog of reports awaiting consideration due to paucity of time. Prior to the exceptional session, held from 5-23 August 2002, 38 State Party reports had been submitted but had not yet been considered by the Committee. At the exceptional session, reports of 11 State Parties were considered[38].

During its lifetime, the Committee has considered reports of up to 13 State Parties per session. In many cases, State Parties have chosen to put forward more than one report for review. At its fourteenth session, the Committee decided that it would review implementation of the Convention in up to a maximum of 8 countries at each of it sessions, although these State Parties could put forward more than one report for combined review. From 1995, the Committee has scheduled the reports of 8 parties for consideration at each session, though during the fifteenth and sixteenth sessions in 1996 and 1997, the Committee considered a 9th country on an exceptional basis. And only 7 countries were considered at the twentieth and twenty-first sessions in 1999 and twenty-seventh session in 2002[39].

The Committee's decision to limit the consideration of reports to 8 State Parties per session, despite the growing backlog of reports awaiting consideration, attracted criticism from several State Parties, a number of which openly suggested that the backlog was more the result of poor working methods than of limited meeting time of the Committee. Some of the critics suggest that the Committee's wide interpretation of its mandate to include, inter alia, discussion of the cycle of the UN World Conferences, has diverted it from its primary task of report consideration. While it may be possible for the Committee to reduce its backlog by considering more reports at each session, this would inevitably affect the quality of report review. Most State Parties' reports are lengthy and detailed and, in most cases, the Committee is also provided with extensive updating information by State Parties shortly before the consideration of their reports, or during the meetings at which the report is reviewed[40].

While the constructive dialogue between the Committee and State Parties should be detailed enough to provide the State Party with sufficient guidance for the practical implementation of the Convention, it is crucial for the Committee to consider methods of reducing the report backlog. First, the entry of Optional Protocol allowing individual complaints under the Convention will place the Committee under even greater time constraints. Second, because the backlog also serves as a disincentive to those State Parties whose reports are overdue. Many State Parties are well aware that there may be a wait of up to three years before the Committee considers their report and that it will, at that time, be necessary to submit additional information to ensure that their reports are updated[41].

The Committee is trying to develop strategies to address the problem of its backlog. The convening of the pre-sessional working group to consider periodic reports at the session prior to that at which the State Party's report will be considered in order to elicit clarifications or ask for more information is a step in the right direction. The Committee at its twentieth session in 1999 recommended that the pre-sessional working group should concentrate on major issues and trends and limit the number of questions and issues. There is a need for the Committee to identify country-specific issues. This would provide for a more focussed and constructive discussion between the Committee and State Parties.

At the eighth and ninth meeting in 1997 and 1998, the chairpersons of human rights treaty bodies suggested that, while the current practice of requiring comprehensive initial reports should be maintained, periodic reports should be focussed and address only a limited range of issues which would be identified by the relevant committee in advance of the preparation of the report. Its pre-sessional working group could identify a limited number of specific issues pertinent to the individual state party. A report would be requested in relation to these issues and the Committee would then conduct its dialogue on the basis of that detailed but targeted or tailored report. This clearer and more tailored focus would also avoid the perception that the Committee has a list of issues that it discusses with all State Parties irrespective of their level of development or specific domestic problems[42].

Addressing the Committee at its twenty-sixth session, the Assistant Secretary and Special Adviser to the Secretary General on Gender Issues and Advancement of Women, called upon the Committee to reform its methods of work, including its reporting procedures and provide guidelines concerning the length of reports from State Parties. She also emphasised the need to adopt reporting guidelines that could streamline the structure and content of reports of State Parties[43].

At its fifty-sixth session, the General Assembly acknowledged the high number of reports awaiting consideration by the Committee, and therefore decided to authorise the committee to hold, on an exceptional basis, an extraordinary session of three weeks duration in 2002 to be used entirely for the consideration of the reports of State Parties in order to reduce the backlog of reports[44].

At its twenty-sixth session the Committee, taking into account the criteria of preference to be given to those State Parties whose reports had been pending for the longest time, the need to give priority to initial reports and desirability of balance of reports in terms of geographic and other factors, decided to invite eleven State Parties to present their report[45]. The exceptional session was held from 5th to 23rd August 2002.

Concluding Comments

At its thirteenth session, in January 1994 the committee adopted the practice of preparing concluding comments on the reports of State Parties. This practice was introduced by the committee to provide concrete suggestions for the implementation of the convention, to make its work more accessible and to bring its practice in line with other human rights treaty bodies. At the thirteenth session, specific procedures were agreed upon for the preparation of concluding comments: that they should cover the most important points raised during the constructive dialogue, emphasising both the positive aspects of the reports and matters on which the committee has expressed concern and should clearly indicate what the committee wished the State Party to focus on in its next report. The comments were to be concise and, where periodic reports were concerned, should take into account the findings of the pre session working group, as well as the constructive dialogue. At the same session the committee decided to include in the concluding comments a section in which the committee's views would be reflected for those state parties that have entered substantive reservations[46].

At its fifteenth session, in January 1996, the Committee decided to dispense with the detailed summary of the constructive dialogue on the reports of State Parties. Summary records were to be retained and the concluding comments of the committee were to be preceded by a brief summary of the presentation of the state party concerned. At its sixteenth and seventeenth sessions, the committee decided that the standard format for concluding comments would be: introduction, positive aspects, factors and difficulties affecting the implementation of the convention, principal areas of concern, and suggestions and recommendation[47].

The procedures and format for concluding comments were revised at the committee's nineteenth session with a view to streamlining, while retaining flexibility. In accordance with the revised format, the concluding comments :[48]

(a) Are preceded by a summary of the State Party's presentation
(b) Usually follow a standard format under four headings: introduction; positive aspects; factors and difficulties affecting implementation of the Convention; principal areas of concern and recommendations.
(c) Include an introduction containing comments on whether the report has followed the Committee's guidelines for the preparation of initial reports; whether it was sufficient or insufficient; whether it incorporates or refers to statistical information desegregated by sex, and the Committee's general recommendations; whether

there are any reservations to the Convention; whether reservations have been withdrawn; whether the State Party has objected to the reservations of other State Parties; whether the State Party has mentioned the implementation of the Beijing Platform for Action and the nature and relevance of the oral presentation. An objective indication of the strength of the report is generally included.

(d) Includes a "positive aspects" section organised in the order of the articles of the Convention. This section notes issues such as the ratification or accession of the Optional Protocol to the Convention, acceptance of the amendment to article 20 (1), the removal of reservations or striking advances in the implementation of the Convention. Concluding comments adopted at the twenty-second session contain longer, more detailed "positive aspects" sections than concluding comments adopted at other sessions.

(e) Describe in the "factors and difficulties" section major overarching reasons why the Convention has not been implemented by the State Party. Any reservations to the Convention and other legal impediments to the implementation of the Convention are also addressed in this section.

(f) Include a "principal areas of concern" section organised in the order of importance of the particular issues to the country under review, and provide concrete proposals from the Committee on the problems identified in the rest of the comments. Include reference to any commitments of the State Party made at the Fourth World Conference on Women. Concluding comments adopted at more recent sessions include three standard paragraphs urging ratification of the Optional Protocol and acceptance of the amendment to article 20 (1) and request dissemination of the Convention, the concluding comments, the general recommendations, the Beijing Platform for Action and the results of the twenty-third special session of the General Assembly, 'Women 2000: Gender, Equality, Development and Peace for the Twenty-first Century.'

(g) Include reference to any commitments of the State Party

made at the Fourth World Conference on Women at Beijing.

(h) Include, where appropriate, specific suggestions to the State Party with regard to possible technical assistance from the Office of the High Commissioner for Human Rights and other parts of the United Nations system, for example, in regard to reservations, review of legislation and law reform.

The Committee also decided that concluding comments would be internally balanced. It would strive to achieve consistency and balance, particularly in terms of praise and expressions of concern, in the concluding comments elaborated at each session. To that end, the Committee would consider the concluding comments comparatively, in an effort to ensure that they were even. Later concluding comments also indicate that the Committee has sought to ensure internal consistency particularly in regard to State Parties from the same region or experiencing similar conditions. Similar language is also used to address several issues, such as the failure of State Parties to provide a definition of discrimination reflective of that in article 1 of the Convention, stereotypical attitudes towards gender roles, concerns and recommendations relating to article 4 (1) on temporary special measures, violence against women and increasingly, women's reproductive health. Notably, although comments adopted since the nineteenth session sometimes note acceptance or implications of International Labour Organisation or regional human rights instruments, it is unusual for other UN human rights treaties to be mentioned. The concluding comments do not reflect the concluding observations/ comments of other human rights treaty bodies on the same State Party; nor do they make reference to recommendations of other human rights mechanisms, such as country-specific or thematic special rapporteurs[49].

It has been recommended that the Committee needs to make some modifications in the current format and content of the concluding comments since the comments are often extremely general, thereby limiting their use in advocacy, planning and implementation and they often identify areas of concern without specifying specific laws or practices or connecting those concerns to specific recommendations. The current pattern of concluding comments should be modified to exclude those parts entitled "positive aspects" and "factors and difficulties impeding implementation." They should include specific information relating to the report or any other documentation and quality of the delegation in the introduction; include in the "concerns and recommendations" section a clear connection between the concerns and recommendations, with recommendations concentrating on concrete proposals that should be as practical and precise as possible. Recommendations, which should be grouped thematically and in order of priority, should clarify whether they relate to policies, practices or legislation, which should be identified. Concluding comments should conclude with a summary of additional information requested, including any deadlines for submission, and should address issues relating to dissemination and the processes or structures that the State Party should establish for follow-up[50].

General Recommendations

Article 21 of the Convention empowers the CEDAW Committee to make suggestions and general recommendations based on the examination of reports and information received by State Parties.

The Committee has adopted 24 general recommendations. Those adopted during the Committee's first ten years were short and modest, addressing issues such as the content of reports and reservations to the Convention. At it tenth session in 1991, the Committee decided to adopt the practice of issuing general recommendations on specific provisions of the Convention and on the relationship between the Convention articles and what the Committee described as "cross cutting" themes. Following this decision, CEDAW issued more detailed and comprehensive general recommendations on substantive matters covered by the Convention which offer State Parties clear guidance on the application of the Convention in particular situations [51]. General Recommendation No. 19 (1992) concerning violence against women and General Recommendation No. 21 (1994) on equality in marriage and family relations are examples of the trend of adopting focussed and detailed recommendations.

In 1997, the Committee adopted the practice of a three-stage process for the formulation of general recommendations. The first stage consists of an open dialogue between the Committee, NGOs and others regarding the topic of the general recommendations. A committee member is then asked to draft the general recommendation, which is then discussed at the next session of the Committee in one of its working groups. At the following session, the revised draft is adopted by the Committee[52].

The Convention is being adapted and updated to include new insights and contemporary issues through the mechanism of general recommendations. It is a means of enlarging the jurisprudence of the Convention The Convention was silent on several issues like violence against women. By formulating General Recommendation, the Convention has provided guidelines to State Parties in identifying the various articles under which violence against women should be reported by the states. However, the general recommendations do not impose any binding obligations on State Parties.

The following general recommendations have been adopted by the CEDAW Committee:

- General Recommendation No. 1, fifth session, 1986, reporting guidelines
- General Recommendation No. 2, sixth session, 1987, reporting guidelines
- General Recommendation No. 3, sixth session, 1987, education and public information programmes
- General Recommendation No. 4, sixth session, 1987, reservations
- General Recommendation No. 5, seventh session, temporary special measures
- General Recommendation No. 6, seventh session, 1988, effective national machinery and publicity
- General Recommendation No. 7, seventh session, 1988, resources
- General Recommendation No. 8, seventh session, 1988, article 8
- General Recommendation No. 9, eighth session, 1989, statistical data
- General Recommendation No. 10, eighth session, 1989, tenth anniversary of the adoption of CEDAW

- General Recommendation No. 11, eighth session, 1989, technical advisory services for reporting
- General Recommendation No. 12, eighth session, 1989, violence against women
- General Recommendation No. 13, eighth session, 1989, equal remuneration for work of equal value
- General Recommendation No. 14, ninth session, 1990, female circumcision
- General Recommendation No. 15, ninth session, women and AIDS
- General Recommendation No. 16, tenth session, 1991, unpaid women workers in rural and urban family enterprises
- General Recommendation No. 17, tenth session, 1991, measurement and quantification of the unremunerated domestic activities of women and their recognition in the GNP
- General Recommendation No. 18, tenth session, 1991, disabled women
- General Recommendation No. 19, eleventh session, 1992, violence against women
- General Recommendation No. 20, eleventh session, 1992, reservations
- General Recommendation No. 21, thirteenth session, 1994, equality in marriage and family relations
- General Recommendation No. 22, fourteenth session, 1995, article 20 of the Convention
- General Recommendation No. 23, sixteenth session, 1997, women in political and public life
- General Recommendation No. 24, twentieth session, 1992, article 12 – women and health
- The Committee is currently drafting the 25th recommendation which will address article 4 (1) of the Convention, on temporary special measures aimed at accelerating de facto equality between men and women.

Relation of CEDAW Committee with Other Treaty Bodies

The CEDAW Committee has been seen both by commentators and by its own members as the 'poor relation' of other treaty bodies, left outside the mainstream of human rights work within the UN and neglected by the international human rights community. Unlike all the other treaty-based supervisory bodies, the CEDAW Committee's secretariat is not provided by the Office of the High Commissioner for Human Rights in Geneva, but by the Division for the Advancement of Women, which also services the Commission for the Status of Women. Therefore, unlike other treaty bodies, the Committee's sessions have never been held at the Office for the High Commissioner in Geneva. Until 1993, when the Division for the Advancement of Women was relocated to the UN headquarters in New York from the UN offices in Vienna, the Committee met alternatively in Vienna and New York. Since its thirteenth session in 1994, the CEDAW Committee's sessions have always been held in New York. The different servicing arrangements for the CEDAW Committee and its geographical separation from other UN treaty bodies has left it outside the mainstream of human rights work within the UN and has meant that the Committee's jurisprudential approach and practices have developed, to a large extent, with little reference to the approach and practices of other treaty bodies. The Committee has been criticised for being out of step with its sister bodies, with critics suggesting that its intellectual and practical development has been slow in comparison[53].

The Committee has been sensitive to these charges. From 1992, it argued that its sessions should be held in Geneva, and should be serviced by the Office for the High Commissioner for Human Rights so that it could interact more closely with other treaty bodies. The Committee's views in this regard were supported by the meetings of persons chairing human rights treaty bodies. Nonetheless, in early 1996, the UN Secretary General informed the Committee's chairperson that, although he had sympathy with the considerations that had motivated the Committee's views, it would continue to be serviced by the Division for the Advancement of Women, so as to provide a strong and unified programme for the advancement of women within the UN [54].

The CEDAW Committee's status as a poor relation of the treaty bodies has been aggravated by its isolation from other international human rights treaty bodies. The only formal mechanism of coordination between the CEDAW Committee and other treaty bodies has been the chairpersons' meetings. The General Assembly in 1985 decided to include the chairperson of the CEDAW Committee in future meetings of chairpersons of the various principal human rights treaty bodies. At the 14th meeting of the chairpersons of human rights treaty bodies in June 2002, chairperson of the CEDAW Committee was elected chairperson \ rapporteur of the meeting. During the meeting, the chairpersons were provided with an opportunity to exchange views among themselves and engage in dialogue with other actors in the field, including the Commission on Human Rights.

In order to bring gender issues into the mainstream of the human rights movement, ad hoc strategies have been initiated. The chairperson of the CEDAW Committee usually attends at least some sessions of the Commission on the Status of Women and the Commission on Human Rights and its Sub-Commission on the Prevention of Discrimination and Protection of Minorities. In 1996, members of the CEDAW Committee and the Committee on the Rights of the Child met to discuss working methods and other areas of mutual concern. Also, in 1996, the Division for the Advancement of Women, the office of the High Commissioner for Human Rights and the United Nations Population Fund (UNFPA) hosted a roundtable of human rights treaty bodies on women's reproductive and sexual health rights at Glen Clove, New York. The Glen Clove roundtable was the first occasion outside the chairpersons' meeting, at which members of all treaty bodies met to discuss a substantive human rights issue. The success of the roundtable, which made concrete recommendations with regard to the treaty bodies, suggests that such meetings should be a regular feature of the future programmes of such bodies. Nonetheless, limited resources and, to a certain extent, institutional jealousies, continue to impose constraints on the efforts to increase collaboration with the other treaty bodies[55].

Except in the case of the Special Rapporteur on Violence against Women, its Causes and Consequences, the CEDAW Committee has yet to consider seriously linkages with the extra-conventional human rights mechanisms – the human rights special procedures system, consisting of special and thematic rapporteurs, representatives, experts and working groups. The Committee should nominate a representative to attend the meetings of the special procedures with the object of creating formal links between the Committee and those non-conventional mechanisms with mandates relating to issues which are of concern to the CEDAW Committee. This would include the special rapporteurs on torture and other cruel, inhuman or degrading treatment or punishment, on internally displaced persons, on religious intolerance and on sale of children, child prostitution and child pornography. The Committee has made an effort to forge a strong relationship with the Special Rapporteur on Violence against Women. The Special Rapporteur agreed in 1999 to brief the Committee periodically and to provide briefing material as well as information on State Parties to be considered by the Committee. Agreement was also reached on providing information to the Committee on country missions[56].

In order to infuse women's concerns into all areas of human rights concerns and make them a part and parcel of human rights considerations, members of the CEDAW Committee have been participating in inter-governmental conference on human rights. Several members of the committee, including the Chairperson, participated in the World Conference against Racism, Racial Discrimination, Xenophobia and Related Intolerance, held in 2001, in Durban, South Africa. The members of the Committee emphasised at the conference that racism, racial discrimination and related intolerance affected women differently than men and stressed the need to integrate a gender perspective into relevant politics, strategies and programmes against racism and racial discrimination. The CEDAW Committee also emphasised the important role that women play in development at the World Conference on Sustainable Development held in 2002.

One of the greatest challenge faced by the CEDAW Committee lies in avoiding the 'ghettoization' of women concerns to bodies created solely to deal with women's issues. The CEDAW Committee needs to avoid creating a parallel universe for women's issues and needs to bring women's concerns into the mainstream of the human rights movement.

Relations With Specialized Agencies

Article 22 of the Convention provides that specialized agencies shall be entitled to be represented during the consideration of the implementation of such provisions of the Convention that fall within the scope of their activities and that the Convention may invite the specialised agencies to submit reports on the implementation of the Convention in those areas.

The CEDAW Committee discussed the role of the specialized agencies and their reports at both its second and third sessions. At the former session, the Committee decided to invite specialized agencies to submit information, but did not determine the status or attention such documents would receive during the Committee sessions. There was debate on whether the Committee should be concerned with such reports when its primary task was the examination of State Parties' reports. Having received reports from the FAO, ILO and UNESCO, the Committee debated their status. It decided that they would be circulated as background papers[57]. Realizing the inadequacy of State Parties' reports, the importance of inputs from specialized organisations was acknowledged by the Committee.

At its seventeenth session in July 1997, the committee pre-sessional working group decided to follow the practice of other treaty bodies, including the Human Rights Committee, the Committee on Economic and Social Rights and the Committee on the Rights of the Child, and invited representatives of specialised agencies and other entities to provide oral information in relation to periodic reports before it. The pre-sessional working group concluded that the practice was a valuable one and recommended that the Committee adopt it as the usual practice for its future sessions. The Committee adopted this recommendation. To provide a similar opportunity for involvement in the consideration of initial reports, the Committee also decided that representatives of specialized agencies and bodies should be invited to meet with the Committee in a closed meeting[58].

While the reports of specialized agencies are becoming more focussed and country-specific and their oral information is useful, several specialized agencies have requested the Committee to provide greater guidance to bodies, which wish to contribute to its work. The Committee should formulate guidelines for this purpose[59].

Relations With NGOs

There is no mention of NGOs in the Convention. However, the CEDAW Committee has developed procedures whereby NGOs can provide valuable inputs to the Committee in the discharge of its functions. The work of the Committee has been developed and enhanced through substantial involvement by international and national NGOs.

At its sixteenth session, an affiliate of International Women's Rights Action Watch (IWRAW), IWRAW (Asia Pacific), in collaboration with the United Nations Development Fund for Women (UNIFEM), organised a training session for NGOs, facilitating the attendance of national NGOs from State Parties reporting at its session. The training session was extremely successful, with CEDAW Committee members finding interaction with the representatives of national NGOs useful. This, combined with the Committee's past experience of the value of NGO input, led the Committee to decide that NGO involvement in its work should be welcomed cautiously, in such a way as to ensure that the independence of experts was not compromised. The Committee decided that from its seventeenth session, the Secretariat should facilitate an informal meeting of NGOs with the Committee outside the Committee's regular time. During such meetings NGOs would be invited to provide country-specific information on the State Parties whose reports were before the Committee. The Committee's decision at the sixteenth session represented a watershed in its relationship with NGOs and provided the basis for more fundamental developments at its seventeenth and eighteenth sessions[60].

The Committee decided at its eighteenth session to increase NGO involvement in the formulation of general recommendations. In 1992, the International League for Human Rights and the IWRAW hosted a conference on violence against women as a contribution to the preparation of General Recommendation No. 19. NGOs have been asked to give their inputs on the general recommendation on temporary special measures to [Article 4 (a)] of the Convention, being currently drafted by the Committee.

During its eighteenth session in January 1998, the CEDAW Committee reached a decision with regard to NGO involvement in the reporting process that moved well beyond its tentative decision at the sixteenth session. Taking advantage of the second IWRAW (Asia/ Pacific)/UNIFEM training programme and the presence of representatives of national NGOs in New York, the pre-sessional working group invited those representatives, as well as those of NGOs, including those working at the international level, to attend its meeting and provide it with country-specific information on those State Parties whose reports were being considered by the working group. The experience proved to be fruitful, with the pre-sessional working groups gaining insights, which enhanced its work. On the recommendation of this group, the Committee plenary decided that representatives of both national and international NGOs would, in future, as a matter of course, be invited to provide country-specific information on State Parties whose reports are being reviewed by the group. Therefore, NGOs are part of the Committee's formal process of preparing recommendations, and formally part of the pre-sessional working group preparation for the review of periodic reports [61].

At its 20th session in 1999, the Committee decided that NGOs could present country-specific information in a working group of the whole. The Secretariat continues to organise informal briefings of the Committee by NGOs outside the Committee's formal meetings. Informal contacts between the NGOs and the Committee and its members are maintained.

NGOs like the IWRAW (Asia Pacific), established for achievement of full potential of CEDAW, play an important role in strengthening the importance of CEDAW and enhancing the effectiveness of the CEDAW Committee. It carries out collaborative projects to facilitate the monitoring and implementation of the Convention regionally and globally.

NGOs play an important role in monitoring and implementing CEDAW by

- Spreading awareness of CEDAW
- Compiling shadow reports to State Party reports submitted to the Committee and assisting the Committee with information
- Lobbying governments, businesses and individuals to implement CEDAW
- Publicising State Party reports and the Committee's concluding comments to a wider national audience

- Providing the Committee with reports on follow-up measures taken by their governments in response to the recommendations contained in the concluding comments

Feminist have often argued that that though CEDAW is a well-meaning effort to recognise and protect women's rights, it has perpetuated the tendency to treat women's concerns as separate from general human rights concerns. However, the charge that women's issues are 'ghettoized' within the United Nations system needs to be viewed in the context that the classic human rights instruments were developed before feminists brought women's concerns to the attention of the international community. There is a growing recognition that women's issues are not separate from the mainstream human rights movement but are a specialised area of the movement. However, the greatest challenge before the CEDAW Committee lies in not creating a 'parallel universe' for women but in bringing gender issues in the mainstream of the human rights agenda.

The CEDAW Committee has taken significant steps to introduce changes in its working methods to make itself an effective instrument for the implementation of the Convention. With the Optional Protocol coming into force, the Committee will have a new avenue for expanding its jurisprudence on women's rights. However, the Committee needs to devise new strategies to deal with the problem of reservations to the substantive provisions of the Convention.

The blame for the failure of international law to protect women's rights cannot be put squarely on CEDAW and its enforcement mechanisms, but on the State Parties' lack of political will to implement their obligations under CEDAW. Most states believe that neglect of obligations imposed by CEDAW will not result in significant national and international political costs. The ultimate criteria for the success of CEDAW is whether it has contributed to a greater awareness and observance of the rights of women in domestic fora. Some steps have been taken in recent years to improve enforcement through dissemination of information and institution building. Women's groups around the world are using the principles enshrined in the Covenant to promote women's rights through court cases and are trying to bring about change in national laws and policies. There are several encouraging examples of invocation of the Convention in domestic courts in countries like Australia (*Aldridge v. Booth*, 1988), Nepal (*Dhangana and another v. Government of Nepal*, 1995), Botswana (*Attorney-General of Botswana v. Unity Dow*, 1995), India (*Vishakha and others v. State of Rajasthan*, 1997, *AEPC v. A.K. Chopra*, 1999). Countries like Panama, Japan and Netherlands have also taken steps to bring their legislation and policies in line with their commitments under the Convention. The Convention is making an impact, though its extent varies from country to country.

CEDAW is a comprehensive bill of rights for women. It has integrated various concerns hitherto expressed in an ad hoc manner. It provides a legal framework for women's rights but it does not automatically confer these rights. However, it legitimises their struggle to realise their rights by providing a set of internationally validated standards. In order to truly exploit the potential of the Convention, women's groups need to build awareness about the provisions of the Convention among national audiences and play an effective role in the reporting and monitoring process.

REFERENCES

1. Charlotte Bunch, "Transforming Human Rights from a Feminist Perspective", in Julia Peters and Andrea Wolper, *Women's Rights. International Feminist Perspective* (London: Routledge, 1995). p. 12.
2. Katarina, Tomasevki, *Women and Human Rights* (London: Zed Books, 1993), p. 100.
3. Anne Gallagher, "Ending the Marginalization: Strategies for Incorporating Women into the United Nations Human Rights System," *Human Rights Quarterly*, Vol. 19, No. 2, May 1997, pp. 296-99.
4. Henry J. Steiner and Philip Alston, *International Human Rights in Context*, (Oxford: Clarendon Press, 1996) pp. 904-05.
5. Anne Gallagher, *op cit.*, pp. 299-302.
6. International Women's Rights Action Watch – Asia Pacific, *CEDAW Convention*, www. iwraw.ap.org
7. Sarah Pritchard, "The Jurisprudence of Human Rights: Some Critical Thoughts and Developments in Practice," *Australian Journal of Human Rights*, Vol. 2, No. 1, 1995.
8. Natalie Hevener Kaufman and Stefanie A. Lindquist, "Critiquing Gender-Neutral Treaty Language: The Convention on the Elimination of Discrimination Against Women," in Julie Peters and Andrea

Wolper (eds.), *Women's Rights. International Feminist Perspectives* (London: Routledge, 1995) p. 114-17.
9. *Ibid.* pp. 122-23.
10. Henry J. Steiner and Philip Alston, *op. cit.*, p. 909.
11. Natalie Hevener Kaufman and Stefanie A. Lindquist, *op. ci t.*, p. 123.
12. Ursula A. O' Hare, Realizing Human Rights for Women, *Human Rights Quarterly*, Vol. 21, No. 2, May 1999, p. 372.
13. Report of the Committee on the Elimination of Discrimination Against Women: General Recommendation No. 12 (8th Session, 1989).
14. Report of the Committee on the Elimination of Discrimination Against Women: General Recommendation No. 14 (9th Session, 1990).
15. Report of the Committee on the Elimination of Discrimination Against Women: General Recommendation No. 19 (11th Session, 1992).
16. *Ibid.*
17. Henry J. Stiner and Philip Alston, *op. cit* p. 919.
18. Aaron Xavier Fellmeth, "Feminism and International Law: Theory, Methodology and Substantive Reform, " *Human Rights Quarterly*, Vol. 22, No. 3, August 2000, pp. 688, 695.
19. Henry J. Steiner and Philip Alston, *op. cit*, p. 919.
20. Katarina Tomasevki, *op. cit*, p. 119.
21. Henry J. Stiener and Philip Alston, *op. cit*, p. 919.
22. United Nations Secretariat, *Ways and Means of Expediting the Work of the Committee*, 25th Session, CEDAW / C / 2001 / 11, 30th May, p. 7.
23. Report of the Committee on the Elimination of Discrimination Against Women: General Recommendation No. 4 (6th Session, 1987).
24. Report of the Committee on the Elimination of Discrimination Against Women: General Recommendation No. 21 (13th Session, 1994).
25. United Nations Secretariat, *op. cit*, p. 7.
26. Roberta Jackson, "The Committee on the Elimination of Discrimination Against Women," in Philip Alston (ed.) *The United Nations and Human Rights* (Oxford: Clarendon Press, 1992), p. 448.
27. Katarina Tomasevki, *op cit*, p. 119.
28. "Report of the Sub-Commission on Prevention of Discrimination and Protection of Minorities on its Forty-third Session, Geneva, 5-30 August, 1991, "UN Document, E/CN/Sub. 2/1991/ 65 of 24 October 1991, pp. 145-46.
29. Ursula A. O' Hare, "Realizing Human Rights for Women, " *Human Rights Quarterly*, Vol. 21, No. 2, May 1999, p. 386
30. Convention on the Elimination of All forms of Discrimination Against Women. Twentieth Anniversary (1979-1999). CEDAW Information Note 5, UN Division for the Advancement of Women, 1999.

31. Optional Protocol to the Women's Convention Comes inti Force, PI/ 1317, WOM/ 1242, 21st Deecember 2000.
32. Ursula A O' Hare, *op cit.*, p. 389.
33. The General Assembly noted the amendment with approval by Resolution A / RES/ 50/202. adopted on 22nd December 1995.
34. Statement by Ms Angela E. V. King. Special Advisor on Gender Issues and Advancement of Women to the CEDAW Committee at its Exceptional Session, 21st August, 2002 at http: // www.un.org/ womenwatch/ daw / cedaw
35. General Assembly Resolution A / RES/ 51/ 66 adopted in 1996.
36. Committee on Elimination of Discrimination Concludes Twenty-Seventh Session, Press Release WOM / 1349, 21 st June, 2002.
37. CEDAW Reporting Process at www. iwraw.ap.or.
38. CEDAW / C / 2002/ EXC / 1.
39. Marie R. Bustelo, "The Committee on the Elimination of Discrimination Against Women at the Crossroads, " in Philip Alston and James Crawford, *The Future of UN Human Rights Treaty Monitoring*, (Cambridge: Cambridge University Press, 2000), pp. 81-84.
40. *Ibid.* p. 85.
41. *Ibid.* 85-86.
42. Marie R. Bustelo, *op cit.*, p. 89.
43. CEDAW, 26th session, A/57/38 (Part I), May 7, 2002.
44. CEDAW/C/2002/EXC/1.
45. *Ibid.*
46. Report of the Secretariat, Ways and Means of Expediting the Work of the Committee, CEDAW/C/2001/11/4, pp. 3-4.
47. *Ibid.*, pp. 4-5
48. *Ibid.*, pp. 5-6.
49. *Ibid.* p. 6.
50. *Ibid.*
51. daw@ un.org.
52. *Ibid.*
53. Marie R. Bustelo, op. cit., p. 81-83.
54. *Ibid*, pp. 82-84.
55. *Ibid.*, pp. 97-100.
56. *Ibid.*, pp. 101-02.
57. Roberta Jackson, "The Committee on the Elimination of Discrimination Against Women," in Philip Alston (ed.), *The United Nations and Human Rights. A Critical Appraisal.* (Oxford: Clarendon Press, 1992), p. 466.
58. Marie R. Bustelo, *op cit.*, pp 103-04.
59. *Ibid.*, p. 104.
60. *Ibid.*, pp 105-06.
61. *Ibid.*, pp. 106-07.

Chapter 3

Women Workers in India

Women in India belong to those marginalised groups of society, which face discrimination in practically every sphere and every stage of their life. The study of women as a category of workers is of crucial importance because the economic role that women play cannot be isolated from their total well being. The process of 'empowerment' of women depends crucially on their economic empowerment. Though a mere increase in work force participation rate of women cannot be a goal by itself, an increase in employment would help in improving their economic and social status. There is also a direct relationship between women's employment and well being of the community. An increase in women's income translates directly into better child health and nutrition status.

The work participation rates for women in India are much lower that that for males. To a certain extent, this is because there is an under-estimation of women's work in the existing data systems. The problem of under enumeration is both because of a conceptual bias and operational problems in data collection systems. Conventional standards for measurement of the labour force followed by data collection systems are based on western concepts which fail to capture women's work in the non monetised sectors, for example, women contributing as helpers in family-based economic activities or doing subsistence production for self consumption or even home based workers. Difficulties in proper enumeration also arise because of biases of the interviewer and respondent at the operational level. Rigid notions about gender roles prevail in our society. Women are viewed primarily as housewives and any economic activities they may perform along with their domestic chores tend to remain under reported either by women themselves or more often by male respondents who speak on behalf of women[1]. The biases and perceptions of the enumerators, who often lack sensitivity and training in conducting interviews, may also lead to inaccuracies.

Economists and feminist scholars have stressed the necessity for proper measurement of women's work because accurate data would provide proper recognition of women's work and help in identification of problems faced by them and would thus be an impetus for changes in policy. Under enumeration of women's work reinforces social prejudices like women are basically 'supplementary earners' or a 'reserve labour force' or that they are mainly housewives and their work does not count [2].

The Census of India and the National Sample Survey Organisation (NSSO) are the two main sources of data on women's employment. The census data has suffered from the problem of under enumeration of women's participation in economic activities. There have also been wide fluctuations in census data on women's work participation rate. This is partly because of the adoption of differing concepts and definitions of 'work' in the various censuses. This has resulted in the census data not being strictly comparable from one census to the other. Data up to the 1951 census was based on the 'income concept' while the subsequent censuses were designed according to 'time' or 'labour force concept'. In the 1961 census, a person was considered a 'worker' if he/she participated in any economically productive work. In the case of regular employment in any trade or service, a person to be treated as 'worker' should have been employed during any of the 15 days preceding the day of enumeration. An exception was made in the case of seasonal work. A person who had put in an hour's regular work a day throughout the greater part of the working season was considered a worker. The 1961 census covered even very marginal work.

The 1971 census made this definition more rigorous. It included only those persons whose main activity in the reference year was participation in any economically productive work. A person engaged in household activities, even if he or she helped in the family economic activity but not as a full time worker, was not treated as a worker in this census. This change in definition, to a certain extent, explains why workforce participation rates for women fell from 27.96 percent in 1961 to 14.15 percent in 1971 census.

The 1981 census divided workers into 2 categories: (1) main workers or those who had worked in some economic activity for a period of 6 months or more (2) marginal workers or those who had worked for less than 6 months. A uniform reference period of one-year preceding the enumeration was adopted for recording activity status in 1981 census, irrespective if whether the activity was seasonal or regular.

The 1991 census followed the same definition of work as the 1981 census. With a view to include persons engaged in unpaid work on farm or in family enterprises, the phrase "including unpaid work on farm or family enterprises" was inserted in the schedule itself. In order to ensure that the economic activity of unpaid workers on farm or in family enterprises was properly enumerated in the 1991 census, the instructions to census enumerators were expanded and emphasis was put on asking probing questions regarding work done at any time at all in the last year or in any of the seasons in the reference period, specifically in the case of women.

The Census of India recognises production for own consumption in cultivation as economic activity. The term cultivation in the census covers only growing certain crops such as cereals, millets, sugarcane etc. Growing of plantation crops, vegetables and other crops for self-consumption are not considered economic activity. Processing of primary commodities for own consumption and own account production of fixed assets are also excluded from the purview of economic activity. In other words, with the exception of cultivation, the census does not include the non-market economic activities as work.

The NSS has a broader definition of 'work'. The NSS, since its 27th Round in 1972-73, has conducted quinquennial surveys on employment/unemployment based on the technique of random sampling in rural and urban areas. According to the 55th Round of the NSS (1999-2000), the term economic activity includes:

(i) all the market activities performed for pay or profit, which results in production of goods and services for exchange

(ii) of the non-market activities:

  (a) all the activities relating to the agricultural sector which result in production (including gathering of uncultivated crops, forestry, collection of firewood hunting, fishing etc) of agricultural produce for own consumption and

(b) activities relating to the own-account production of fixed assets. Own account production of fixed assets include construction of own houses, roads, wells etc, and of machinery, tools etc. for household enterprise and also construction of any private or community facilities free of charge.

Unpaid helpers who assist in the operation of an economic activity in the household farm or non-farm activities were also considered as workers.

While both market and non-market activities for the agriculture sector are included in the definition of work, for the non-agriculture sector only market activities are included.

The NSS employment surveys define three different levels of employment: usual status, current weekly status and current daily status. The corresponding reference time periods are one year, one week and each day of the week.

Although there have been refinements in the definition of the term 'work' and the degree to which women's work goes under enumerated has reduced, the problem of inaccurate measurement still persists. Several studies have shown that there is still large scale under enumeration of women workers. The 1991 census itself acknowledged such possibilities by initiating special steps to ensure better enumeration of women workers. Yet, a study conducted to verify the accuracy of the 1991 census workforce estimates in some villages by the Self Employed Women's Association (SEWA) showed that the census workforce count was way below the physical count made by SEWA [3].

Both the census and the NSS deviate from standard international practice for the measurement of workforce. Neither the census nor the NSS take into account primary activities (other than agriculture) for household consumption, or processing of primary products for household consumption. Though both the census and NSS data are helpful in arriving at a broad picture of the pattern of the workforce participation, they need to be substantiated by micro-level studies to arrive at an accurate picture. Moreover, since both data systems use different definitions of 'work', they are not strictly comparable.

To understand the macro level picture of women's employment in India, we have looked at data from two sources:

1. Census of India. While the 2001 census data is not yet released, some provisional data has been made available and is useful for analysing trends at an aggregate level.
2. NSSO data. The 55th round of the NSS (July 199-June 2000) has reported on the Employment and Unemployment Situation in India 1999-2000, and this forms a useful source of data for meaningful analysis.

Census Data

The Work Participation Rate (WPR), which is defined as the percentage of total workers to the total population is the basic variable that we look at to analyse trends from 1981 to 2001. We have excluded data pertaining to Jammu and Kashmir and Assam given the non-availability of data from these states for some previous censuses. This leads to a small change in data as reported here v/s overall data as per the Census 2001. Also, data from Kachchh, Rajkot and Jamnagar, where Census could not be held in 2001 has not been excluded from previous censuses, but this is not expected to affect the analysis.

Table 1 : Work Participation Rate*

	Total Workers			*Main Workers*			*Marginal Workers*		
	2001	*1991*	*1981*	*2001*	*1991*	*1981*	*2001*	*1991*	*1981*
	Percentage of total population								
Total	39.4	37.5	36.7	30.7	34.2	33.5	8.7	3.3	3.2
Male	52.0	51.6	52.6	45.5	51	51.6	6.5	0.6	1
Female	25.8	22.3	19.7	14.9	16	14.1	11.0	6.2	5.6
Rural	42.2	40.1	38.8	31.3	35.8	34.8	10.9	4.3	4
Male	52.5	52.6	53.8	44.7	51.9	52.6	7.8	0.7	1.2
Female	31.3	26.8	23.1	17.1	18.8	16.1	14.2	8	6.9
Urban	32.2	30.2	30	29.3	29.5	29.2	2.9	0.7	0.8
Male	50.8	48.9	49.1	47.4	48.6	48.5	3.4	0.4	0.5
Female	11.6	9.2	8.3	9.2	8.2	7.3	2.4	1	1

* Excluding Assam and Jammu & Kashmir

Source : Census of India

As can be seen from the Table 1, though the rate of growth in WPR for women is higher than that for men over the last two decades, women still lag behind males in terms of WPR (25.8 per cent for women compared to 52 per cent for men as per 2001 Census). While the WPR for males has been mostly stagnant over the last two decades, the WPR for females has shown a better growth, rising from 19.7 in 1981 to 25.8 in 2001.

The increase in female WPR is mainly due to increase in proportion of female rural marginal workers which registered significant increase from 6.9 (1981) percent to 14.2 percent (2001); this trend is also true for male rural marginal workers.

The 2001 Census results show a marked change in the composition of marginal workers:

- In 1991, 99 per cent of total men workers were main workers; this ratio fell to 87.5 per cent in 2001 and correspondingly the ratio of marginal workers to total workers for men increased from 1 per cent in 1991 to 12.5 per cent in 2001
- For women, the ratio of marginal workers to total workers increased from 28 per cent in 1991 to 43 per cent in 2001. Correspondingly, the ratio of main workers to total workers for women reduced from 72 per cent in 1991 to 57 per cent in 2001
- The increase in the ratio of men marginal workers in 2001 had a substantive change in the composition of marginal workers. In 1991, 91 per cent of marginal workers were women, and this ratio fell to 61 per cent in 2001

This change in composition of marginal workers shows the growing "feminization of the labour force," implying that men are now working under many of the same conditions that women worked earlier in – lack of job security and low wages.

Some other interesting data that emerges from the 2001 Census (provisional data) is that in rural areas while the proportion of workers engaged as cultivators among males (42.2) exceed those among females (36.50), in the category of agricultural labourers the proportion of workers among females (43.4) far exceed the males (27.5). There is larger proportion of female workers engaged in Household Industries than males both in rural as well as urban areas.

Table 2 gives details of classification of working population across various parameters. It is observed that:

- the compounded annual growth rate (CAGR) for female workers is significantly higher at 3.50 per cent (1991-2001) as compared to 1.98 per cent for males in the similar period, and this is the case for the previous two decades also
- the CAGR for marginal workers is significantly higher than the growth rate for main workers in 1991-2001. As analyzed above, men were the main contributor to the higher growth in marginal workers in this decade
- urban growth rates in working population have been consistently higher than the rural growth rates over the last three decades, reflecting the decreasing share of agriculture in India's GDP over time.

Table 2 Classification of Working Population *

	2001	*1991*	*1981*	*1971*
		millions		
Total workers	389	306	242	181
CAGR	2.44%	2.37%	2.97%	
Of which:				
Rural	299	242	195	149
CAGR	2.16%	2.16%	2.73%	
Urban	90	64	47	32
CAGR	3.41%	3.21%	4.03%	
Male	266	219	179	144
CAGR	1.98%	2.00%	2.19%	
Female	123	87	63	36
CAGR	3.50%	3.38%	5.62%	
Main	304	279	221	175
CAGR	0.85%	2.37%	2.35%	
Marginal	86	27	21	6
CAGR	12.20%	2.44%	14.09%	

* Excluding Assam and Jammu & Kashmir
CAGR = Compounded Annual Growth Rate
Source : Census of India

In the light of the above, it is interesting to note that eCENSUS India Issue No. 7: 2002 28 FEBRUARY 2002, makes, *inter-alia*, the following observations:

- The percentage increase in the female workers between 1991 and 2001 was a whopping 40.6 percent when the female population during the corresponding period increased by 21.7 percent. Significantly higher rate of growth of female workers as compared to growth of female population clearly brings out better capture of women's work at the Census 2001 especially in certain parts of the country.
- It may be noted that while the percentage decadal growths of female population in rural and urban areas were 18.3 and 31.7 respectively, corresponding percentage in the decadal growth recorded for female workers were 37.6 percent and 66.1 percent.
- Out of the net addition of 85 million workers between 1991 and 2001 Censuses, 60 million (about 70 percent) came from marginal worker category. Among the females, the net accretion of 36 million total workers, 28 million (77 percent) were marginal workers.
- The significantly large increase in the number of female cultivators and agricultural labourers during 1991-2001 is largely perhaps due to improved coverage of female workers.
- The preliminary data on workers and their categories have already sprung up several surprises, which needs to be further analysed in the context of the liberalization of economy in the early nineties.

Comparison with NSSO Rates: A comparison of the WPR as per the provisional results of the Census of India 2001, was made with the WPR estimated on the basis of sample survey by National Sample Survey Organisation (NSSO) in India. At the all India level, as the following table would show, the difference between the two sets of returns is marginal:

Statement showing Work Participation Rate as returned in 2001 Census (Provisional) and as given by NSSO

	Work Participation Rate (WPR)			
	Persons/ Males/ Females	As per2001 Census (Provisional)	As per NSSO*	Difference
India	Persons	39.26	38.85	0.41
	Males	51.93	54.1	-2.17
	Females	25.68	22.45	3.23

Note: SSO (National Sample Survey Organisation) estimates WPR on the basis of sample survey in India. The figure quoted above refers to 55th Round (July 1999). The WPR refers to Usual Status (i.e., Principal Status and Subsidiary Status).

NSS Data

As per the NSSO, compared to the census population or the projections thereof, population estimates from the NSSO surveys are, in general, on the lower side. This difference arises mainly due to the differences in methods and coverage adopted by the NSSO in comparison to the census operation. However, the ratio obtained from the survey are much closer to the ratios obtained using the census figures. Given that we will mainly be using the NSSO ratios (and not absolute numbers) in this study, the analysis is expected to be relevant and meaningful.

NSS Data would also help us look at sectoral trends in employment of women. We will look at WPR trends across status of employment, geographical, literacy, age and industry level distributions.

NSS Definitions

Usual activity status refers to the activity status of the person during the reference period of 365 days preceding the date of survey.

The activity status over which the person spent relatively longer time (i.e. major time criterion) during the 365 days preceding the date of survey is considered as the ***principal usual activity status*** of the person.

A person whose principal usual status was determined on the basis of the major time criterion could have pursued some economic activity for a relatively shorter time (minor time) during the reference period of 365 days preceding the date of survey. The status in which such economic activity was pursued was the ***subsidiary economic activity status*** of that person.

WPR Trends

In Table 3 estimates are presented for two categories viz. (a) "usually employed" in the principal status (ps workers) and (b) "usually employed" *only* in a subsidiary status (ss workers). The two categories constitute the total usually employed (or "all" workers).

Table 3 : Number of persons employed per 1000 persons according to usual status

NSS Round (year)	*Category of worker*	*Rural*			*Urban*			*All*		
		M	*F*	*P*	*M*	*F*	*P*	*M*	*F*	*P*
55	ps	522	231	380	513	117	324	520	203	365
(1999-00)	ss	9	68	37	5	22	13	7	56	32
	all	*531*	*299*	*417*	*518*	*139*	*337*	*527*	*259*	*397*
50	ps	538	234	390	513	121	327	532	206	375
(1993-94)	ss	15	94	54	8	34	20	13	80	45
	all	*553*	*328*	*444*	*521*	*155*	*347*	*545*	*286*	*420*
43	ps	517	245	385	496	118	315	512	217	369
(1987-88)	ss	22	78	49	10	34	22	19	68	43
	all	*539*	*323*	*434*	*506*	*152*	*337*	*531*	*285*	*412*
38	ps	528	248	391	500	120	320	521	218	374
-1983	ss	19	92	54	12	31	20	17	78	46
	all	*547*	*340*	*445*	*512*	*151*	*340*	*538*	*296*	*420*
32	ps	537	248	395	497	123	319	529	224	371
(1977-78)	ss	15	83	49	11	33	22	14	73	52
	all	*552*	*331*	*444*	*508*	*156*	*341*	*543*	*297*	*423*
27	ps									
(1972-73)	ss									
	all	*545*	*318*	*	*501*	*134*	*	*	*	*

ps = principal status; ss = subsidiary status * : proportions not derived for NSS 27th round

Source : NSS Report No.458 : Employment and Unemployment Situation in India, 1999-2000

From the table, we can observe the following trends in WPR :

- While the WPR (all persons) has fallen by 2.3 per cent in 1999-00 v/s 1993-94 (and for the first time below 40 per cent), the WPR for women (ps+ss) has shown a sharper fall of 2.7 per cent in the same period
- The percentage of women employed in subsidiary status (ss workers) as a proportion of the percentage of all women employed (ss+ps) is much higher at 21.62 per cent vs 1.35 per cent for men (1999-00); and within women the rural ratio at 29.44 per cent is higher than the 15.83 per cent in urban areas. This would be primarily be explained by women's contribution towards agriculture activities under the subsidiary status, though the ratio (rural) has declined to 29.44 per cent from 40.17 per cent in 1993-94.

Comparison with Census Data

The significant difference in NSS data trends when compared with the Census data trends lies in the WPR for women; while the Census data shows a growth in WPR from 19.7 per cent (1981) to 25.8 per cent (2001), the NSS data shows a fall from 29.6 (1983) to 25.9 per cent (1999-00). Though the NSS ratios almost coincide (NSS 55th round and Census 2001), these differ widely in the previous years.

For analysis of the current WPR trends, we will take advantage of the ready availability of data classified on varying parameters (age, geography etc.) in the NSS 55th round to look at variations in WPR for women across these parameters.

NSS WPR Trends : Geographical Distribution

WPR varies considerably across States/U.T.'s both for rural and urban persons. For rural female population, the ratio varies from a high of 47.8 per cent (Andhra Pradesh) to a low of 7.3 per cent (Tripura), leaving aside Delhi with a ratio of 2.9 per cent as an outlier. Other states with a high rural female WPR (> 40%) are Gujarat, Himachal Pradesh, Maharashtra, Meghalaya, Mizoram, Nagaland and Tamil Nadu.

For urban female population, Mizoram (25.9%) has the highest WPR ratio, while J&K (6.2%) has the lowest ratio. It is also observed that high rural female WPR need not necessarily imply a high urban female WPR, though in most cases both move in tandem vis a vis the all India averages.

The state wise variations are covered in the NSS Report No.458: Employment and Unemployment Situation in India, 1999-2000.

Table 4 : Number of employed per 1000 persons according to usual status taking both principal and subsidiary statuses into consideration by sex and residence for States and Union Territories during 1999-2000

State / U.T	*Employed persons per 1000 population*					
	Rural			*Urban*		
	Male	*Female*	*Person*	*Male*	*Female*	*Person*
Andhra Pradesh	605	478	542	511	178	348
Arunachal Pradesh	422	310	369	399	100	267
Assam	529	151	349	522	112	332
Bihar	492	173	338	432	75	266
Goa	539	181	359	498	106	309
Gujarat	584	413	499	536	135	345
Harayana	475	202	346	506	98	314
Himachal Pradesh	536	471	203	499	130	322
J&K	548	327	442	478	62	281
Karnataka	595	380	487	545	178	366
Kerela	553	238	387	558	203	373
Madhya Pradesh	536	382	462	488	134	319
Maharashtra	531	434	484	532	137	346
Manipur	495	253	380	445	211	330
Meghalaya	557	418	486	393	197	296
Mizoram	555	440	499	471	259	363
Nagalan	518	441	482	393	199	305
Orrisa	551	299	423	475	145	317
Punjab	530	280	410	549	125	353
Rajasthan	500	388	446	486	138	323
Sikkim	502	241	380	519	200	375
Tamil Nadu	594	430	513	563	215	393
Tripura	504	73	303	494	75	295
Uttar Pradesh	481	201	345	490	94	304
West Bengal	534	160	349	567	117	350
A&N Islands	547	180	371	632	206	422
Chandigarh	784	128	635	547	136	351
D&N Haveli	582	354	470	656	112	404
Daman & Diu	655	300	503	549	186	376
Delhi	520	29	308	528	105	332
Lakshwadeep	497	115	285	432	179	308
Pondicherry	560	287	425	555	169	352
All India	**531**	**299**	**417**	**518**	**139**	**337**

Source: NSS Report No.458 : Employment and Unemployment Situation in India, 1999-2000

WPR Trends : Age Composition

Table 3 shows the per 1000 distribution of usually employed persons by age group for all workers.

Table 5: Per 1000 distribution of usually employed by age group

Age Group	*Rural*		*Urban*	
	Male	*Female*	*Male*	*Female*
0-4	—	—	—	—
5-9	2	3	1	2
	3	*5*	*1*	*3*
10-14	22	37	11	29
	30	*46*	*15*	*33*
15-19	94	90	67	78
	107	*100*	*77*	*82*
20-24	122	118	122	105
	126	*126*	*124*	*114*
25-29	134	137	145	126
	128	*137*	*146*	*130*
15-29	350	345	334	309
	361	*363*	*347*	*326*
30-34	122	139	139	137
	121	*131*	*142*	*138*
35-39	121	129	139	159
	115	*115*	*132*	*142*
40-44	98	101	122	117
	88	*96*	*113*	*111*
30-44	341	369	400	413
	324	*342*	*387*	*391*
45-49	85	85	97	93
	80	*86*	*94*	*93*
50-54	66	62	70	65
	66	*62*	*65*	*64*
55-59	50	45	43	42
	50	*45*	*45*	*42*
45-59	201	192	210	200
	196	*193*	*204*	*199*
60 & above	85	53	45	48
	86	*51*	*47*	*47*
All	1000	1000	1000	1000

Figures in italics are corresponding figures for 1993-94, NSS 50th Round

Source: NSS Report No.458 : Employment and Unemployment Situation in India, 1999-2000

The table shows a significant concentration of the usually employed in the age bracket of 15-44. The proportion of usually employed females in this age bracket is 69 per cent in rural and 73 per cent in urban areas.

Chart 1
Per 1000 distribution of usually employed age group: Comparison between NSS 50th and 55th rounds

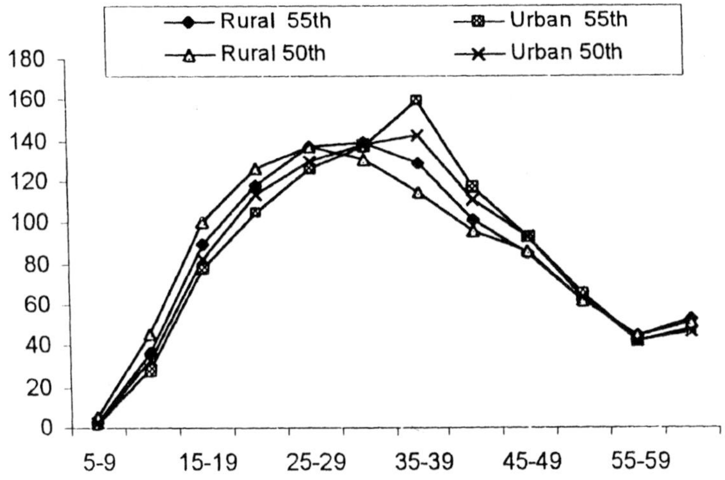

Chart I shows that the age distribution of the usually employed has remained mostly similar, except for a blip in the Urban 55th round 35-39 age group. A pictorial representation of age distribution in the NSS 55th Round is as below :

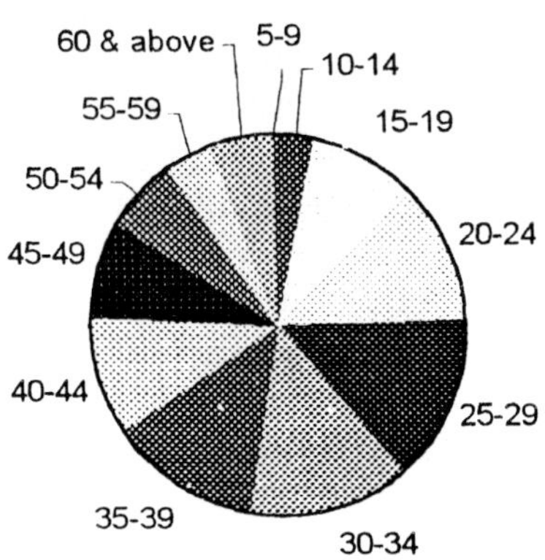

55th Round : Rural Female

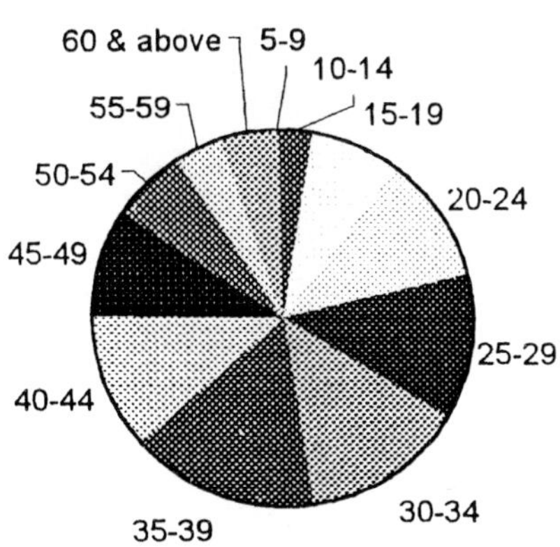

55th Round : Urban Female

WPR Trends : Literacy

Table 6 : Per 1000 distribution of usually employed of age 15 Years and above by education category (all workers)

Education Category	*Rural*		*Urban*		*Total*	
	Male	*Female*	*Male*	*Female*	*Male*	*Female*
Not Literate	396 *437*	739 *785*	160 *184*	439 *489*	278 *311*	589 *637*
Literate and upto Primary	273 *291*	155 *142*	219 *258*	176 *197*	246 *275*	166 *170*
Middle	163 *137*	62 *43*	188 *173*	103 *84*	176 *155*	83 *64*
Secondary	93 *75*	28 *19*	169 *155*	88 *76*	131 *115*	58 *48*
Higher Secondary	42 *33*	9 *6*	94 *87*	55 *47*	68 *60*	32 *27*
Graduate & above	33 *26*	6 *4*	168 *143*	139 *106*	101 *85*	73 *55*
All	1000	1000	1000	1000	1000	1000

Figures in italics are corresponding figures for 1993-94, NSS 50th round

Source : NSS Report No.458 : Employment and Unemployment Situation in India, 1999-2000

This table highlights the glaring divergence in male and female worker literacy levels :

- As per NSS 55th round data, 58.9 per cent of female workers are not literate, as against 27.8 per cent of male workers falling in this category. This ratio varies significantly between rural and urban workers
- 73.9 per cent of rural female workers are in the non literate category; only 1.5 per cent have studied till higher secondary or above
- While the overall female non literate ratio has decreased as compared to the NSS 50th round, the rate of decrease is much faster for male workers than for female workers
- The higher non literate ratio amongst female workers is to be seen in the light of the broad industry division of labour (below) where a significant proportion of female workers are employed in agriculture.

WPR Trends : Broad Industry Groups

Table 7 : Changes in the distribution of male and female workers in broad industry groups between 1983 and 1989-2000

Rural *(Percent)*

Year	*NSS*	*Male*			*Female*		
		Primary	*Secondary*	*Tertiary*	*Primary*	*Secondary*	*Tertiary*
1983	38th	77.5	10.0	12.2	87.5	7.4	4.8
1999-2000	55th	71.4	12.6	16.0	85.4	8.9	5.7

Urban *(Percent)*

Year	*NSS*	*Male*			*Female*		
		Primary	*Secondary*	*Tertiary*	*Primary*	*Secondary*	*Tertiary*
1983	38th	10.3	34.2	55.0	31.0	30.6	37.6
1999-2000	55th	6.6	32.8	60.6	17.7	29.3	52.9

Source : NSSO Reports

As seen from the above report, the primary sector is the main employer of women in the rural areas, with the proportion having come down marginally over the last two decades.

In the urban areas, the proportion of women employed in the tertiary sector has increased to more than 50 per cent, reflecting the increasing employment of women in the growing service sector of the economy.

The table highlights the status of agriculture as the dominant employment category in rural India; 85.4 per cent of all rural female workers and 71.4 per cent of all rural male workers are employed in this sector.

In urban India, manufacturing, trade, hotel and restaurant and services sectors are the main employers. The top ten manufacturing industries that employ women in large numbers are:

a) Tobacco
b) Cotton textiles
c) Cashewnut Processing
d) Machine tools and parts
e) Matches, explosives and fireworks

f) Clay, glass, cement, iron and steel
g) Drugs and medicines
h) Grain mill and bakery
i) Garments

WPR Trends : Industrial Distribution

Table 8 : Per 1000 distribution of usually employed by broad industry division (all workers)

Education Category	*Rural*		*Urban*		*Total*	
	Male	*Female*	*Male*	*Female*	*Male*	*Female*
Agriculture	714	854	66	177	390	516
	741	*862*	*90*	*247*	*416*	*555*
Mining & quarrying	6	3	9	4	8	4
	7	*4*	*13*	*6*	*10*	*5*
Manufacturing	73	76	224	240	149	158
	70	*70*	*235*	*241*	*153*	*156*
Electricity, water Etc.	2	0	8	2	5	1
	3	*0*	*12*	*3*	*8*	*2*
Construction	45	11	87	48	66	30
	32	*9*	*69*	*41*	*51*	*25*
Trade, hotel & Restaurant	68	20	294	169	163	95
	55	*21*	*219*	*100*	*110*	*61*
Transport, storage & communications	32	1	104	18	80	10
	22	*1*	*97*	*13*	*49*	*7*
Services	61	37	210	342	116	190
	70	*34*	*264*	*350*	*132*	*192*
All	1000	1000	1000	1000	1000	1000

Figures in italics are corresponding figures for 1993-94, NSS 50th round

Source : NSS Report No. 458 : Employment and Unemployment Situation in India, 1999-2000

WPR Trends : Organized and Unorganized Sectors

The data for this analysis is obtained from census data till 1991 (latest census data is not available presently)

It is observed from Table 9 that :

- The growth in total employment in the organized sector during the decade 1981-91 (16.85%) was much slower than the growth in total employment in the unorganized sector (39.96%) and we expect that this trend would have continued in the decade 1991-2001, though actual data is not available

- In the same time frame, growth in female employment in the unorganized sector was staggeringly high (101.09%, i.e. the number of female unorganized workers more than doubled in 1981-91). By way of comparison, the growth in female employment in the organized sector was lower at 35.37 per cent
- As seen in the charts above, in 1991, 96 per cent of females were employed in the unorganized sector, and this ratio was 90 per cent for men. It can be seen that unorganized sector is the major provider of employment in India.
- The following charts show pictorially the disparity in male – female employment in both organized and unorganized sectors

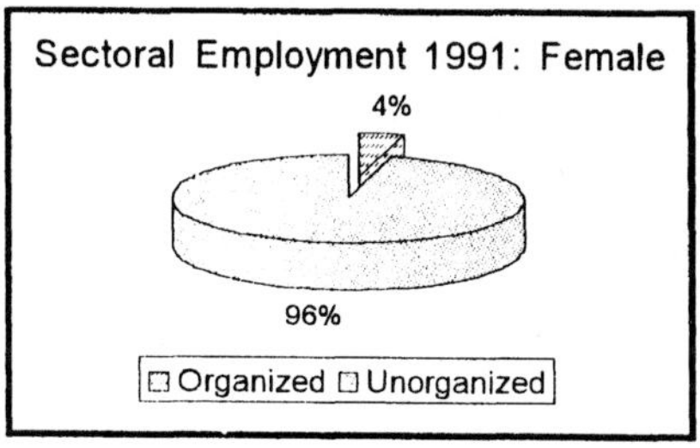

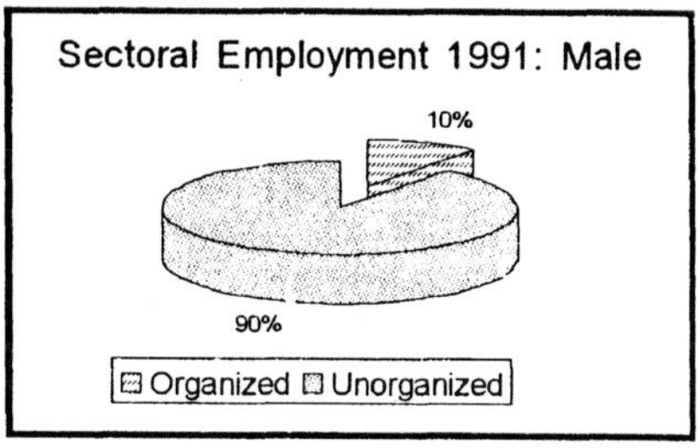

The share of women in the organized sector was at 14 per cent in 1991, and this is em.1stimated to have grown to 17.2 per cent in 1999 as per the Tenth Five Year Plan document. Though the ratio has increased, it still continues to be sharply lower as compared to the ratio for men.

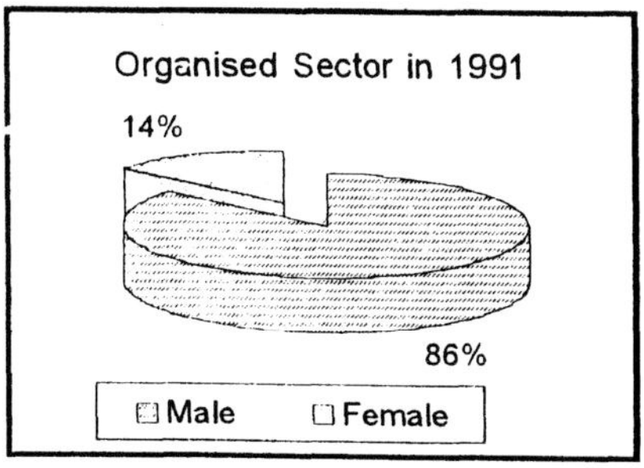

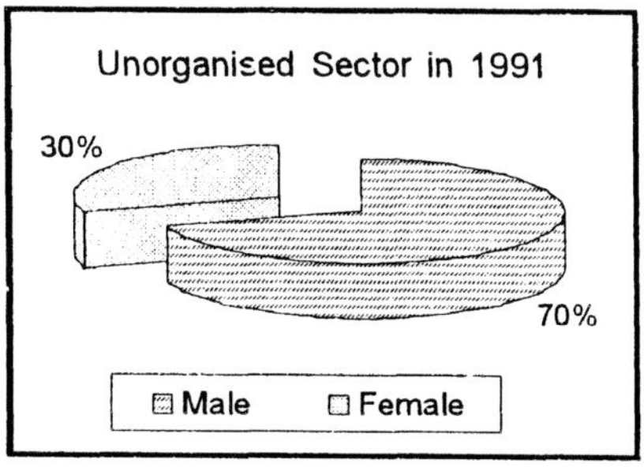

Table 9 : Employment in the Organized and Unorganized Sectors during 1971 to 1991 (in Lakhs)

Year	*Male*			*Female*			*Total*		
	Organized Sector	*Unorganized Sector*	*Total*	*Organized Sector*	*Unorganized Sector*	*Total*	*Organized Sector*	*Unorganized Sector*	*Total*
1971	155.6	1336.16	1491.76	19.3	294.15	313.45	174.9	1630.21	1805.11
1981	200.86	1625.75	1826.61	27.93	427.59	455.52	228.79	2053.34	2282.13
1991	229.53	2014.11	2243.64	37.81	859.86	897.67	267.34	2873.87	3141.21

Source : Sarla Gopalan, Women and Employment in India, 1995

In the unorganized sector, the share of women in total employment at 30 per cent is relatively highèr than their share in the organized sector, predominantly due to their contribution in agriculture and related activities.

Within the organized sector, the share of women workers in the public sector has shown a steady increase over time as can be seen in Table 9.

Table 10 : Women in the Public Sector

Millions

Year	*Women*	*Men*	*Total*
1981	1.5	14	15.5
per cent of Total	9.7%	90.3%	
1991	2.4	16.7	19.1
per cent of Total	12.6%	87.4%	
1999	2.8	16.6	19.4
per cent of Total	14.4%	85.6%	

Source : Tenth Five Year Plan 2002-07, 2002

The same is true for women in the Government, increasing from 1.2 million (11% of total) in 1981 to 1.6 million (14.6% of total) in 1997.

However, in the decision making levels of Government, the ratio of women in lower than the overall ratio as can be seen from Table 10. The share of women IAS and IPS officers at 7.2 per cent of total in 1997 is significantly lower than the 14.6 per cent share of women in Government.

Table 11 : Representation of Women in Premier Services (1987-2000)

Service	*1987*	*1997*	*2000*
1981	1.5	14	15.5
IAS	339	512	535
per cent of Total	7.50%	10.20%	10.40%
IPS	21	67	110
per cent of Total	0.90%	2.20%	3.30%
Total	360	579	645
per cent of Total	5.40%	7.20%	7.60%

Source : Tenth Five Year Plan 2002-07,2002

WPR Trends : Employment Status

Table 12 : Changes in the distribution of Employment Status categories over time

Rural

Year	NSS Round	Male			Female		
		Self-employed	*Regular*	*Casual*	*Self-employed*	*Regular*	*Casual*
1983	38th	60.5	10.3	29.2	61.9	2.8	35.3
1987-88	43rd	58.6	10.0	31.4	60.8	3.7	35.5
1993-94	50th	57.9	8.3	33.8	58.5	2.8	38.7
1999-2000	55th	55.0	8.8	36.2	57.3	3.1	39.6

Urban

Year	NSS Round	Male			Female		
		Self-employed	*Regular*	*Casual*	*Self-employed*	*Regular*	*Casual*
1983	38th	40.9	43.7	15.4	45.8	25.8	28.4
1987-88	43rd	41.7	43.7	14.6	47.1	27.5	25.4
1993-94	50th	41.7	42.1	16.2	45.4	28.6	26.2
1999-2000	55th	41.5	41.7	16.8	45.3	33.3	21.4

Source : NSSO Reports

In the rural areas, there has been an increase in the proportion of casual labour over time and this trend is true for both male and female workers. This seems to be a fall out of fragmentation of land holdings and increase in landless households, increasing the pressure on casual labour.

In the urban areas, we have seen an increase in the proportion of women in regular employment and a corresponding fall in women employed as casual labour.

In summary, WPR trends vary significantly across various parameters, and a look at each of these gives us insight towards better understanding the status of women workers in India.

Gender-based Disparity In Wages

To quote the report of the National Commission on Labour:

"There is increasing inequality in the labour market, and wage differentials present among various groups and various sectors of the economy. There are large inter-industry and intra-industry wage differentials. In different sectors of the economy, a worker will be paid differently though he may be doing the same kind of job. Even in the same industry, different units may pay different wages for the worker who is having the same measurable skills." Though this observation is directed by the Commission more towards the organised sector, intuitively is seems apt to describe the gender-based disparities in wages.

The NSSO data for 1987-88 and 1993-94 provides a useful framework for understanding the disparities. Table 13 gives women's wages as a proportion of men's wages in the same industry across various education categories for urban India. This Table shows that women workers in urban India are subject to negative gender based wage discrimination across all industry divisions.

- At an aggregate level, women workers in urban India received 83 per cent of the wages paid to men workers in 1987-88, and this ratio has declined to 79.8 per cent in 1993-94
- This ratio is more weighted against the women workers at the lower end of the literacy spectrum; non literate women workers received 59 per cent of the wages paid to non literate male workers in 1987-88, and this ratio declined to 57.8 per cent in 1993-94
- Construction work, which mostly involves manual labour, shows a high level of wage disparity at the lower literacy categories (where most workers are employed). Non literate women workers in construction received 52.4 per cent of the wages paid to men workers in this category in 1987-88, and this ratio declined to 46 per cent in 1993-94

Table 13 : Gender based Wage Differentials of Regular Wage/Salaried Employees Aged 15-59 by Industry and Education, Urban India, 1987-88 and 1993-94

(Female wage as a percentage of male wage)

Industry Division	*Not literate*	*Literate upon middle*	*Secondary*	*Graduate and above*	*All Levels*
1987-88					
Agriculture	79.1	73.3	97.7	105.1	69.6
Mining	69.9	83.8	132.7	74.3	68.1
Mfg.2	43.9	43.8	66.5	78.4	43.8
Mfg.3	64.8	68.3	81.5	77.4	76.2
Utilities	94.2	71.4	79.5	77.2	87.6
Construction	52.4	60.2	44.1	73.6	70.5
Trade	43.4	86.9	82.3	113.5	81.5
Transport	115.9	104.3	87.5	94.9	115.4
Finance	103.2	171.0	64.9	77.4	86.8
Services	57.2	66.8	82.8	82.0	78.1
All industries	59.0	67.1	83.9	81.6	83.0
1993-94					
Agriculture	92.0	89.4	114.2	92.9	90.8
Mining	77.1	22.8	82.3	67.8	67.8
Mfg.2	46.6	51.5	54.7	88.5	53.0
Mfg.3	68.3	50.3	70.6	78.6	73.8
Utilities	44.2	-	79.5	86.9	89.3
Construction	46.0	59.7	106.9	47.7	54.1
Trade	59.3	87.1	89.0	85.7	99.5
Transport	117.0	75.1	94.9	84.5	103.7
Finance	48.2	60.0	74.5	80.5	84.3
Services	56.6	54.8	88.2	76.1	72.0
All industries	57.8	56.8	88.3	77.2	79.8

Source : Gender Based Discrimination in the Urban Labour Market, Sudha Deshpande and Lalit K. Deshpande, in Gender and Employment in India, Edited by T.S. Papola, Alakh N. Sharma,1999

In the rural areas also the disparity is stark. In 1987-88, rural women workers employed in agriculture were paid 73.05 per cent of the wages paid to men workers in this category, and the ratio was at 57.85 per cent in the rural construction industry sector.

Table 14 : Male-Female Wage Ratio on Agriculture and Non-Agriculture

(Female wage as a percentage of male wage)

States	*1964-65*	*1974-75*	*1977-78*	*1987-88*	*1993-94*
Agriculture					
All India	59	67%	67%	77%	67%
Andhra P.	45	77%	67%	71%	71%
Bihar	91	91%	91%	91%	83%
Gujarat	83	83%	91%	91%	91%
Harayana		77%	91%	71%	77%
Karnataka	63	63%	71%	71%	77%
Kerela	56	71%	67%	71%	71%
M.P.	77	67%	77%	83%	83%
Maharashtra	50	56%	59%	67%	63%
Orissa	67	71%	77%	71%	77%
Punjab	67	53%	63%	38%	91%
Rajasthan	67	71%	71%	91%	83%
Tamil Nadu	83	67%	67%	67%	59%
U.P.	83	77%	71%	77%	83%
West Bengal	77	77%	91%	77%	77%
Non Agriculture					
All India	63	56%	48%	71%	53%
Andhra P.	71	59%	56%	67%	59%
Bihar	91	59%	59%	83%	77%
Gujarat	50	83%	56%	91%	59%
Harayana		71%	45%	45%	45%
Karnataka	59	63%		77%	63%
Kerala	48	48%	40%	63%	43%
M.P.	71	59%	59%	91%	63%
Maharashtra	48	50%	45%	67%	56%
Orissa	59	59%	77%	71%	71%
Punjab	45	38%	38%	56%	56%
Rajasthan	53	56%	83%	91%	63%
Tamil Nadu	56	56%	53%	59%	48%
U.P.	40	59%	50%	77%	71%
West Bengal	71	50%	33%	53%	59%

Source : Jeemol Unni, 'Women Workers in Agriculture: Some Recent Trends,' T.S Papola and Alakh N. Sharma, Gender and Employment in India, 1999.

At an all India level, the ratio of female wage earnings to male wage earnings in agriculture was at 59 per cent in 1964-65, and this increased to 77 per cent in 1987-88, and thereafter the ratio has again shown a decline in 1993-94.

As seen in Table 14, for the all India non-agriculture side the ratio has shown a declining trend (except in 1987-88), falling from 63 per cent in 1964-65 to 53 per cent in 1993-94. This all India data when looked at in conjunction with the data for urban India in Table 13 seems to point that the women in rural India get a raw deal in wages; the urban all industries ratio is at 79.8 per cent in comparison to the 67 per cent ratio for all India agriculture and 59 per cent ratio for all India non agriculture categories in 1993-94.

There are disparities at state level also, with Maharashtra and Tamil Nadu lagging behind in both agriculture and non agriculture wage ratios as seen in Table 14.

Looking across select occupational groups, one observes similar trends in Table 14. In the non-literate category, the disparity is stark with women workers receiving 59 per cent of the wages paid to men workers in this category, and this ratio was lower at 57.8 per cent in 1993-94. Spinners/weavers in this literacy segment were the worst affected, receiving 48.6 per cent of the wages paid to men workers in this category in 1987-88, and this ratio was 51.9 per cent in 1993-94.

Table 15: Gender based Wage Differentials of Regular Wage/ Salaried Employees Aged 15-59 in Selected Occupational Groups by Education, Urban India, 1987-88 and 1993-94

(Female wage as a percentage of male wage)

Occupational Group	*Not literate*	*Literate upon middle*	*Secondary*	*Graduate and above*	*All Levels*
1987-88					
Nursing	78.1	-	100.4	85.5	99.1
Teachers	96.9	73.8	77.4	81.3	78.0
Clerical	67.8	92.7	90.5	92.2	90.6
Housekeepers, etc.	61.9	62.2	94.7	82.1	63.1
Spinners/Weavers	48.6	52.2	61.1	79.4	49.7
All occupations	59.0	67.1	83.9	81.6	83.0
1993-94					
Nursing	77.7	82.0	108.3	85.5	91.1
Teachers	151.2	37.1	82.7	71.4	69.4
Clerical	91.9	78.9	88.9	87.4	89.6
Housekeepers, etc.	60.3	79.6	63.6	87.5	56.3
Spinners/Weavers	51.9	68.0	111.5	133.9	60.4
All occupations	57.8	56.8	88.3	77.2	79.8

Source : Gender Based Discrimination in the Urban Labour Market, Sudha Deshpande and Lalit K. Deshpande, in Gender and Employment in India, Edited by T.S. Papola, Alakh N. Sharma, 1999

While women are often paid lower wages than men for same or similar type of work, gender-based discrimination in wages often occurs covertly through a division of labour on the basis of gender. Gender related segregation in occupations is one the prominent and endurable aspects of labour markets the world over. Gender-based segregation exists in traditional as well as modern societies. The phenomenon exists in different forms, namely, horizontal segregation and vertical segregation. The former refers to concentration of women and men in different types of jobs without reference to job hierarchies, while the latter concerns itself with concentration of men in higher level and women in lower level ones, both within and between occupations and industries[4].

In India also there is a clear gender-based division of labour in all the sectors of economy. The gender-based division of labour has extended from household work to work outside the home. Women are generally concentrated in low-skilled, low paid jobs. Agriculture is the most important activity of the women workforce in the rural areas, with women engaged as cultivators and labourers. A very strict division of labour on the basis of gender characterises agricultural activity. Though the pattern of women's participation in agriculture varies greatly among regions, crops, farming systems, castes and classes, women are primarily involved in those activities which require less skills, more back-breaking and low paying work. There is a clear segregation of labour, with women rarely engaged in ploughing but almost exclusively performing operations like transplanting, weeding, harvesting and threshing. It is also observed that men generally perform mechanized operations, while women mainly do operations needing manual work. Recent technological changes have eliminated many jobs done by women. Men have begun to substitute women in activities in which machinery has displaced manual labour.

In other sectors also women are concentrated in low-skilled and low-paying jobs. For example, in the building and construction industry, women workers are engaged only in unskilled occupations. No women workers are engaged in skilled or semi-skilled occupations as masons, electricians, carpenters, foremen, fitters, *bhistis*, floor grinder, sinkers etc. They are only employed in unskilled jobs and low paying jobs as labourers, helpers or coolies. With the introduction of new labour replacing machinery, there will be reduction in employment opportunities, particularly for women because they are only engaged in manual work.

Even in industries in which women are employed in large numbers like textiles, drugs and medicines, export-oriented industries like garments, hosiery, electronics and food processing, gender-based division of labour can be seen. The garment sector has become the fastest growing export sector in the country. Women are employed both in factories and in home-based work. The garment industry of Delhi promotes a gender-based division of labour and jobs are segregated into those suitable for men and those suitable for women. The division is not constant but created and recreated to the detriment of women. Women as a group receive much lower wages than men and have less control over the work they do. Women also do more routine and monotonous work and use skills which can be easily learnt and cannot be used elsewhere [5]. Even in the garment industry of Calcutta, the division of work between men and women is very clear in each firm. Women form the bulk of workers but the men occupy all the skilled and better paid jobs. There are no instances of men and women both performing the same tasks. This is because in this region the designing and cutting work is traditionally done by men and there is a long-standing system of training male apprentices. There are few opportunities for poor women to get such training. In the garment industry in Chennai, there are some instances of a mixed workforce working on the same task in a given unit, but the long term tendency is towards gender-wise segregation of workers and tasks[6].

In Ludhiana's export-oriented hosiery industry women workers are employed in only 4 processes, namely, winding on hand winding machines, embroidery, checking and packing and manual button stitching. Women tend to be engaged in processes in which they use their traditional skills and for which no special training is required. The replacement of hand-wheels by power winders has displaced a large number of women workers. Even in button stitching, women workers are engaged only where machines cannot be used. In the checking and packing department, the presence of women workers is negligible. A majority of women doing embroidery work in this industry are home-based workers. An analysis of the nature of work performed by women shows that they are employed in those processes where they are indispensable and relatively cheaper to engage[7].

Women are at the bottom of the ladder in terms of employment, earnings and status in the marine food processing industry, which is fully export oriented. The growth of the marine products processing industry is a recent phenomenon. The industry became significant by the end of the 1980 as an important source of foreign exchange. The industry has a distinct preference for recruiting single women[8].

In the marine products processing industry in Andhra Pradesh, women are recruited from Kerala on the argument that local women do not possess traditional skills in food processing. Hired as contract labour, the migrant women are young and rarely return to work once they get married. The migrant women are basically employed as graders, while local women are employed, depending on the workload, primarily to do peeling work. Hence, there is a perceptible division of labour between the migrant and local women. Comparatively, the migrant women earn marginally better than the local women, who are generally paid on a piece-rate basis. But both the migrant and the local women are clearly disadvantaged when the work they perform is compared to that done by men. Tasks performed by men do not involve cleaning, processing and grading the prawns. Men do not work standing for endless hours in puddles of water. The tasks performed by men, like unloading of prawns, crushing of ice, attending to the refrigeration plant and the freezing operations, are not continuous activity functions performed in continuous cycles for 8 hours. The women, on the other hand, work continuously, repeatedly performing the same activity in short time cycles, whether they are doing peeling, grading or deveining work. This gender-based division of labour is based on perceptions that it is appropriate for women to perform monotonous and time-consuming tasks that require patience, perseverance and dexterity[9].

However, despite such clear differences that distinctly require greater work intensity and attention, the tasks performed by women are placed low in the hierarchy of skill levels. Though the work performed by women working as graders is the critical task that enhances the value of the product, they are not even paid the minim um wages. The tasks performed by them are placed below the compressor/machine operators, whose contribution to effective addition to the product is negligible. Moreover, the peeling operation does not even find mention in the wage notification. The very perception of viewing skills used by women as 'traditional' skills emanating form housework, is the convenient argument that permits the devaluation of the skill in the eyes of both men and women[10].

In the electronics industry in the Santa Cruz Electronic Export Processing Zone (SEEPZ), Mumbai, women constitute a significant section of the workforce. Employers prefer employing young, unmarried women. While women are employed in the assembly operations, which is the main work in these electronic units, men are employed mainly as loaders, security staff, drivers, supervisors and as maintenance staff. Men are rarely employed in the assembly operations. Women are preferred for their nimble fingers, for their dexterity and their ability to handle minute components. More specifically, employers prefer to hire women because they have the patience required for such intricate work. They can sit for long hours, concentrating on the task at hand, unaffected by the tediousness involved in repetitive tasks. Women are also more willing to put up with low wages, the difficult regimen of work and are not disposed to unionise[11].

However, women's skills are not perceived as technical skills, but as skills perpetually practiced by women within home. The outcome of such a perception is that most assembling work is seen as unskilled work, despite the much-lauded qualities of patience, dexterity and concentration. Further, as women in this industry are recruited fresh from school, without any experience or technical diplomas, and as training on the job is minimal, the label of 'unskilled' is easily affixed. Women who work in assembly units do not find much of a market for their skills and no growth opportunities[12].

A study conducted in the pharmaceutical industry of Mumbai also shows that women's jobs are largely in the low-grade categories. Women, who are mainly employed as packers, checkers, labelers, bottle-washers, are invariably in the lower most grades. This also means that on an average women earn less than men do[13].

In the electric fan industry of Calcutta, male and female tasks are clearly segregated and there are no instances of overlap in any units. Skilled jobs such as armature winding, which were earlier performed exclusively by women, have now been taken over by men. Wage settlements in the seventies and eighties improved the wages and resulted in pushing out women because wages had improved sufficiently to attract male workers and also because more skilled workers were available for work. Women now play a minor role in this industry and perform only unskilled jobs[14].

Women receive less wages than men partly because women often hold low-level, low-paid jobs in female-dominated occupations. Women are still disproportionately represented in relatively low-paid jobs. In urban India women are concentrated in 2 types of occupations: (i) in professional, technical and related occupations more as teachers, clerks and nurses (ii) in service occupations as maids, cooks, domestics and sweepers[15].

The labour market parallels the subordination of women in the household and relegates women to low-paid end of the occupational ladder. Thus, wage discrimination against women can be seen at 3 levels: (1) employment of women in low-paid jobs with little scope for upward mobility (2) payment of lower wages than men for same or similar work. (3) Viewing women's skills as traditional skills and placing them low in the hierarchy of skills.

NOTES AND REFERENCES

1. A.V. Jose (ed.), *Limited Options. Women Workers in Rural India*, (Geneva: ILO, 1989) p. 4.
2. Aanchal Kapur (ed.), *Women Workers' Rights in India : Issues and Strategies. A Reference Guide*, (New Delhi: ILO, 1999) pp. 4-5.
3. S.S. Suryanarayanan, "Gaps and Biases in Data Relating to Employment of Women," in T.S. Papola and Alakh N. Sharma, (eds.), *Gender and Employment in India*, (New Delhi: Vikas Publishing House, 1999) p. 83.
4. Sandra Rothboeck and Sarthi Acharya, "Gender-Based Segregation in the Indian Labour Market, " *Indian Journal of Labour Economics*, Vol. 42, No. 4, October-December 1999, p. 581.
5. Vijay Rukmini Rao and Sabha Hussain, "Invisible Hands – The Women Behind India's Export Earnings," in Nirmala Banerjee (ed.), *Indian Women in a Changing Industrial Scenario*, (New Delhi: Sage, Publications, 1991) pp. 153-54.
6. Nirmala Banerjee, "The More it Changes the More it Remains the Same," in Nirmala Banerjee (ed.), *Indian Women in a Changing Industrial Scenario*, (New Delhi: Sage Publications, 1991) p. 257.

7. Manjit Singh and K. Gopal Iyer, "Women Workers in Ludhiana Export Hosiery Industry," in Chetṉa Kalbagh (ed.), *Women and Development* (New Delhi: Discovery Publishing, 1991) pp. 192-93.
8. K. Padma, "Work, Unionisation and Gender in Marine Food Processing Units," in Cherian Joseph and K.V. Eswara Prasad, *Women, Work and Inequity. The Reality of Gender* (Noida: National Labour Institute, 1995) p. 16.
9. *Ibid*. pp. 55-56.
10. *Ibid*. p. 56.
11. Minakshi Thorat, "Labour Administration, enforcement and Gender," in *Women, Work and Inequity. The Reality of Gender*, Cherian Joseph and K. V. Eswara Prasad (Noida: National Labour Institute, 1995). pp. 211-12.
12. *Ibid*.
13. Sujata Gothoskar, "Struggles of Women in the Pharmaceutical Industry in Bombay," in Sujata Gothoskar (ed.), *Struggles of Women at Work*, (New Delhi: Vikas Publishing House, 1992) p. 138.
14. Nirmala Banerjee, *op. cit.*, pp. 288-89.
15. Sudha Deshpande and Lalit K. Deshpande, "Gender-Based Discrimination in the Urban Labour Market," in T.S. Papola and Alakh N. Sharma (eds.), *Gender and Employment in India*, (New Delhi: Vikas Publishing House, 1999) pp. 234-36.

Chapter 4

Women Workers in the Textile Industry

The textile industry, one of the oldest industries in the country, is India's single largest industry. After agriculture, it is the largest employer, providing employment to approximately 21 million people. Though going through a period of recession, the textile industry in 2000-2001 contributed about 14 percent to industrial production and 27 percent to the country's export earning[1].

The structure of the textile industry is extremely complex. It can be broadly divided into three sectors: handloom sector, mill sector and powerloom sector. It is estimated that in the year 2000, around 12 million people were employed in the handloom sector. A majority of these were generally self employed. Around 1 million were employed in the mill sector and, as per official estimates, 6.6 million were employed in the powerloom sector. However, industry estimates put this figure at around 8 million[2].

Since the textile industry is a highly labour intensive industry, the study of employment of women in this industry assumes significance. However, women workers constitute a small percentage of total workers in this industry. In 1995, women workers accounted for only 10.7 percent of the total workforce in this industry. Indeed the textile industry is very much male dominated. A comparison with other Asian countries revealed a significantly higher percentage of women workers. Examples are Taiwan, China, with 54 percent of female employment, the Republic of Korea with 51 percent, and Malaysia with 48 percent, all in 1995[3].

The textile industry in India also provides a typical example of the division of labour on the basis of gender and a valuable case study on the impact of affirmative action on the employment of women. In the textile industry today, women are to be found mainly as winders and packers. Women's gradual loss of their livelihood as spinners is documented in various studies. According to the Report of the Commission on the Status of Women, 1975, out of the 200 different operations in the textile industry, women are found in only four or five today, whereas in the pre-war years they were to be found in about 80.

This chapter will discuss the trends and nature of women's employment in the textile mills of Mumbai and the powerlooms of Bhiwandi, Thane district. Though the textile mills of Mumbai, plagued by sickness, are downing their shutters, they were once the largest source of employment in the city. This chapter will analyse the trends in women's employment in the mill sector, the nature of production organisation, division of labour on the basis of gender and working conditions. Two National Textile Corporation (South Maharashtra) mills – Apollo Textile Mills and New City of Bombay Manufacturing Mills – were selected for conducting the study. These two mills were selected because in comparison to other NTC (S M) mills, these mills were almost fully operational and would hence provide a better understanding of the dynamics of the production process. These two mills have also been identified as 'revivable' mills.

These two mills provide employment to 51 women (both workers and staff). Since the number of women workers in these mills is not high, it was decided to include all of them in the study. The research methodology included an open-ended questionnaire designed to elicit the required information, as well as unstructured interview of managers, supervisors and trade union officials, and observation of the working environment. The workers were interviewed at their workplace.

To have a historical perspective on the change in working conditions over time, data in a specific format was also sought and obtained from the management of these two mills.

In Bhiwandi, women working in the powerloom industry were also studied. Five powerlooms, which provide employment to 18 women workers were a part of the study.

By selecting NTC mills in Mumbai and powerloom units in Bhiwandi, this study attempts to analyse the situation of women workers in both the organised and unorganised sectors of the textile industry.

Women Workers in Temxtile Mills of Mumbai

The textile industry of Mumbai, developed in the 1850s, was one of the main industries employing women. The first factories were spinning mills, which spun cotton into coarse yarn for domestic handicraft production and for exports abroad. Women formed a quarter of the workforce[4]. Subsequently this figure oscillated between one-fifth and one-fourth. In 1919, women constituted 20.3 percent of the labour force. This proportion rose to 22.9 percent in 1930, but from that year onwards there was a steady decline in their proportion from 18.9 percent in 1934 to merely 14.9 percent in 1939[5]. In absolute numbers the peak year for the employment of women in Mumbai's textile mills was 1926. Between 1926 and 1939 the average daily employment of women in the mills went down from 35, 541 to 21, 757, that is, a reduction of over 11, 000 or 34 percent. Since then the decline in women's employment has been constant, so that in 1947 they constituted 11.17 percent of the labour force, in 1955, 8.47 percent, in 1965, 3.83 percent, in 1975, 1.97 percent, in 1980, 1.6 percent and in 2001, a mere 1.1 percent. (Table 1).

In order to understand the causes behind the decline in the proportion of women workers in Mumbai's textile mills, it is necessary to discuss the process right from the beginning.

Since the inception of the textile industry of Mumbai, women worked in only two sections of the mills. Eighty percent of the women workers worked in the winding section, which was a hand operated process involving no machinery, and 20 percent worked in the reeling section, where machinery with moving parts was involved. Women were restricted to only two departments in the mills because during this period they were reluctant to work with male workers. It is reported that mill owners had offered women work in departments where there were male workers but the women had refused. Thus, in the beginning division of labour on the basis of gender was necessary since women were not willing to work with men. The reason why women's labour was segregated to only two departments was that there were not sufficient women workers to work other departments on an exclusively women basis[6].

Table 1 : Women Workers as Percentage of Total Textile Workers in Mumbai

Year	*Total Number of Workers*	*Women Workers*	*Percentage*
1884	39716	8816	22.20
1895	73865	18275	24.74
1899	80498	18952	23.54
1910	102275	21581	21.10
1915	113495	22296	19.64
1920	140898	28717	20.38
1925	146244	32396	22.15
1930	127578	29163	22.86
1934	128420	24319	18.94
1939	145691	21757	14.93
1947	205491	22962	11.17
1951	196363	18421	9.38
1955	203391	17219	8.47
1961	208000	11100	5.34
1965	192786	7386	3.83
1970	174167	4231	2.43
1975	167819	3308	1.97
1980	250000	4992	2.00
2002	40000	450	1.13

Source : Till 1947, Morris D. Morris, Emergence of an Industrial Working Class, Oxford University Press, 1955; till 1975, Mira Savara, Changing Trends in Women's Employment – A Case Study of the Textile Industry in Bombay, Himalaya Publishing House, 1986; 1980 and 2001 figures: Rashrtiya Mill Mazdoor Sangh

The inadequate supply of women workers in Mumbai's textile industry was related to the nature of labour supply to the cities during this period. In the initial stages of the textile industry there was a shortage of labour in the urban areas. The majority of labour was drawn from Ratnagiri, an underdeveloped region of Maharashtra, where land was unproductive. The practice was for the males to migrate, leaving his wife and family behind to look after the land. This fits the general tendency that the more unproductive the land, the more they tend to be basically women's concerns. Thus, the fact that Ratnagiri was a backward area with low agricultural productivity meant that there was a tendency of male migration to the cities and female headed farms in Ratnagiri[7].

Women workers in the cities were primarily widows or from families who had no land. A survey was conducted on 1462 workers (26.7 percent of whom were women) in Mumbai's mills in 1927-28. This survey indicated that 12 percent of the women workers were below the age of 20 years, 54 percent were in the age group of 25-30 years, 28 percent were in the age group of 35-50 years and 6 percent were over 50 years. Whereas 74 percent of the men working in the textile mills were married and only 3 percent widowed, of the women working in textile mills, 44 percent were widows and 55 percent married[8].

The first labour laws to develop in India related to the working conditions of women and child workers in the textile industry. While the Factories Act, 1881, restricted the hours of work for children, an amendment to the Factories Act in 1891 provided for a one day weekly holiday and a half-hour lunch break for all workers. Women workers were not allowed to work before 5 AM or after 8 PM and could work for a maximum of 11 hours. The legislation, passed in response to women's social role as housewife, was an attempt to create the conditions which would enable women to combine the roles of both housewife and worker. The legislation did not lead to any changes in the employment of women. This was because women workers had been working on a piece rate basis and tended to work a shorter working day in any case. More important, during this period, in the late 1890s there was a shortage of labour for the mills. Therefore, female labour had to be employed whenever available[9].

When electricity was introduced in the mills in 1904, working hours of males were extended beyond daylight and working days of up to 14 hours became common. This forced the government to pass a law restricting the hours of work for men to 12 hours. The hours of work for women remained 11 hours. Legislation relating to maternity was passed in 1929 and for provision of crèches in 1934. While maternity benefits were paid regularly by 1934, the starting of crèches did not proceed very fast. The 1934 Act made it compulsory for those mills that employed over 50 women to provide crèches. But in practice very few mills started crèches. As late as 1943, only 24 mills out of 66 mills had crèches in their premises. There was no retrenchment of women workers due to these laws. But the effect of these laws was that it made the hiring of women workers more burdensome and more expensive than before. However, it is essential to stress that the social reasons for passing these laws was not only concern for the needs and problems of women, but primarily the needs of the production process for increased discipline and reduced turnover of labour. In 1922, night work for women was prohibited through an amendment of the Factory Act, 1911. Though there was no immediate impact of this legislation, this restriction played a very important role in altering the pattern of women's employment[10].

The increasing competition faced by Mumbai's textile mills in the late 1920s from Japanese mills in the export market forced the Mumbai mills to launch a process of rationalisation and greater productivity drives. Rationalisation occurred in the weaving and reeling and winding departments and both men and women's jobs were affected. Cheese winding machines were introduced in Mumbai's cotton textile mills in 1925, changing the winding process from one entailing some amount of hand labour to one using machines. Soon after this more dramatic changes were introduced by the use of Universal winding machines. The introduction of these machines simplified the winding and reeling process, compressing them into one. As these machines wound straight into the cheese or the beam, which could be dyed, reeling yarn into hanks for dyeing became unnecessary. Prim winding too was introduced at the same time, speeding up the winding process. The introduction of new machines made the work process simpler and more monotonous. A number of the same actions had to be performed in the same amount of time as before and additionally the number of spindles under one women's supervision increased[11].

With the introduction of rationalisation, productivity increased and the existing labour force was no longer necessary. Around 5100 workers were retrenched. Separate figures for women workers are not available. Workers began to join trade unions hoping that the unions would be able to defend their jobs. The process of rationalisation did not make the process of production more complicated. The argument that women did not have the necessary skills to work on the new machines did not apply to the textile industry. In fact, the work process became more simplified. The effect of rationalisation was to reduce the number of women required by the machines, not to displace women with men for reasons of different skill levels required[12].

In 1928 there was a general strike in the textile industry over the issue of rationalisation and retrenchment. The strike ended after six months, with a government undertaking to set up a tripartite committee to investigate the issue of rationalisation in the industry. The committee, consisting of government, management and trade union representatives, ultimately developed a formula for retrenchment and a recruitment policy that was acceptable to all parties. It was decided that those workers with shorter years of service in the industry would be the first to be retrenched with payment of gratuity dependent on the number of years of service that a worker had put into the mill[13].

In 1935 the Bombay Mill Owners Association started the *Badli* (temporary) Control System. The system was devised with the purpose of giving regular, even though limited, employment, to the *badli* or temporary workers. The *badli* labour schemes involved giving special *badli* cards to a selected number of workers who were assigned to different departments according to the requirements. The *badlis* were asked to present themselves each morning to the mill when they were used to fill the temporary vacancies. Whenever a permanent vacancy arose in any occupation, the senior most *badli* worker would get the permanent workers post. The scheme thus ensured that workers who were retrenched would be the first to be re-employed[14]. The *Badli* labour schemes of the different mills were centralised in one pool in 1950 with the starting of the Government Decasualisation Scheme. Labour recruitment into the industry thus became an insulated one.

In the 1930s most mills began to run a night shift. Thus, there was ample opportunity for retrenched workers to get employment in the textile industry and there was little opposition from the male workers to the formula developed by the committee. However, since women could not work in the night shift, there was no potential for the re-absorption of the excess female workforce. The only way of protecting the rights of the female workforce was by either breaking down the existing gender division of labour or allowing women to work in the night shift. However, despite the fact that the process of rationalisation equally affected women, the issues regarding women's employment were never taken up. The trade unions failed to take up the cause of women workers primarily because of the lack of adequate representation of women in union activities.

Women resisted the reduction of employment in their ranks because there was little opportunity for them to get alternate employment in the organised sector. Women workers insisted they would share the available work amongst themselves. Thus, there was no immediate large-scale retrenchment of women workers. There was instead a slow and gradual decline in the female workforce. The mill owners followed a policy of very limited new recruitment of women. When women workers retired, women rarely filled up their vacancies. Thus, the decline represented the rate of retirement of women workers, who left the industry when they were too old to work anymore. The very limited recruitment of women workers since the 1930s is reflected in the age of the women workers and by the fact that a far greater percentage of women worked a longer period in the industry. In 1940, 58 percent of the women had worked for less than 10 years but in 1955, only 14 percent of the women had worked under 10 years, indicating a fall in the new recruitment of women in the textile mills[15].

The prohibition of women from working in the night shift resulted in a one-sided breakdown of the traditional division of labour on the basis of gender. While women rarely worked in departments other than winding, men began to be gradually employed in the winding department, which was earlier run exclusively by women workers. Since women worked in the first shift, to begin with men were recruited to work in the second and third shift in the winding department. Gradually they also began to work in the first shift of the winding department[16].

Women Workers in National Textile Corporation (NTC) South Maharashtra (SM) Mills

The textile industry began to go through a period of recession from the late 1970s and early 1980s. Obsolete machinery and poor capacity utilisation hampered the performance of the mills. The textile policy and the reluctance of the mill owners to make investments deeply affected production. The competition faced from the powerlooms also affected the mill sector. The textile mills in Mumbai experienced a prolonged eighteen months strike. After the strike ended, a number of mills closed down. The mills, which reopened, decided to go in for rationalisation that resulted in reduction of the workforce. There were around 2,50,000 textile mill workers in Mumbai till 1980. After the strike, the figure declined to 1,23,000. After this the number of textile workers continued to decline and it is estimated that there are now only 40,000 textile workers in Mumbai.

As a result of the growing recession in the textile industry, the government decided to take over a large number of textile mills. The National Textile Corporation, a public sector undertaking, was set up with the main objective of managing the affairs of the sick textile undertakings taken over by the government. It was formed under the provisions of the Sick Textile Undertakings (Nationalisation) Act of 1974. NTC consists of 119 mills under 9 NTC subsidiaries and 1 holding company. It is now possible that a large number of these NTC mills may be shut down.

Table 2 : Employment in National Textile Corporation (South Maharashtra) Ltd.

As on 30.09.2001

Mills	*No. of Male Employees*	*No. of Female Employees*	*Total*	*Percentage of Women Employees*
Apollo	892	16	908	1.76
Bharat	893	6	899	0.67
Digvijay	932	5	937	0.53
Jupiter	788	17	805	2.11
Mumbai	859	17	876	1.94
New Hind	920	28	948	2.95
Aurangabad	211	14	225	6.22
Barshi	349	20	369	5.42
Chalisgaon	957	9	966	0.93
Dhule	853	19	872	2.18
Nanded	652	18	670	2.69
Elephinstone	753	15	768	1.95
Finlay	1379	15	1394	1.08
Gold Mohur	1085	1	1086	0.09
Madhusudan	597	14	611	2.29
New City	1194	36	1214	2.97
P. Process	476	1	477	0.21
Corp. Office	118	26	144	18.06
Total	13908	277	14179	1.95

Source : NTC

There are 18 mills under NTC (SM). Out of a total of 14,169 employees, there are 13, 908 male employees and only 277 female employees. Female employees constitute a mere 1.95 percent of the working population. (Table 2) Apollo Mills Ltd and New City of Bombay Manufacturing Mills were the two NTC (SM) mills selected for conducting the study.

The Morarkas established Apollo Mills in 1920. The mill was takenover by M\S Rajputana Textile (Agencies) Pvt Ltd. They later ceased to be the managing agents and the company was thereafter managed by a Board of Directors, with the controlling share holding with the Morarkas. In 1972 the Government of India appointed the Maharashtra State Textile Corporation Ltd. as Authorized Controller. In 1974 the management of Apollo Mills was vested with the NTC and its name has been subsequently changed to Apollo Textile Mills.

All the machines were in a dilapidated condition at the time of the takeover and consequently productivity and quality levels were extremely poor. The amount of Rs. 378.75 lakhs was invested since the mill was nationalised. However, the partial modernisation proved to be ineffective and the mill continued to incur losses. The main reasons for the losses are low capacity utilisation/low productivity and consequent low production value. The mill is a spinning/grey composite mill, having the installed/commissioned capacity of 36472 ring spindles and 133 plain looms. The current capacity utilisation for spinning is 79.5 percent and for weaving is 87.9 percent. It has been identified as a revivable mill and the investment required for plant and machinery renovation amounts to Rs. 23.38 crores. The revival plan has been submitted to the Board of Industrial Finance and Reconstruction (BIFR) for final approval.

Apollo Mill, as of 31st March 2001, has an on-roll strength of 908 employees. There are only 16 female employees and they constitute 1.7 percent of the workforce. Out of the 16 female employees, 10 fall under the category of workers and 6 fall under the category of staff and officers.

New City of Bombay Mfg Mills was established in the year 1905 with a spindleage of 56,260 and 623 looms. In 1983, the management of the mill was taken over by the Government of India. Subsequently the mill was nationalised with effect from 1994 and the mill became one of the units of NTC (SM).

After the take over, most of the spindles and looms were recommissioned and started with full utilisation. In the course of time, the uneconomic spindles and looms were stopped because

Table 3 : Growth of Number of Men and Women Workers employed in New City Mill

	Regular		*Badli*		*Total*			*Women workers as % of total No. of workers*		
	Men	*Women*	*Men*	*Women*	*Men*	*Women*	*Total*	*Regular*	*Badli*	*Total*
	1	2	3	4	5	6	7	8	9	10
Unskilled										
1981-82	408	33	1077	4	1485	37	1522	7.48	0.37	2.43
1991-92	611	5	332	1	943	6	949	0.81	0.30	0.63
2001-02	313	5	194	1	507	6	513	1.57	0.51	1.17
Skilled										
1981-82	1500	48	0	0	1500	48	1548	3.10		3.10
1991-92	888	30	0	5	888	35	923	3.27	100.00	3.79
2001-02	490	17	21	5	511	22	533	3.35	19.23	4.13
Total										
1981-82	1908	81	1077	4	2985	85	3070	4.07	0.37	2.77
1991-92	1499	35	332	6	1831	41	1872	2.28	1.78	2.19
2001-02	803	22	215	6	1018	28	1046	2.67	2.71	2.68

of lower productivity and quality. Since most of the machines were in a poor condition at the time of takeover, the productivity and quality levels were poor. Though partial modernisation has been undertaken, it has proved to be inadequate and the mill continues to make losses. Most of the machines are obsolete and require immediate replacement. This mill is also a spinning/grey composite mill having the installed/commisioned capacity of 38,728 ring Spindles, 107 plain looms and 124 automatic looms. The current capacity utilisation for spinning is 85 percent and for weaving is 90 percent.

New City Mill has also been identified as a revivable mill and the investment required for the modernisation amounts to Rs. 47.62 crores. The same has also been submitted to the BIFR for final approval.

New City Mill, as on 31st March 2001, has an on-roll strength of 1214 employees. The mill has a total of 36 female employees, who constitute 2.9 percent of the workforce. Out of the 36 female employees, 33 fall under the category of workers and 3 fall under the category of staff and officers.

Table 4 : Number of Persons Employed in Supervisory Jobs in New City Mill

	Men	*Women*	*Total*	*Women as % of total*
	1	2	3	4
1981-82	78	0	78	0.00
1991-92	46	0	46	0.00
2001-02	43	0	43	0.00

Table 5: Number of Persons Employed in Managerial Positions in New City Mill

	Men	*Women*	*Total*	*Women as % of total*
	1	2	3	4
1981-82	24	0	24	0.00
1991-92	22	0	22	0.00
2001-02	14	0	14	0.00

Table 6 : Number of Persons Employed in Clerical Jobs in New City Mill (e.g : clerks, accountants, store-keepers, stenos etc.)

	Men	*Women*	*Total*	*Women as % of total*
	1	2	3	4
1981-82	191	3	194	1.55
1991-92	89	3	92	3.26
2001-02	61	2	63	3.17

Table 7 : Number of Persons Employed in Security Jobs in New City Mill

	Men	*Women*	*Total*	*Women as % of total*
	1	2	3	4
1981-82	31	0	31	0.00
1991-92	23	0	23	0.00
2001-02	20	1	21	4.76

Table 8: Number of Persons Employed in Menial Jobs in New City Mill (e.g. sweepers, orderlies etc.)

	Men	*Women*	*Total*	*Women as % of total*
	1	2	3	4
1981-82	17	4	21	19.05
1991-92	9	3	12	25.00
2001-02	6	3	9	33.33

Table 9: Growth of Number of Men and Women Workers Employed in Apollo Mill

	Regular		*Badli*		*Total*			*Women workers as % of total No. of workers*		
	Men	*Women*	*Men*	*Women*	*Men*	*Women*	*Total*	*Regular*	*Badli*	*Total*
	1	2	3	4	5	6	7	8	9	10
Unskilled										
1981-82	438	2	315	0	753	2	755	0.45	0.00	0.26
1991-92	200	0	120	0	320	0	320	0.00	0.00	0.00
2001-02	117	0	80	0	197	0	197	0.00	0.00	0.00
Skilled										
1981-82	1456	28	678	8	2154	36	2190	1.89	1.17	1.64
1991-92	1002	18	89	3	1091	21	1112	1.76	3.26	1.89
2001-02	468	8	88	2	556	10	566	1.68	2.22	1.77
Total										
1981-82	1894	30	993	8	2907	38	2945	1.56	0.80	1.29
1991-92	1202	18	209	3	1411	21	1432	1.48	1.42	1.47
2001-02	585	8	168	2	753	10	763	1.35	1.18	1.31

Table 10: Number of Persons Employed in Supervisory Jobs in Apollo Mill

	Men	*Women*	*Total*	*Women as % of total*
	1	2	3	4
1981-82		Information Not Available		
1991-92	40	—	40	0.00
2001-02	24	—	24	0.00

Table 11: Number of Persons Employed in Managerial Positions in Apollo Mill

	Men	*Women*	*Total*	*Women as % of total*
	1	2	3	4
1981-82		Information Not Available		
1991-92	23	—	23	0.00
2001-02	14	—	14	0.00

Table 12: Number of Persons Employed in Clerical Jobs in Apollo Mill (e.g : clerks, accountants, store-keepers, stenos etc.)

	Men	*Women*	*Total*	*Women as % of total*
	1	2	3	4
1981-82		Information Not Available		
1991-92	87	2	89	2.25
2001-02	63	3	66	4.55

Table 13: Number of Persons Employed in Security Jobs in Apollo Mill

	Men	*Women*	*Total*	*Women as % of total*
	1	2	3	4
1981-82		Information Not Available		
1991-92	27	—	27	0.00
2001-02	22	—	22	0.00

Table 14: Number of Persons Employed in Menial Jobs in Apollo Mill (e.g. sweepers, orderlies etc.)

	Men	*Women*	*Total*	*Women as % of total*
	1	2	3	4
1981-82	Information Not Available			
1991-92	5	—	5	0.00
2001-02	2	—	2	0.00

Tables 3 to 14 gives the data on of men and women workers employed in New City Mill and Apollo Mill from 1981 to 2002. This data has been obtained from NTC.

As a precursor to understanding the role of women in the textile mill environment, we need to look at the production process. The process is summarized as follows :

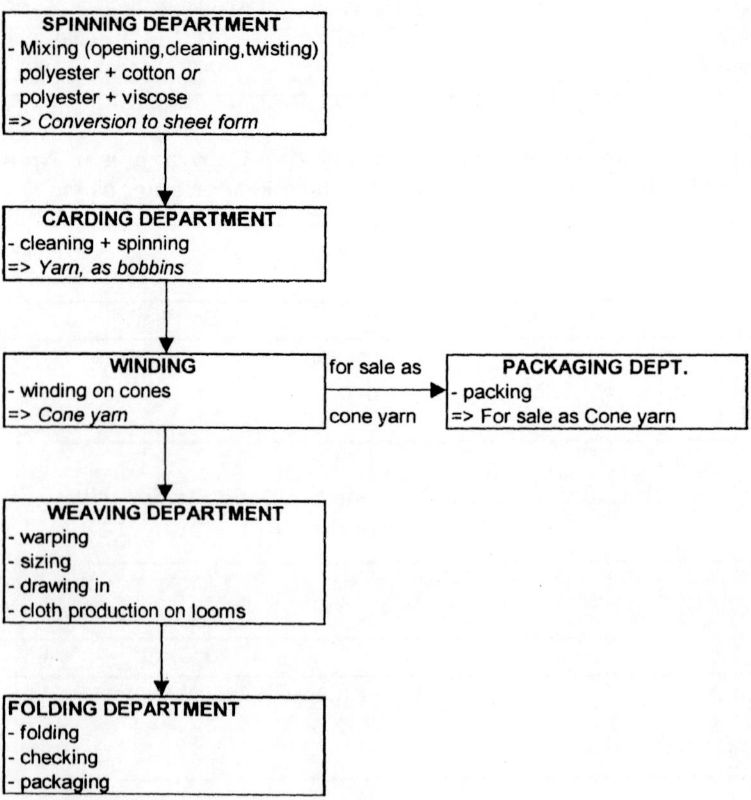

The division of labour on the basis of gender in the mills is apparent even to a casual observer. A majority of the women workers in the two mills work in the winding department. Eighty-six percent of women workers work in the winding section while the rest are employed in unskilled jobs as sweepers. In both the mills there are no women in managerial or supervisory positions. In the winding section, no woman worker has ever been promoted to the post of jobber or supervisor. Women workers who fall under the category of 'staff and officers' work as clerks or telephone operators. Out of a total of eight women working as 'staff and officers', three work in the Research and Development department. Even here they work at very junior levels as testers or typists cum clerks.

As mentioned earlier, though there has been a breakdown of this traditional gender-based division of labour, it has been a completely one-sided one. While women rarely work in any department other than winding, men are now employed in the winding section in large numbers. To begin with, the winding department was run exclusively by women. However, because of the prohibition of women workers from working in the night shift men began to be employed in the winding departments to work in the other two shifts. Gradually male workers began to work in the first shift also. As a result, male workers are now in a majority even in the winding section. In the two mills, women workers constitute merely 32 percent of the workforce in the winding section. Thus, while men have taken over areas traditionally associated with women workers, women workers are not employed in any other departments of the mills. The explanation given by managers and supervisors for the absence of women workers from other departments is that the work is too strenuous for women. However, a close observation of the production process shows that this explanation is not satisfactory. The work done by male workers in other sections of the mill, for example carding, weaving and folding sections, can also be done by women workers.

Since 86 percent of the female workers are employed in the winding section, a study of their age, number of years in the mills, marital status, educational background, wages, economic background has been done.

Table 15: Job-wise Growth in Number of Men and Women Workers in New City Mill

Name of job	*Number of workers employed*								
	1981-82			*1991-92*			*2001-02*		
	Men	*Women*	*Total*	*Men*	*Women*	*Total*	*Men*	*Women*	*Total*
1	2	3	4	5	6	7	8	9	10
Wender	1		1						
W/Ward	1		1						
Winder	1		1	12	6	18			
Mazdoor	5		5	9		9			
Tenter	2		2	11		11		No Workers Recruited in 2001-02	
Todo Draver	9		9						
Doffer Gaiter	1		1	12		12			
Weaver	5		5						
Asst.Tenter				2		2			
Fitter				4		4			
P/V Mixer				3		3			
Wheel Boy				2		2			

The very limited recruitment of women workers since the 1970s is reflected in the age of the women employed in the mills and by the fact that a majority of them have worked for a very long period in the industry. The majority of women workers in the winding department in both the mills belong to the 50 plus age group (68.1 percent). Twenty percent of them belong to the 40-50 age group and 12 percent belong to the 30-40 age group. Sixty-eight percent of the women have worked in the mills for 20 years or more, 12 percent have worked for 15-20 years and 20 percent have worked for 10-15 years. Table 15 gives an indication of the limited recruitment of women in the textile mills.

In the sample, 64 percent of the women workers were widows, 24 percent were married, 8 percent were separated from their husbands and 4 percent were unmarried. Forty-eight percent of the women had more than 2 children, 44 percent had 2 or less than 2 children and 4 percent were childless.

Education does not appear to play an important role in women's recruitment in this industry. While 44 percent of them were illiterate, 32 percent had studied up to standard 5th, 20 percent had studied up to standard 7th and only 4 percent had studied up to standard 10th.

A majority of women workers in these mills had worked elsewhere on an average for 2-4 years. While most of them had worked in the textile industry in the spinning, packing, reeling or winding departments of private mills, some had worked in home-based industries like the beedi industry.

Women workers in the winding department are paid on a piece rate basis. Since older women workers tend to be less productive, they draw lower wages. The average basic salary in this department is Rs. 323.03. In comparison to skilled workers in other departments like spinning and weaving, their wages are on the lowest end of the spectrum. (see Table 16). While most women in the winding section on an average draw a gross salary of Rs 4000, they do not take home on an average more than Rs 2000 since a majority of them have taken loans from the cooperative societies of the mills at 15 percent interest.

Table 16: Changes in Wage/Salary Structure : Job-Wise Apollo and New City Mills

Name of the job		*Wage Rate*	*Rs.*
	1981-82	1991-92	2001-02
Spinning Jobber	574.13	574.13	588.13
Spinning Helper	461.52	470.52	470.52
8 Sider	461.52	461.52	461.52
Doffer Gaitler	306.29	311.39	311.39
Mazdoor	282.53	314.25	314.25
Winder	335.19		323.03
Fitter	340.08	387.14	431.34
Tenter	373.62	489.14	549.54
Weaving Jobber	491.92		561.15
Weaving Helper	397.58		482.47
Weaver	347.32		395.49
Boiler Attendant	402.14	448.5	475.02

Economic necessity was the main reason for women's entry in the industry. All the women interviewed had taken up work due to this reason. The average family size in our sample was 5.4 persons. The average number of earners per family was 2.2 persons. Women's contribution to the family income was crucial. While in some cases they were the sole earners, in a majority of cases they were the highest earning member of the family. This is contrary to the common notion of viewing male workers as the main providers and female workers as merely supplementing the family income.

Both New City and Apollo Mills have closed down the crèches in their premises given the dwindling numbers and age profile of the women workers. When the crèches were operational, 42.03 percent of the women workers had used the facility and 58.97 percent had not used the facility. The main reasons given by women for not using the creche was that their children were looked after by relatives or that their homes were very far from the mill and hence they could not bring their children along.

All the women workers in the sample are union members. They are all members of the Rashtriya Mill Mazdoor Sangh. However, none of them are involved in the union activities. They are all passive members of the union. They did not feel that they had benefited in any way by joining the union. However, they were hopeful that if they were ever in any trouble, the union would come to their aid.

Women workers are now virtually non-existent in the textile mills of Mumbai. The decline in women's employment has been gradual but steep. From constituting a quarter of the workforce, they now constitute a mere 1.1 percent of the workforce in Mumbai's mills. In comparison, women constitute 13 percent of the workforce in mills in Tamil Nadu, followed by Andhra Pradesh (11.40 percent), Madhya Pradesh (11.40 percent), Kerala (10.10 percent) and Karnataka (8.20 percent).[17]

Powerloom Sector of Bhiwandi

The decentralised powerloom sector plays an important role in production of cloth in India. It not only contributes significantly to the cloth production in the country but also provides employment to millions of people. As per official estimates, 6.6 million people are employed in the powerloom sector. However, industry estimates put this figure at around 8 million. The powerloom sector produces a wide variety of cloth, both grey as well as processed with intricate designs. The contribution of the powerloom sector to the total cloth production of the country is to the extent of 59.15 percent. It also contributes significantly to the export earnings of the country. While much of the yarn production takes place in the mill sector, 78 percent of the cloth production takes place in the powerlooms and handlooms[18]. The estimated number of powerlooms in this sector in the country at various stages till 30th September, 2001 is contained in Table 17.

Table 17: Growth in the Powerloom Sector

(as of 30th Sep. 2001)

Year	*No. of Powerlooms*
1996-97	1415844
1997-98	1534398
1998-99	1599114
1999-2000	1629853
2000-2001	1655367
2001-2002	1665722

Source : Ministry of Textiles

Table 18 : Statewise Distribution of Powerlooms

State	*Total Powerloom Units*	*% of Total*	*Powerlooms*	*% of Total*
Andhra Pradesh	6,458	1.99	42668	3.14
Assam	261	0.08	2726	0.20
Bihar	1,442	0.44	2870	0.21
Goa	18	0.01	122	0.01
Gujarat	30,924	9.51	301678	22.22
Harayana	2,653	0.82	9982	0.74
Himachal Pradesh	159	0.05	1302	0.10
Karnataka	19,692	6.06	56530	4.16
Kerala	499	0.15	2273	0.17
Madhya Pradesh	15,510	4.77	34421	2.54
Maharashtra	156,376	48.09	540578	39.82
Orissa	767	0.24	3223	0.24
Punjab	3,455	1.06	21980	1.62
Rajasthan	3,919	1.21	31471	2.32
Tamil Nadu	56,921	17.51	233842	17.22
Uttar Pradesh	25,028	7.70	65366	4.81
West Bengal	810	0.25	4220	0.31
Delhi	124	0.04	1102	0.08
Union Territories				
Chandigarh	11	0.00	42	0.00
Dadra & Nagar Haveli	20	0.01	464	0.03
Pondicherry	117	0.04	830	0.06
Total	325,164	100.00	1357690	100.00

Source: Survey of Socio Economic Conditions of Powerloom Workers of Bhiwandi, Maharashta Institute of Labour Studies, 1997

In a survey conducted by the Ministry of Textiles in 1995, the total number of powerlooms in India was estimated to be 13,57,590. Maharashtra accounted for 39.82 percent of the total number of the powerlooms in the country. (see Table 18) Bhiwandi, the single largest powerloom centre in Maharashtra, has 2,32,000 authorised powerlooms and accounts for 17.10 percent of the total powerlooms in India. The number of unauthorised powerlooms in Bhiwandi is also quite large[19].

Growth of Bhiwandi Powerloom Centre

According to the report of the Powerloom Inquiry Committee (1960), the first powerloom was installed in Ichalkaranji town of Maharashtra in 1904. The First World War brought prosperity to the industry, In the 1930s, small entrepreneurs purchased looms discarded by the mills in Mumbai and converted them into powerlooms. The Second World War also gave a boost to the powerloom sector. The mill sector was unable to meet the increasing wartime demand for cloth. This accelerated the pace of growth of the powerloom sector. In the post independence period, technological and labour problems faced by the mills created opportunities for the powerloom sector and helped it prosper[20]. In order to overcome policy restrictions on ceiling of loom capacity and labour costs and the onslaught of trade unions, mill owners resorted to subcontracting much of their production to the powerlooms. This contributed substantially to the growth of powerloom sector. Being in the informal and unorganised sector, powerlooms have learnt to function outside the legal framework. Production in this sector takes place under exploitative conditions. Combining family and wage labour, working hours in the powerlooms are as long as 12 hours with low wages and no social security benefits[21].

Bhiwandi, a part of Thane district, is situated at a distance of 51 kms from Mumbai. The growth of Bhiwandi powerloom centre passed through three different phases of development. Initially it grew as a handloom centre (1860-1930). The growth of Bhiwandi as a handloom centre was accelerated with the migration of weavers from Bengal in the 1880s. Till 1923 there was no electricity in Bhiwandi. The first powerloom in Bhiwandi was established in 1930[22].

This was followed by a period of transition in which handlooms were gradually replaced by powerlooms. The years after the First World War were marked by economic depression. The textile industry in India had also received a setback. Many mills in Mumbai were forced to shut down. In order to fill the vacuum in the textile market, many handloom weavers replaced their handlooms with powerlooms by buying second-hand looms from the mills. Gradually handlooms disappeared from the scene in Bhiwandi[23]. During the post-independence period, Bhiwandi grew only as a powerloom centre.

The imposition of excise duty on powerlooms and the progressive rising rate of the duty led to the fragmentation of bigger powerlooms into smaller ones. Since units having up to 4 powerlooms were completely exempted from excise duty, powerloom owners with more than 4 looms split the ownership of their establishment. This fragmentation took place in the case of 70 to 75 percent of the total powerloom units[24].

In 1951, there were about 3000 powerlooms operating in Bhiwandi. In 1960, the figure reached to 16, 500 and by 1982 there were 1,20,000 powerlooms in Bhiwandi. Nearness to Mumbai, the main market of raw material yarn and shortage of power supply in Mumbai helped Bhiwandi to grow as the nearest possible powerloom centre[25].

The powerloom industry of Bhiwandi flourished during the eighteen-month long strike in Mumbai's mills. The textile mills outsourced their production to the powerloom centres in Bhiwandi, Solapur, Jalgaon and Madanpura. The powerlooms were provided working capital and raw material by the mill owners. These centres were now producing cloth under the brand names of the mills. New powerlooms were set up and employment increased[26].

Bhiwandi produced cheap cloth and profits were possible because of an evasion of excise duty, low electricity costs (sometimes at no cost at all because unscrupulous owners shamelessly stole power) and, most importantly, the presence of cheap migrant labour. Weavers, largely from Andhra Pradesh, flocked to Bhiwandi. They came from very poor rural areas and were willing to work and live in appalling conditions. They are usually paid on a piece rate basis. The workers live in small dormitories of about 20 beds. The workers get none of the benefits due to them under law, such as dearness allowance, bonus, gratuity or provident fund. Since the industry remains unorganised, it has been difficult to sustain a labour movement here[27].

The powerloom sector of Bhiwandi is now going through a lean phase. The dumping of cheap and high quality cloth from countries like Korea and China has dealt a blow to Bhiwandi. Another huge blow came when the Maharashtra State Electricity Board (MSEB), reacting to the charge that Bhiwandi was a 'power thief', changed its existing tariff for the powerlooms. In its revision of tariffs, the MSEB imposed a staggering hike of 71.42 percent. The special-category status for powerlooms was removed and it was merged with the general motive power category. The minimum unit consumption slab was reduced from 500 units to 300 units[28]. During the past year, almost 25 percent of the powerlooms have been sold as scrap and a large number of workers have been pushed into unemployment. Today Bhiwandi is in the grip of reverse migration[29].

Women Workers in the Powerloom Sector

The powerloom sector, a highly labour-intensive sector, employs women in very small numbers. A survey on the working and living conditions of workers in the powerloom sector was conducted in the 1988 in 11 states on an all-India basis, by the Labour Bureau, Ministry of Labour. In the first stage of sampling, 305 units were covered and in the second stage of sampling, 410 units were covered.

Table 19 shows that there were a total number of 3,369 workers employed in the 305 sampled units. Of these 169 were women. It shows that there were only 5 women workers for every 100 male workers. In Tamil Nadu and Andhra Pradesh, the employment of women workers in the powerloom industry was in comparison to other states on the higher side, that is, 18.8 and 17.8 percent respectively. Out of a total of 169 workers, 86 were from Tamil Nadu. In comparison, in Maharashtra the employment of women in the powerloom industry was the lowest at 0.2 percent, followed by Gujarat and Harayana at 2 percent. Maximum number of women workers were working as winders/twisters.

Table 19: Proportion of Women Labour in Poweloom Industry

State	*Total no. Of units Covered*	*% of units employing Women workers*	*Total no. of workers in the unit*				*% of women workers to all workers*	*% of women workers to total no. of women workers covered in the industry*
			Men	*Women*	*Children*	*All*		
Andhra Pradesh	10	40	67	16	7	90	17.8	9.47
Gujarat	40	10	977	20		997	2.0	11.83
Haryana	10	10	96	2		98	2.0	1.18
Karnataka	20	30	180	16	1	197	8.1	9.47
Madhya Pradesh	10		25			25		
Maharashtra	120	2.5	778	3	1	782	0.4	1.78
Punjab	10	10	210	13		223	5.8	7.69
Rajasthan	10		103			103		
Tamil Nadu	45	62.2	358	86	13	457	18.8	50.89
Uttar Pradesh	20		213		2	215		
West Bengal	10	40	169	13		182	7.1	7.69
Total	305	16.7	3176	169	24	3369	5.0	100.00

Source : Statistical Profile on Women Labour (Fourth Issue) 1993, Labour Bureau, Ministry of Labour, Government of India.

Table 20 shows the occupation and gender-wise average daily wage rates of time rated workers. In the powerloom sector, women were working only as weavers, winder/twisters and helpers/ coolie/packers. The average daily wage rates of women workers varied from a minimum of Rs. 12.50 to a maximum of Rs. 33 at an All-India level, depending upon the occupations in which such workers were working. In Tamil Nadu, women workers were observed to be drawing a higher wage in comparison to their male-counterparts in the same occupation.

Table 21 shows occupation and gender-wise average daily earnings of piece-rated workers. Women workers were found working only in three occupations: (1) weaver (2) winder/finisher (3) warper/sizer and their daily earnings varied from Rs. 8.75 to Rs. 16.91 per day at All-India levels.

Table 20 : Average Daily Wage Rate of Time Rated Workers by Occupation and Sex in Powerloom Industry

Occupation	*Average daily Earnings (including DA)—(Rs.)*							
	Men		*Women*		*Children*		*All*	
	Min.	*Max.*	*Min.*	*Max.*	*Min.*	*Max.*	*Min.*	*Max.*
Weaver	25.79	29.52	20.00	33.00			28.28	29.80
Winder (Robin/Pern/ Twister)	17.91	19.00	13.70	14.21	8.71	9.13	16.39	17.52
Warper/Folder/Sizer	29.92	30.33					29.92	30.33
Dyer	25.74	27.00					25.74	27.00
Master/Jobber/Maistry/ Designer	37.70	41.37					37.70	41.37
Folder/Finisher/Clipper	26.29	28.21					26.29	28.21
Helper/other Labourer/ Coolie/Checker	19.28	20.63	12.50	12.50			18.31	19.47

Source : Statistical Profile on Women Labour (Fourth Issue) 1993, Labour Bureau, Ministry of Labour, Government of India.

Of the units where women workers were employed, 20 percent were such where working hours varied from 8 to 12 hours. For women workers, spread over was up to 10 hours in about 55 percent of units. In rest of the units, spread over of shifts for women workers was even more than 10 hours to 14 hours in violation of various labour laws[30].

Out of the total number of 305 units surveyed, women were employed in only 51 units. But only 5 units were observed to be providing maternity benefits under the Employee State Insurance Scheme. No unit was found providing maternity benefits under the Maternity Benefits Act, 1961.[31]

Table 21: Average Daily Earnings of Piece Rated Workers by Occupation and Sex in Powerloom Industry

Occupation	*Average daily Earnings (Rs.)*							
	Men		*Women*		*Children*		*All*	
	Min.	*Max.*	*Min.*	*Max.*	*Min.*	*Max.*	*Min.*	*Max.*
Weaver	29.64	42.70	14.54	16.91			29.49	42.45
Winder (Robin/Pern/ Twister)	21.00	22.82	8.75	10.79	8.60	9.40	14.29	15.55
Warper/Folder/Sizer	32.22	44.84	10.00	12.00			34.21	43.85
Dyer	23.11	27.59					23.11	27.59
Master/Jobber/Maistry/ Designer	26.29	32.22					26.29	32.22
Folder/Finisher/Clipper	23.25	23.25					23.25	23.25
Helper/other Labourer/ Coolie/Checker	17.80	21.91					17.80	21.91

Source : Statistical Profile on Women Labour (Fourth Issue) 1993, Labour Bureau, Ministry of Labour, Government of India.

Women Workers in Powerlooms of Bhiwandi

Women workers are employed in very small numbers in Bhiwandi's powerlooms. Moreover, there is a clear division of labour on the basis of gender. Women workers in Bhiwandi work only in the mending/clipping section of the powerloom units.

The five powerloom units included in the sample produce nylon/polyester viscose cloth and have on an average 35 powerlooms each. After the yarn is purchased, the production process involves warping, beam drawing and weaving. Once the grey cloth is produced, women workers are engaged in mending any defects in the cloth and clipping the superfluous threads in the grey cloth. With the introduction of new machines, the quality of grey cloth produced is much better and very little mending work is required. In all the units surveyed, women workers were mainly engaged in semi-skilled operations as clippers.

There were a total number of 275 workers employed in the 5 units surveyed. Out of these 18 were women. Women workers formed 6.5 percent of the workforce in the sampled units. Since there are no muster rolls in these units and no employee records are maintained, it is difficult to get information about the workers. In all the units in the sample, workers are hired by a contractor who pays them their wages. A majority of women workers live in Bhiwandi, while a small minority come from Thane city. The working conditions in the powerloom units are terrible. In all the units, women worked in cramped conditions, with poor lighting and no ventilation. Since the sheds in which they worked were covered with tin roofs, it becomes unbearably hot in the summer. Most women complained of spells of nausea, dizziness and headaches. There were no separate toilet facilities for women in the units. The only toilet provided by the units were makeshift *kutcha* toilets. Most women workers avoided using these common toilets. In fact, some women workers preferred to walk back home (which could be a one hour walk back and forth) to use the toilet. If they were absent for even an hour, their wage was deducted.

All the women workers in the sampled units were paid on a time-rate basis. While 58 percent of the women were paid on a monthly basis, the remaining 42 percent were paid on a weekly basis. The women workers work for 8 hours every day and are on an average paid Rs. 45 per day. Their wages fall on the lower end of the spectrum primarily because of the division of labour on the basis of gender. Women are confined to the lowest paying jobs.

The workers in Bhiwandi's powerlooms do not enjoy the benefits of any paid leave, weekly off, dearness allowance, provident fund, medical assistance under the Employee State Insurance Scheme or maternity benefits. If any monetary assistance is provided by the owner in case of an illness, it is duly deducted with interest from their salary. There is no job security for these women working in the powerlooms. The fear of losing their jobs is constant. Even women who have been working for more than 10 years in the present unit did not feel their jobs were secure. In the course of conducting the interviews, most women workers appeared extremely nervous if the owner or supervisor walked in, despite assuring them that the owner had granted permission to conduct the interview.

The majority of women in the powerloom units belonged to the 30-40 age group. (55 percent), 20 percent belonged to the 20-30 age group and 25 percent belonged to the 40-50 age group. Out of the sample, 14.02 percent women had been working in the present unit for less than 1 year, 25.78 percent from 1 to 3 years, 32.21 percent for 3 to 5 years, 21 percent for 5 to 10 years and 7 percent for 10 to 15 years. Most women had previous experience in the powerloom sector and had on an average worked for 1-3 years in some other powerloom unit.

In the sample, 48 percent of the women workers were married, 35 percent were widows, 15 percent had been deserted by their husbands and 2 percent were unmarried. Economic necessity was the major cause for women's entry into this sector. All the women interviewed had taken up work for this reason. Women's contribution to the family income was crucial. In a majority of cases in the sample, the women were either the sole earners or the highest earning member of the family. Most women working in the looms had 3-4 children and the average family size was of 5-6 persons.

A survey was conducted on the social and economic conditions of powerloom workers of Bhiwandi in 1997 by the Maharashtra institute of Labour Studies. The sample constituted a total number of 50 units and 250 workers. The survey shows that women work as semi-skilled workers in the clipping departments of powerlooms. They constitute a mere 3.87 percent of the total workforce.

An analysis of women workers in the textile industry shows that women are employed in very small numbers throughout the industry. The prevalence of gender-based division of labour is also seen throughout the industry, both in the organised and unorganised sectors. Women workers are generally confined to only the winding/mending sections. They are generally concentrated in the lowest paying jobs. In order to improve the status of women workers in this industry, there is a need to launch intensive skill upgradation programmes. Both in the mills of Mumbai and powerlooms of Bhiwandi, women workers constitute a negligible percentage of the working population. In the unorganised powerloom sector, they enjoy none of the social security benefits legally due to them and all labour laws are openly flouted. There is an urgent need to improve the enforcement of labour laws in the powerloom sector of Bhiwandi.

NOTES AND REFERENCES

1. Ministry of Textiles, Annual Report 2000-2001, (New Delhi, Government of India, 2001), www. texmin. nic.in.
2. *Ibid.*
3. Labour Practices in the Footwear, Leather, Textiles and Clothing Industries (Geneva: ILO, 2000), www.ilo.org.
4. Morris D Morris, *The Emergence of the Industrial Labour Force in India* (OUP: Bombay, 1965), p.4.
5. Radha Kumar, "Factory Life: Women Workers in the Bombay Cotton Textile Industry, 1919-1939," in Sujata Gothoshkar (ed.), *Struggles of Women at Work* (Vikas Publishing House: New Delhi, 1992), p. 123.
6. Mira Savara, *Changing Trends in Women's Employment – A Case Study of the Textile Industry in Bombay,* (Himalaya Publishing House : New Delhi), p. 22.
7. *Ibid.*
8. *Ibid*, p. 16.
9. *Ibid.*, p.124.
10. *Ibid.*, p. 126.
11. Radha Kumar, *op cit*, p. 125.
12. Mira Savara, *op cit*, p. 35.
13. *Report of the Textile Labour Inquiry Committee*, (Bombay: Government of India, 1940), p. 208.
14. *Report of the Badli Labour Inquiry Committee – Cotton Textile Industry, 1967*, (Government of Maharashtra: Bombay, 1968), p.44.
15. Mira Savara, *op cit*, p. 62.
16. *Ibid.*
17. Ajit Kumar, 'Spinners Hike Output to Overcome Loss', *The Indian Express*, September 27, 1999.
18. Ministry of Textiles, Annual Report 2000-2001, *op cit*.
19. Maharashtra Institute of Labour Studies, *Survey of Socio-Economic Conditions of Powerloom Workers of Bhiwandi* (Mumbai : Unpublished, 1997), p. 2-3.
20. Indian National Textile Workers' Federation and The Ambedkar Institute for Labour, *Socio-Economic Study of the Powerloom Workers in the Bhiwandi Centre* (Mumbai : Unpublished, 1986), pp1-2.
21. Uma Ramaswamy and Sarath Darala, "Women in the Indian Textile and Garment Industry, " in Ludgera Klemp and Bernd Reddies (eds.), *Women Textile Workers Demand Justice. On the Situation of Textile and Garment Industry in the Countries of the South* (Friedrich Ebert Foundation: Duseldorf, 1992), p. 21.
22. Socio-Economic Study of the Powerloom Workers in the Bhiwandi Centre, *op cit*, pp. 9-10.
23. *Ibid*, p. 10.

24. *Ibid*, pp. 10-11.
25. *Ibid*, p. 11.
26. Sharit Bhowmick and Nitin More, "Coping with Urban Poverty. Ex-Textile Mill Workers in Central Mumbai, " *Economic and Political Weekly*, Vol. XXXVI, No. 52, December 29 2001, p. 4822.
27. Freny Manecksha, "Bhiwandi's *Bunkar Biradari*: From Boom to Bust, "*Humanscape*, November 2000 at www. humanscapeindia.net.
28. *Ibid*.
29. M. H. Lakdawala, "Bhiwandi: Gloom Town," *Islamic Voice*, Vol. 15, No. 172, April 2001.
30. Labour Bureau, *Statistical Profile on Women Labour (Fourth Issue)*, (New Delhi: Government of India Press, 1993), p. 81.
31. *Ibid*.

Chapter 5

State Action for Women Workers

Given the poor status of women workers, it is undeniable that the government will have to play a crucial role in the protection and promotion of their rights. State intervention in the form of legislation, policy framework and promotional programmes is a prerequisite in ensuring and advancing women workers' rights. This chapter will examine the constitutional; judicial, statutory and developmental measures adopted for the promotion of rights of women workers.

The need for safeguarding the rights of women found its expression in the Indian Constitution. The Constitution of India guarantees certain fundamental rights (Part III of the Constitution) which are justiciable and enforceable by the courts. The Constitution, which is the basic law of the land, mandates equality before law. Article 14 of the Constitution guarantees equality before law and equal protection of the law.

The principle of equality enshrined in the Constitution was put to test in the *Air India v Nargesh Meerza case.*[1] In this case, the Supreme Court considered the validity of the service regulations governing the airhostesses in Air India and Indian Airlines. According to Regulation 46 and 47, an airhostess would be retired in the following cases: (1) on attaining the age of 35 years. Under Regulation 47, the Managing Director had the discretion to extend the age of retirement by 1 year at a time beyond the age of retirement up to the age of 45 years if an airhostess was found to be medically fit. (2) On marriage if it took place within 4 years of service (3) on first pregnancy. On the other hand, assistant flight pursers who were males retired at the age of 55 or 58. Both categories constituted the same cabin crew.

The court upheld the validity of different retirement ages for air hostesses and air flight pursers because it ruled that the difference was not on the ground of sex only and also upheld the regulation on question of bar of marriage before 4 years of service.

The condition that the services of airhostesses would be terminated on first pregnancy was held by the court to be unreasonable and arbitrary and thereby clearly violating Article 14.

The court also held that the power given to the managing director to use his discretion to extend the age of retirement violated Article 14 of the Constitution. According to the court, this conferred a wide and uncontrolled discretion on the managing director and hence violated Article 14 on the ground of excessive delegation of powers. The court struck down the regulation and the effect of this was that airhostesses would retire at the age of 45 years if found medically fit.

In 1989, the government directed both Indian Airlines and Air India to eliminate discrimination and permit air hostesses to fly till the age of 58. Indian Airlines complied with the directive immediately but Air India did nothing till 1993, when they increased the age limit, but only till the age of 50. In July 2003, the Supreme Court upheld Air India's policy banning air hostesses from flying after 50. The court ruled that the age limit will allow women to "fulfill their marital obligations." The air hostesses long struggle for gender equality has suffered a serious setback with this judgement.

Article 15 of the Constitution provides that the state shall not discriminate against any citizen on grounds of religion, race, caste, sex or place of birth. Article 15 provides for a particular application of the general principle of equality embodied in Article 14. The framers of the Constitution were aware that mere prohibition of discrimination would not be enough to alleviate the status of women. Thus Clause 3 of Article 15 empowers the state to make 'any special provisions for women and children.' This clause empowers the state to make laws in favour of women.

In *Government of Andhra Pradesh v. P.B. Vijaykumar,*[2] the Supreme Court considered the validity of Rule 22-A of Andhra Pradesh State and Subordinate Services Rules which provided for preference to women in direct recruitment.

Rule 22-A provides for preference being given to women to the extent of 30 percent of the posts other things being equal. This is clearly not reservation for women in the normal sense of the term. Reservation normally implies a separate quota, which is reserved for a separate category of persons. Within that category, appointments may be made in order of merit. Rule 22-A did not provide for this kind of reservation. It is a rule for a very limited affirmative action. It operates, first of all, in respect of direct recruitment to posts for which men and women are equally suited. Secondly, it operates only when men and women are equally meritorious. This is an express condition of Rule 22-A, thus limiting its action.[3]

The court held that the rule was within the ambit of Article 15 (3) and Article 16. Delivering the landmark judgement, Justice Sujata Manohar observed that the "insertion of clause (3) of Article 15 in relation to women is a recognition of the fact that for centuries women of this country have been socially and economically handicapped. As a result, they are unable to participate in the socio-economic activities of the nation on a footing of equality. It is in order to eliminate this socio-economic backwardness of women and to empower them in a manner that would bring about effective equality between men and women that the clause is placed in Article 15. Its object is to strengthen and improve the status of women. An important limb of this concept of gender equality is creating job opportunities for women....".[4]

Article 16 (1) of the Constitution guarantees equality of opportunity to all citizens in matters relating to employment or appointment to any office under the state. Article 16 (2) provides that no citizen shall be discriminated against in respect of any employment or office under the state on grounds of religion, race, caste, sex, descent, and place of birth or residence. It may be noted that under Article 16 the guarantee against discrimination is limited to employment and appointment under the state. Article 15, however, is more general and deals with all cases of discrimination, which do not fall under Article 16.

In *C.B. Mutthamma v. Union of India case,*[5] the petitioner, a senior member of the Indian Foreign Service, alleged that she was denied promotion to Grade I service owing to long standing practice of hostile discrimination on the basis of gender. The court ruled that a provision in service rules of the IFS which required a female employee to obtain the permission of the government in writing before her marriage is solemnised and denying her the right to be promoted on the ground that the candidate was a married woman was discriminatory and hence unconstitutional.

In *Bombay Labour Union v. International Franchise case*,[6] a rule requiring an unmarried woman to give up her position when she married was challenged. The rule applied only to a particular department of the company. The justification offered by the company for this rule was the need to work in teams, the need for regular attendance and greater absenteeism among married women. The Supreme Court held that here there was no evidence that married women were more likely to be absent than unmarried women and struck down the restriction.

In *Maya Devi v. State of Maharashtra case*,[7] a requirement that married women obtain their husband's consent before applying for public employment was challenged as violating Article 14, 15 and 16. The Supreme Court held that the consent requirement was unconstitutional.

Neera Mathur v. Life Insurance Corporation case is yet another example of prejudice against women in employment.[8] In this case the petitioner had applied for the post of an assistant in the LIC and having been successful in both the written test and personal interviews was asked to fill a declaration form and submit it to the corporation. On 25th May 1989 she was also examined by a lady doctor of the LIC and was found medically fit for the job. Having successfully undergone a short training programme, she was given an appointment letter, dated 25th September 1989, and put on probation for 6 months. Her appointment was to be confirmed, subject to her obtaining satisfactory work report from the corporation. The petitioner took maternity leave from 9th December 1989 to 8th March 1990. In the meantime, the petitioner on February 1990 was discharged from the service during the probation period.

Moving the High Court under Article 226 of the Constitution, the petitioner challenged the order of discharge on the ground that that it was not a discharge simplicitor but was based on some discrepancy in the declaration made by her before joining the service. The LIC resisted this contention by pointing out that the petitioner's work was not satisfactory and under the terms of the appointment, she was discharged without notice and without assigning any reasons. The respondent also pointed out that the petitioner had deliberately withheld the fact of being pregnant at the time of filing the declaration form. Having found favour with the LIC, the High Court observed that that "the petitioner's work during the period of probation was found to be not satisfactory".[9]

On appeal, the Supreme Court issued an interim mandamus, directing LIC to reinstate the appellant in the service within 15 days of the order. The Supreme Court observed" We have nothing on record to indicate that the petitioner's work during the period of probation was not satisfactory. Indeed, the reason for termination seems to be different. It was the declaration given by her at the stage of entering the service. It is said that she gave a false declaration regarding her pregnancy with a view to suppress the fact that she was pregnant at the time of appointment. It seems to us that the petitioner cannot be blamed in this case as she was medically examined by the doctor who was on the panel of LIC and was found fit for the job." Hence the petition was allowed. The result was undoubtedly favourable for the petitioner but in this case the court lost the opportunity to scrutinise the gendered nature of the service rule.[10]

Article 19 of the Constitution guarantees the following 6 freedoms: (a) Freedom of speech and expression (b) Freedom of assembly (c) Freedom to form associations (d) Freedom of movement (e) Freedom to reside and settle in any part of the territory of India (f) Freedom of profession, occupation, trade or business. Article 23 prohibits traffic in human beings and forced labor.

The framers of the Indian Constitution also incorporated provisions relating to workers in Part IV of the Constitution dealing with Directive Principles of State Policy. The Directive Principles that concern women workers directly are: Article 39 (a) – the right to an adequate means of livelihood for men and women equally; Article 39 (d) – equal pay for equal work for both men and women. Article 39 (c) – protection of the health and strength of workers – men, women and children – from abuse and entry into vocations unsuited to their age or strength; Article 42 – just and humane conditions of work and maternity relief; and Article 43 – provision of work, a living wage, conditions of work ensuring a decent standard of life and full enjoyment of leisure and social and cultural opportunities, and the promotion of cottage industries.

Labour Legislation and Women Workers

The Constitution of India, the supreme law of the land, mandates equality before law and equal protection of law. The Indian government has also enacted specific laws to redress the problems of workers. Since women workers are particularly vulnerable to exploitation, many legislative provisions, which address the problems of women workers, are included in almost labour laws. Table 1 gives an overview of the laws and the provisions specifically applicable to women workers.

For clarity of discussion, labour laws affecting women can be classified into three categories: (I) Laws which pertain specifically to women workers (II) Laws which are general in nature but have special features for the protection of women workers (III) Laws which are general in nature but are more relevant to women workers because they form a large section of the workforce in certain occupations.

Table 1: Laws and Provisions specifically applicable to Women Workers

EMPLOYMENT OF WOMEN – PROTECTIVE LEGAL PROVISIONS		
S.No.	*Name of Enactment*	*Protective Provisions*
1.	The Bidi & Cigar Workers (Conditions of Employment) Act, 1966.	Provisions of creches for the benefit of women workers in the industrial premises wherein more than fifty female employees are ordinarily employed.
2.	The Plantation's Labour Act, 1951	Provision of creches in every plantation wherein fifty or more women workers (including women workers employed by any contractor) are employed or where the number of children of women workers (including women workers employed by any contractor) is twenty or more. Women workers are provided time off for feeding children.
3.	The Contract Labour (Regulation & Abolition) Act, 1970	Provision of creches where twenty or more women are employed as contract labour. Not to be required to work beyond 9 hours between 6 am and 7 pm with the exception of midwives and nurses in plantations.

(*Contd....*)

(Contd....)

S.No.	*Name of Enactment*	*Protective Provisions*
4.	The Inter State Migrant Workmen (Regulation of Employment & Condition of Service) Act, 1979	Provision of creches for the benefit of women workers in establishments wherein twenty or more women are ordinarily employed as migrant workmen and in which employment of migrant workmen is likely to continue for three months or more.
5.	The Factories Act, 1948	Provision of creches in every factory wherein more than thirty women workers are ordinarily employed.
6.	The Mines Act, 1952	Employment in mines below ground prohibited. Provision of separate toilets and washing facilities for women workers.
7.	Maternity Benefits Act, 1961	Maternity benefits to be provided on completion of 80 days working. Not required to work six weeks immediately following the day of delivery or miscarriage. No work of arduous nature, long hours of standing likely to interfere with pregnancy/normal development of foetus or which may cause miscarriage or is likely to affect health to be given for a period of six months immediately preceding the period of one week before delivery. One medical certificate, advance maternity benefit to be allowed. Rs.250.00 as Medical bonus to be given when no prenatal confinement and postnatal care is provided free of charge.
8.	Equal Remuneration Act, 1976	Payment of equal remuneration to men and women workers for same or similar nature of work protected under the Act and also under the provisions at Sl.No.4. No discrimination permissible in recruitment and service conditions except where employment of women is prohibited or restricted by or under any law.
9.	Employees' State Insurance (General) Regulation, 1950	Claim for maternity benefit becomes due on the date medical certificate is issued for miscarriage, sickness arising out of pregnancy, confinement or premature birth of child. Claim for maternity benefit becomes due on the (General Regulation 1950) the date medical certificate is issued for miscarriage, sickness arising out of pregnancy, confinement or premature birth of child.

(Contd....)

(Contd....)

S.No.	*Name of Enactment*	*Protective Provisions*
10.	Beedi Workers Welfare Fund Act, 1976	Appointment of women member in the Advisory and Central Advisory Committee is mandatory under the Acts at Sl.Nos.10-13.
11.	Iron Ore Mines, Manganese Ore Mines and Chrome Ore Mines labour Welfare Fund Act, 1976.	-do-
12.	Lime Stone and Dolomite Mines Labour Welfare Fund Act, 1976	-do-
13.	Mica Mines Labour Welfare Fund Act, 1946.	-do-
14.	The Building and Other Construction Workers (Regulation of Employment and Conditions of Service) Act, 1976	Representation of a woman member on Building and other Construction Worker Welfare Boards. Provisions for maternity benefit to female beneficiaries of the Welfare Fund. Provision for creches where more than 50 female construction workers are ordinarily employed.
15.	Industrial Employment (Standing Orders) Act, 1946.	Provision regarding safeguards against sexual harassment of women workers at their work places.

(I) Laws Pertaining Specifically to Women Workers

These include the Maternity Benefit Act and Equal Remuneration Act.

Equal Remuneration Act, 1976

The ILO Convention No. 100 of 1951 relating to equal remuneration for men and women was ratified by the Government of India in 1958. To give effect to the constitutional provisions and also to ensure the enforcement of ILO Convention No. 100, the Equal Remuneration Ordinance was promulgated in 1975. The above ordinance was subsequently replaced by the Equal Remuneration Act, 1976.

The preamble of the Act lays down that the Act is intended to provide for the payment of equal remuneration to men and women workers and for the prevention of discrimination, on the ground of sex, against women in the matter of employment or any other matter which is connected to or is incidental to employment. This Act imposes a statutory obligation on the employer to prevent discrimination against women in terms of payment of remuneration to them and to ensure equality in respect of terms and conditions of employment in comparison to their male counterparts.

The fundamental premise behind the Equal Remuneration Act is that men and women doing same or similar work must get equal wages. An employer is punishable in the event of discrimination against women in respect of wages, recruitment, promotion or transfer.

The Act applies to all manners of employment notified in the schedule and to the workers employed therein. The list of classes of employment listed in the schedule under the Act is extensive and includes industries from the formal and informal sector.

The term 'remuneration' is defined as the basic wage or salary inclusive of any additional emoluments payable in either cash or kind.

The term "same work or work of similar nature" means work in respect of which skill, effort and responsibility required are the same, when performed under similar working conditions, by a man or a woman and the difference, if any, between the skill, effort and responsibility required of a man and those required of a woman is not of practical importance in relation to the terms and conditions of employment.

The Act lays down that no employer shall pay to any worker a remuneration, whether payable in cash or kind, at rates less favourable than those at which remuneration is paid by him to the worker of the opposite sex for performing the same work or work of a similar nature.

The Act was amended in 1987 to prohibit discrimination not only in initial recruitment but also in any condition of service subsequent to recruitment such as promotion, training or transfer. In 1987, the fines for non-compliance under Section 10 were increased from Rs. 500-1000 to Rs. 10,000-20,000. The jail term was also increased from 1 month to 2 years. However, these punitive measures have not really improved the situation. The text of the Equal Remuneration Act is contained in Annexure V.

The interpretation and application of the Equal Remuneration Act came into focus in the *Air India v. Nargesh Meerza case*[11] in which the Supreme Court ruled that the application of the Equal Remuneration Act could not be unconditional. If men and women are employed under different conditions of service then they could not be seen to belong to one class of service. The court observed that differences in the conditions of work could only be seen as discriminatory if the employers had similar work agreements.

The Supreme Court adopted a different stand when an issue pertaining to discrimination in payment of remuneration came up before it in the *Mackinnon Mackenzie and Co v. Audrey D' Costa case.*[12] In this case the petitioner, a lady stenographer, claimed that the remuneration being paid to her was less than the remuneration paid to male stenographers for similar type of work. The employer claimed that the lady stenographer, who was working as a confidential stenographer, was not doing the same or similar type of work and hence there was no discrimination on account of sex.

The court rejected this argument and held that the work being performed by the women as confidential stenographers was almost the same as that of male stenographers even though women were not employed in the general pool of stenographers consisting of male employees only. Thus the court ruled that both men and women should get equal remuneration.

The Supreme Court in this case opined that in order to ascertain whether the work done by the male and female workers was the same or of similar type, the authority should take a broader view. Moreover, in deciding whether any differences in work were of practical importance or not, the concerned authority should take an equally broad approach because the very concept of similar work would imply differences in details.

It has been suggested that the Act should be amended so that the phrase 'same work or work of similar nature' should be replaced by the phrase 'work of equal value.' In this context, the Shramshakti report of 1988 pointed out that measuring value of work and equating them is a far more difficult task than identifying 'same work or work of similar nature.' There is a tendency to categorise tasks generally done by women as being of a slightly inferior nature, warranting lower rates of wages. This is seen even in the fixation of minimum rates of wages. To avoid this, the Shramshakti report recommended that it would be advantageous if a group of activities in any industrial occupation are broad-banded into one category, on the basis of inquiries and studies, so that the present situation is remedied.[13]

The piece rate system has also been one method of paying lower wages to women without contravening the provisions of the Equal Remuneration Act since a large number of women workers are paid wages under the piece rate system. The Shramshakti report pointed out that the piece rate system was an institutionalised mechanism to pay lower wages to women. While the time rate system follows the Minimum Wages Act, there are no such regulations for the piece rate system. Therefore, women put in long hours of work to earn a pittance, which may be a fraction of what they would have earned under the time rate minimum wage. The National Commission on Labour in its report on women and child workers has recommended that the Act must amended to remove the incompatibility between the piece rate and the time rate system of fixing wages.[14]

Enforcement of Equal Remuneration Act

There are several mechanisms for the enforcement of the Equal Remuneration Act. Some of these are provided for in the realm of the law, while other agencies that implement the Equal Remuneration Act were constituted under the previous labour laws. Section 7 of the law provides for the appointment of inspectors by an appropriate authority in order to ensure that employers are complying with the provisions of the Act. At present, the inspectorate carrying out such inspections is the office of labour commissioner that was instituted under previous labour laws. However, the Equal Remuneration Act is just one of the laws under its purview and the pressures of work have made the law machinery inadequate. The Labour Ministry and the Central Advisory Committee regularly monitor the situation regarding enforcement of the provisions of the Equal Remuneration Act. The special cell calls for annual returns from the state governments in order to monitor implementation of the Act. In most cases response from state governments has not been encouraging.[15] The number of convictions under the Equal Remuneration Act is very low. Table 2 gives an overview of the position of enforcement of the Act.

One of the main problems facing the implementation of the Equal Remuneration Act is inadequate training of inspectors in determining what is 'work of same or similar nature'. There is also a lack of gender-sensitisation amongst those who enforce law. Inspectors fail to identify cases of discrimination, which are rampant in industries like electronics and garments. The National Commission on Labour in its report on women and child workers has highlighted the need to formulate guidelines for inspectors and other authorities to detect violations of the Act. The Commission has also stressed the urgent need for initiating a process of gender sensitization of officials. The Commission in its report has recommended the creation of a separate inspecting

Table 2: Position of Implementation of the Equal Remuneration Act, 1976

Spheres	*Inspection*	*Violation Detected*	*Violation Rectified*	*Prosecutions Launched*	*Convictions*	*Acquittals*
State/UTs						
1996*	15315	2145	17	260	173	-
1997*	18716	1869	169	243	158	-
1998*	15862	460	233	151	-	-
Central						
1997	4195	4722	4223	1144	537	27
1998	4056	4115	3879	1086	450	24
1998-99	3968	3935	3981	968	500	10
1999-2000*	2431	2652	2367	394	196	6
2000-2001*	4121	4265	3886	775	267	112

* Provisional

agency to detect and identify the discrimination and unequal emoluments for same or similar kind of work. This is necessary because the existing inspecting agency is overburdened with the enforcement of general labour legislation.

Before the Act was amended in 1987, complaints could be filed either by registered trade unions or by individuals. Since the 1987 amendment, the Act has provided for the involvement of social organizations in enforcement. The following social welfare organisations have been recognised under the Act for the purpose of filing complaints in courts against employers:

- The Centre for Women's Development Studies, New Delhi
- Self Employed Women's Assocaition, Ahemdabad
- The Working Women's Forum (India), Chennai
- The Institute of Social Studies Trust, New Delhi

Section 6 of the Equal Remuneration Act provides for the setting up of one or more Advisory Committees for rendering advice to the government with regard to the extent to which women may be employed in such establishments or employments where there are gender-based wage disparities. With regard to composition of the Advisory Committees, it has been explicitly provided that it shall consist of not less than 10 persons, of which at least half shall be women.

Accordingly, the union and state governments have set up various advisory boards. The Central Advisory Committees which have been set up under the Equal Remuneration Act have met 7 times between 1989 and 1999, but their recommendations are far too general to help in the implementation of the Act. Further, the committees have no specific roles to play and are not given any powers to influence the methods by which the problems associated with the Act can be solved. The result is that the 'action taken' reports of the committee are characterised by a lack of understanding of the factors that lead to wage disparities. In the light of this experience, the character of the committees needs to undergo a change. For example, the Advisory Boards constituted under the Minimum wages and Bonded Labour Acts have a fair amount of discretionary powers to influence matters of implementation and also determine the process of fixation of wage rates. The National Labour Commission, in its report, has recommended that the Act should be suitably amended to give these committees appropriate powers. The power of these committees should be focussed on the identification of discriminatory practices and the enforcement of the Act. For this purpose, they should be given appropriate powers to monitor the functioning of the Labour Commissioner's Office to monitor the Act. Moreover, the terms of reference of these committees should include a review of all labour laws that are incompatible with the principle of equal remuneration.

It has been over 2 decades since the Equal Remuneration Act was formulated and adopted, yet the practice of paying lower wages to women for the same or similar work is still rampant. The Shramshakti report of 1986 made the following observations: "Virtually nowhere did we find equal wages being paid to men and women for the same work – not in any occupation. Even in states where women's status is not that low, like Nagaland, Manipur and Assam, women do not receive equal wages. It is not only private employers who practice this discrimination. Cooperatives are also at fault. Even when the government is the employer, the payment to women is less than that to men for the same work. The dismally few exceptions to this rule were found in Himachal Pradesh. As many times as we probed, as many times as we witnessed women doing exactly the same labour and putting in the same hours as men, nowhere were we given a satisfactory answer as to why they are being paid less."

While the Equal Remuneration Act is a step in the right direction, in practice it has failed to achieve its goals. There is a need to build greater awareness about the provisions of the Act. In some cases, employers have been known to confuse this Act with the Minimum Wages Act, 1948. Several provisions of the Act need to be amended as suggested above. Enforcement of the Act needs to be improved, including training of labour inspectors.

The Maternity Benefit Act, 1961

The Maternity Benefit Act, 1961, provides for special benefits to women workers for certain periods before and after childbirth.

The Act applies to all women workers in industrial and non-industrial undertakings, mines or plantations, to persons employed for exhibition of equestrian, acrobatic or other shows and to shops where more than 10 persons are employed. However, the Act does not apply to any factory or establishment governed by the Employees' State Insurance Act. Where a factory/ establishment is governed under the Employees' State Insurance Act but a woman employee is not qualified to claim maternity benefits, then such an employee is entitled to claim maternity benefit under this Act.

The Act has a very limited scope and coverage since it applies to only those undertakings/establishments where more than 10 persons are employed. It does not apply to the unorganised sector where a majority of women are employed, for example, home-based workers, construction workers etc.

A women is entitled to maternity benefits only if she has worked in an establishment for a period of at least 80 days during the 12 months immediately preceding the date of her expected delivery. It has been suggested that this eligibility criteria should be removed.

A woman worker is entitled to 6 weeks' leave with full pay before the delivery and 6 weeks' leave with full pay after delivery. The woman can, at her option, take full 12 weeks' leave with full pay after her delivery. If the worker has a miscarriage, she is entitled to get 6 weeks' leave with full pay after the miscarriage. If a worker falls sick due to pregnancy, delivery or miscarriage or because of delivering a premature baby, she is entitled to take one extra months' paid leave.

The worker can refuse to do any work which is physically tiring or which involves standing for long hours, carrying loads etc, or any kind of work which can endanger the proper growth of the foetus. A worker can request for light work during one month before the 6 weeks pre-delivery leave, and also if she doesn't take the above 6 weeks leave.

Under the Act, a worker returning to work after giving birth is entitled to 2 nursing break everyday till the baby is 15 months old. These nursing breaks are in addition to other normally given breaks.

If the employer does not have any facilities for pre and post-natal care, the woman worker is entitled to a medical bonus of Rs. 250. This amount is highly inadequate and needs to be increased to at least Rs. 1000.

The administration of the provisions of this Act in respect to firms and establishments engaged in exhibition of equestrian, acrobatic and other performances is controlled by the Central Government, whereas in respect to all other establishments it is looked after by the concerned State Governments. The Act provides for the post of inspector to monitor the compliance of this Act. The inspector is entitled to receive complaints and undertake examination of all relevant records for the purpose of investigating a complaint.

The Shramshakti report noted that one of the causes often cited for the poor employment rate for women is the incidence of maternity benefits and the consequent reluctance on the part of employers to hire women workers. It highlighted that the average expenditure incurred as maternity benefits is not large but even so, one can visualise a psychological, if not a financial barrier in the minds of the employer in recruiting women as employees. Whatever may be the cause and motivations, the Shramshakti report has recommended that the 'burden' of maternity benefits in respect of women employees must be borne by all the employers and not only by the individual employer who has women in his or her employment. It is seen that in respect of establishments covered by the Employees State Insurance Act, 1948, the expenditure incurred in providing maternity benefits is borne by the Corporation and not by the individual employer concerned. It is necessary to provide a method by which this responsibility for providing maternity benefits is equally shared by all employers. For this purpose, the Shramshakti report recommended the establishment of a Central Fund out of which the benefits may be provided. All employers should pay to this fund a percentage of the wages (of both men and women workers) as monthly contribution.

The Group on Women Workers and Child Labour of the National Commission on Labour has recommended in its report that 15 days paternity leave of absence to accompany the maternity leave of female employees.

II. General Labour Laws with Specific Sections for Women Workers

Most labour laws are general in nature but have specific provisions for the protection of women workers. These provisions pertain either to women's reproductive and caring role and include provisions for maternity or creche facilities or are aimed at protecting them against conditions which are considered unsuitable for women, including carrying heavy loads, working underground or prohibition of night work. Some such general laws will be discussed in this section.

Factories Act, 1948

This Act provides for the health, safety and welfare of workers in factories. A factory is defined as any premise where a manufacturing process is carried out with the aid of power and where 10 or more workers have worked on any day of the preceding year. If the manufacturing process is carried out without the aid of power, the number of workers must be 20 or more.

The definition of worker includes those who are directly employed as well as those who are employed through a contractor.

The Act prohibits the employment of women and children in any part of a factory for pressing cotton in which a cotton opener is at work.

The Act lays down that in every factory where more than 30 women workers are employed, creches should be provided. It is now being recommended that creches should be provided in factories employing more than 10 workers, regardless of whether they are men or women.

The Act also prescribes separate and adequately screened washing facilities for male and female workers.

In line with ILO Conventions No. 103, 89 and 45, which were ratified by the Indian Government, the Factories Act, 1948, prohibits night work for women workers. Section 66 of the Factories Act lays down that it is illegal to make women work between 7 PM and 5 AM.

The issue of prohibition of women from working in the night shift is a controversial one. There is no doubt that legal prohibition of night work has restricted women's employment. Industries, which follow the shift system, avoid employing women workers because they can work only in the general shift and it becomes difficult to rotate workers and therefore gives rise to resentment among male workers.

The Report of the Committee on the Status of women in India, 1974, recommended the extension of work period up to 10 PM provided transport facilities and adequate security is provided to women workers. It also recommended that for the retrenchment of women workers, prior permission should be taken.

The recent Chennai High Court judgment permitting women to be employed in night shifts in factories has received mixed response. The verdict was in response to a public interest litigation filed by women employees, groups and trade unions challenging Section 66 of the Factories Act.

Justice E. Padmanabham, who passed the order, indicated that it was in keeping with the constitutional guarantee of equal opportunity. The court ruled that the bar on night shifts for women results in denial of livelihood and therefore, is a restrictive and not an affirmative action. The court ruled that in the night shift, women should be employed only in batches of not less than 10 or not less than two-thirds of the total night shift strength and factories should provide proper and safe transport facilities, amenities and forums for redress of grievances of sexual harassment.

As mentioned earlier, a blanket ban on night work for women does limit employment opportunities for women but these restrictions can be lifted only if adequate transport and security facilities are provided. Otherwise it could open the doors for exploitation, particularly sexual exploitation. The National Commission on Labour has recommended that night work should be allowed on a case to case basis only. A committee to be nominated by the Ministry of Labour should examine the case of each industry for permitting night work.

Mines Act, 1952

The Mines Act applies to all excavation-related industries, including oil exploration, crude conditioning and even open cast workings.

The Act prohibits the employment of women in any part of the mine that is below the ground. Additionally, no woman can be employed above ground except between 6 AM and 7 PM. It is also mandatory to provide a woman worker at least 11 hours of gap between the termination of employment on any given day and the resumption of employment on the next day. While the Central Government has the power to vary the timings of employment of women, at no event can a woman be made to work between 10 PM and 5 AM.

III. Laws Which are General in Nature but are more Relevant to Women Workers

There are some laws, which are general in nature but are more relevant to women workers because they form a large section of the workforce in certain sectors. Some such laws are discussed below:

Minimum Wages Act, 1948

The Minimum Wages Act is one of the most relevant laws for women workers because the Act is primarily designed for the protection of workers in the unorganised sector, where the majority of women work.

The Minimum Wages Act stipulates that a person must be paid at least that amount of wages as is fixed by the government. However, different minimum wages are fixed for different industries. The employer is bound to pay the minimum wage even if the employee has agreed to work for less than the minimum wage. The Act provides that minimum wages can be fixed according to the nature of the work on the basis of the hour, by the day or by the month. The Act also provides that wages payable under the Act has to be paid in cash. But in case of agricultural operations, payments can be paid partly in cash and partly in kind but total value of the non-cash remuneration must, when added to the cash payment, add up to at least the minimum wage.

While the Act provides a mechanism for fixing and revising minimum rate of wages, it does not give any guidelines as to the basis on which the minimum wages are to be fixed or revised. This has been the subject of considerable criticism and discussion over the years. The Shramshakti report recommended that in fixing minimum wages, the basic minimum needs of the workers and his/her family for sustenance should be kept in view so that the wage prescribed is a just wage.

In some notifications of the wages under the Act, there is a tendency to classify work as "light work usually done by women" and "heavy work usually done by men." Such notifications are highly objectionable and have been criticised as a device to circumvent the law and perpetuate the practice where women workers' wages are fixed at lower levels than those of men workers. The Shramshakti report has recommended that specific occupations must be listed out and minimum rates of wages notified against these so that it is possible to verify whether women-related occupations are ranked lower in the matter of wages.

In a large number of scheduled employments and occupations, the practice is to fix minimum rates of wages on the basis of piece rates. In determining the output, no scientific or equitable procedure is followed, resulting in women workers, particularly in home-based occupations, having to put in long hours of work, supplemented by the efforts of other family members, to earn a pittance of a wage which may be a fraction of the time-rated wage. The problem becomes worse when sufficient raw material is not provided to them to enable them to earn more piece-rated wages. The Shramshakti report recommended that the time spent by the home worker in collecting raw materials and returning the finished product should be kept in view in fixing piece-rate wages. There should also be a provision for a fallback wage to guarantee a regular income even in the off-season, when material availability may be low.

In respect to home-based workers, by and large, the employer is saved from incurring not merely expenses relating to setting up a factory, installing equipment but also expenses for supervision and control. Through the mechanism of rejection, at various levels, and the consequent loss of wages to the woman worker for the labour she has already put in, unfair control is being exercised at no cost to the employer. The Shramshakti report has suggested that the home-worker should be recompensed to an extent for this element of self-supervision, as well as provision of work space and sometimes a part of the material inputs. The report recommended that a premium of 25 percent of the notified minimum rate of wages, either time-rate or piece-rate should be paid to home workers as compensation.

Minimum rates of wages are fixed/revised in respect of jobs, which are included in the Schedule. Section 27 of the Minimum Wages Act empowers the appropriate government to add employments to the schedule by notification after prior publication. Though governments have been periodically adding employments to the schedule, there are still certain employments, which have not, been added to the schedule. Even where an employment is added to the schedule, there are time lags in the fixation of minimum rates of wages for that employment and under the scheme of the Act, other benefits of the Act also do not accrue to the workers by mere scheduling, but only after minimum rates of wages have been fixed. In order to ensure that wages at an irreducible minimum level is payable, the Shramshakti report has suggested that a national or at least a regional minimum wage is fixed and this rate, which will have to be periodically revised, made widely known through the media.

In setting up advisory boards and committees for fixing/ revising minimum rates of wages, the Shramshakti report has also recommended that there must be at least one woman member to represent the interests of women workers on wage fixation/ revision committees and not less than two women workers on the advisory boards to represent the interest of women workers.

The National Commission on Labour in its report on women and child workers has made the following recommendations for the enforcement of the Minimum Wages Act:

1. At present complaints are filed by an inspector, as per Section 22B of the Act. It has been suggested to give such authority to selected social welfare associations for filing such complaints, especially for female workers. Two or three such associations may be selected in each state.
2. At present the Labour Commissioner is designated by the state government as the authority to hear and decide the claims arising out of payment of less-than-minimum rate of wages. In general the claims recovery process takes too long. Therefore, it is suggested that Section 20 be amended so that all Class I labour officers be empowered to hear and decide such cases.

Beedi and Cigar Workers (Conditions of Employment) Act, 1966

The Beedi and Cigar Workers Act, 1966 is very significant for women workers because after agriculture, the beedi and tobacco processing sector employs the largest number of women workers in the country. Moreover, apart from the Minimum Wages Act, 1948, the Beedi and Cigar Workers Act is the only law which deals with home-based workers in a detailed manner. Hence this Act is very significant for women workers because the majority of home-based workers in beedi rolling are women.

The term employee is defined as a person employed directly or indirectly to do any skilled, unskilled, manual and clerical work and includes contract workers and home workers.

The Act provides that if more than 30 women are employed, a creche for children below 6 years of age has to be provided. Provisions of the Maternity Benefit Act also apply to beedi and cigar establishments.

According to the Shramshakti report, the main deficiency in the implementation of the Act is the reluctance and failure on part of the employer to register women workers in his books. As a result, women beedi workers do not get the benefit that should accrue to them under the law. Even wages do not get paid to them but to the male member of the household whose name alone, in most cases, figures in employers' books. Employers have learnt to circumvent the law by adopting the contract system. According to the Shramshakti report, the manufacturers have adopted the contract system in beedi production. Any given manufacturer employs between 2 to 600 contractors. Large contractors in turn hire subcontractors. Despite the statutory minimum wage fixed in each state, contractors set their own lower wage rate when contracting women to do work. The raw materials they deliver to the workers are almost always under weight. Therefore the women always produce fewer beedis than the number the contractor has assigned them. The women have to pay from their wages for the number of beedis lacking - usually 10-30 percent of their daily wage. On top of this, contractors practice a fixed deduction of Rs. 2 per week and then proceed to reject 5-20 percent of the beedis as defectively rolled. They indiscriminately make this rejection claim even from women who have been rolling beedis for 20 years.

Since the minimum wage for beedi rolling varies from state to state, the beedi industry shifts from place to place. The National Commission on Labour has recommended that a national minimum wage should be fixed for beedi rolling and should be adopted by all states.

Plantations Labour Act, 1951

This Act is of special relevance to women workers as they account for 50 percent of the workforce in plantations. The Act generally applies to tea, coffee, rubber and cinchona plantations. It can be extended by notification by the state government to any other plantations.

The Act imposes a duty on the employer to provide creche facilities in every plantation where 50 or more women workers are employed.

The definition of the term 'family' in the Act includes "where the worker is a male, his parents dependent on him." Such a definition reflects a clear paternalistic bias in the statutes. The Shramshakti report also suggested that the Act should be suitably amended and a female workers' parents should also be treated as her family.

Sexual Harassment at the Workplace

An important aspect of providing women safety and security at the workplace is providing her with protection against sexual harassment. There is no act specifically prohibiting sexual harassment at the workplace. Section 509 of the Indian Penal Code prohibits any word, gesture or act intended to insult the modesty of a woman. Under the IPC, sexual harassment has been dealt with as criminal offence.

In 1997, in the *Vishakha and others v. State of Rajasthan case,*[16] the Supreme Court, in a landmark judgement, while referring to Article 14, 19 and 21, held that sexual harassment of working women amounts to violation of right to equality, right to life and liberty and the right to practice a profession, occupation or trade. While referring to Article 51 (c) and Article 253, the court held that gender equality includes protection from sexual harassment and right to work with dignity.

The Supreme Court in this case has laid down guidelines to determine what constitutes sexual harassment. As per the Supreme Court guidelines, sexual harassment at the workplace includes unwelcome sexually determined behaviour such as:

- physical contacts and advances
- a demand for sexual favours

- sexually coloured remarks
- showing pornography
- any other unwelcome physical, verbal or non-verbal conduct of a sexual nature

In 1999, in the *Apparel Export Promotion Council v. A. K. Chopra case,*[17] the Supreme Court further developed the jurisprudence on sexual harassment by ruling that actual molestation or even physical contact is not required to establish a case of sexual harassment if the background of the entire case establishes the genuineness of the complaint.

As a result of these guidelines, the issue of sexual harassment at the workplace has been highlighted and will help women workers in seeking redress.

While India has a plethora of labour laws, their outlook tends to be paternalistic and also tends to ignore women's experiences. On the one hand, there is a need to improve the scope and content of these laws in order to make the provisions clear, precise and gender-sensitive, on the other hand the implementation and enforcement of these laws also needs to be improved, particularly in the unorganised sector where the majority of women workers are employed. It is also to necessary to widen the enforcement machinery to bring in more persons who can carry out inspections and monitoring of the acts. Moreover, an immediate programme of gender-sensitisation of law enforcers must be carried out since labour officers generally have little understanding of the issues of concern to women workers. Penalties of violation of these laws also need to be increased and participation of workers in the enforcement of law needs to be encouraged.

Status of CEDAW in the Indian Legal System

India ratified CEDAW in 1993 but made reservations on the articles relating to cultural and customary practices [5 (a)] and to equality in marriage and family relations [16 (1)].

In response to questions on India's First Report on CEDAW, the Secretary, Department of Women and Child Development, stated that international conventions and treaties ratified by India do not automatically form part of Indian law and need to be incorporated into Indian law through enabling legislation before the implementation and enforcement of their provisions. However, the Constitution of India incorporates in letter and spirit the provisions of various articles of CEDAW, especially that of Article 1 and 2. In fact, the Constitution of India, which predates CEDAW, is strongly influenced by the UDHR. The principle of gender equality is firmly established in the Indian Constitution.[18]

Despite the constitutional safeguards and legislative provisions, discrimination against women is endemic. In order to ensure that the legal and constitutional safeguards actually reach women, the government has set up a statutory National Commission for Women in 1992, charged with the responsibility of overseeing the working of such safeguards and reviewing laws and regulations which are discriminatory to women.

The Department of Women and Child Development is the nodal agency for implementation of the various articles of CEDAW. This Department, in this capacity, coordinates with other ministries and departments for its implementation.

The Supreme Court has taken a positive stand in emphasising the importance of CEDAW. In the *Vishakha v. State of Rajasthan* case, the Supreme Court referred to the importance of international norms, particularly CEDAW, in providing guidelines for protecting the rights of women. The court held: "It is now accepted rule of judicial construction that regard must be had to international conventions and norms for construing domestic law where there is no inconsistency between them and there is a void in the domestic law. In the absence of domestic law occupying the field, to formulate effective measures to check the evil of sexual harassment of working women at all workplaces the contents of conventions are significant for the purpose of interpretation of gender equality rights to work with human dignity in Article 14, 15, 19 (1) (g) and 21 of the Constitution. Any international convention not inconsistent with the fundamental rights and in harmony with its spirit must be read into these provisions to enlarge their meaning and content and to promote the constitutional guarantees."

In the *AEPC v. A. K. Chopra* case also the Supreme Court referred to CEDAW in providing guidelines for protecting the honour and dignity of women.

In response to a question by the CEDAW Committee on the measures taken by the Indian Government to popularise CEDAW, the Secretary, Department of Women and Child Development, informed that the CEDAW text has been circulated widely to various ministries and departments. Sensitisation workshops have been held by national level institutions such as the National Institute for Public Cooperation and Child development (NIPCCD) and its regional centres to bring the provisions of CEDAW closer to state-level and government functionaries and NGOs.[19] Some NGOs like Sakhi have been conducting seminars and workshops for promoting awareness about CEDAW amongst women activists and lawyers. However, awareness about CEDAW continues to poor not only amongst the general public but also amongst women groups and lawyers.

Developmental Efforts of the State

In the years following independence, despite the presence of constitutional safeguards and enactment of various laws, it became apparent that advancement of women's status would require intervention from the state. There have been various shifts in policy towards women in the last 50 years from the concept of 'welfare' in the seventies to 'development' in the eighties and now to 'empowerment' since the nineties.

In the seventies, there was a realisation that the extreme deprivation suffered by women required comprehensive examination. In 1971, the Committee on the Status of Women in India (CSWI) was appointed by the government to study, investigate and recommend measures to improve the conditions of women. The CSWI submitted its report in 1974.

The CSWI report played a seminal role in raising very fundamental questions regarding the role, impact and trajectory of government policy in India. The report highlighted the disturbing features of the aggravation of social and economic inequalities faced by women at work. It drew attention to the decline in numbers and proportion of women workers in industry and the wage disparities between men and women. The CSWI concluded that labour laws concerning women had remained restricted to the attitude of protection and welfare and had not reflected the shifting emphasis towards equality and greater employment opportunities for women. In was on CSWI recommendation that the in 1976, the Equal Remuneration Act was passed and in 1986, the Factories Act was amended to extend the right to creche facilities to a relatively larger number of women employed in factories.[20]

The approach in the 1st to 4th Five Year Plans was based on the belief that industrialisation and development would generate conditions for women to develop alongside. Policy programmes specifically for women were directed at provision for welfare activities. The Fifth Five Year Plan (1974-79), which emphasised the need of income, coincided with the International Women's Decade and the submission of the CSWI report. The 5th Plan saw a major shift in approach towards women's development, with 'welfare' giving way to 'development.' It made the following recommendations in the area of training and employment:[21]

- reservation of a definite quota for women for training within the industry in order to arrest their retrenchment as a consequence of modernisation.
- reservation of a definite quota for women for training of apprentices under the National Apprentices Act.
- development of programmes of vocational training in close relation with industry and resources located in the area.
- development of training programmes in production and market organisation to develop self-employment.
- vocational training programmes for both illiterate and semi-literate women workers.
- development of training-cum-production centres in small scale or cottage industries in both rural and urban areas to provide employment to women near their homes.

A new awareness was growing in the government that women, and particularly working women, as a group, had been adversely affected by the nature of the economic processes accompanying industrialisation. This new concern was again reflected in the approach of the Working Group on Employment of Women and the incorporation of an emphasis on women in the reports on agriculture and rural development for the 6th Plan (1980-85). For the first time a chapter on women and development was included in the 6th Five Year Plan. Through the 6th and 7th Plans, the government introduced a number of beneficiary-oriented programmes, which extended direct benefits to women as part of poverty alleviation policies. In the 8th and 9th Plans (1992) onwards, there was a shift in approach from 'development' to 'empowerment'.[2] The 9th Five Year Plan listed empowerment of women as a major plan objective and included a Women's Component Plan in the plan of all Central Government ministries/ departments and of State Governments/UT Administrations.

The new approach of the Government of India, which marks the period following the debate in Parliament on the CSWI Report, is reflected not only in the Five Year Plans but also in a series of policy statements. In 1978, the National Plan of Action for Women was prepared by a National Committee on Women, constituted by the Government of India. It identified the problems constraining participation of women as wage employees and enjoined Central and State Government departments/agencies to:[23]

- ensure equal opportunities for women's participation where women are employed in significant numbers
- ensure special facilities for women where their participation is negligible
- in rural areas, at first point of entry, give preference to women
- maximum age of entering government service be raised up to 35 years of age to encourage women who have dropped out of employment to fulfil child bearing responsibilities to re-enter employment.

Following the National Plan of Action, a separate Department of Women and Child Development (DWCD) was established under the newly created Ministry of Human Resource Development. This department continues to function as the nodal agency for the advancement of women.

In 1988, the National Perspective Plan for Women 1988-2000 was unveiled. The Plan recognised the need to bring women's concerns into the mainstream. "A parallel sub-stream of women's development, even if possible, will only perpetuate discrimination and subordination." The Plan envisioned an "alternate strategy of national development which will provide not just an additional space for women, but create a democratic, egalitarian, secular, cooperative social structure." It also outlined the initiatives required and advocated a series of strategies. In the field of employment it made the following recommendations:[24]

1. Women's participation in trade union activities needs to be encouraged.
2. The maximum age for employment of women in the organised sector should be 35 years.
3. Special entrepreneurship training programmes should be organised.
4. Expansion of creche facilities and extension of ESI and Maternity Benefits Act to the unorganised and agriculture sector.

A National Commission for Women was set up in 1992. It functions as a national apex statutory body to review the constitutional and legal safeguards for women, recommend remedial legislative measures, facilitate redressal of grievances and advice government on all policy matters affecting women.

The government employment programmes affecting women workers can be divided into 3 categories:

I. Wage employment programmes
II. Self-employment programmes
III. Programmes exclusively for women

I. Wage Employment Programmes

The two main wage employment programmes are Jawahar Rozgar Yojana and Employment Assurance Scheme.

1. Jawahar Rozgar Yojana

The government has introduced wage employment programmes since the 6th Five Year Plan. The first such programme was the National Rural Employment Programme. Later, the Rural Landless Employment Guarantee Programme was introduced. In 1989, these two were merged to form the Jawahar Rozgar Yojana (JRY). The JRY aims at generating gainful employment for unemployed rural men and women and to create sustainable employment by strengthening the rural economic infrastructure.

The target group for JRY consists of people below the poverty line, especially those belonging to scheduled castes/scheduled tribes and freed bonded labour. Thirty percent of the employment opportunities are reserved for women. JRY aims at improving the quality of life through increased accessibility to wages. It is a centrally sponsored scheme and is implemented by state governments. The central government's fund share is 80 percent, while states spend 20 percent.

Table 3 shows that the annual Central allocation for JRY has been gradually decreasing. Similarly, the States' share of allocation has also been declining.

Table 3: Financial progress of JRY

(Rs. in crores)

Year	*Allocative*			*Release*			*Expenditure*
	Centre	*State*	*Total*	*Centre*	*State*	*Total*	
1993-94	3248.56	810.86	4059.42	3229.66	653.43	3883,09	3878.71
1994-95	3502.56	874.36	4376.92	3497.63	873.14	4370.77	4268.33
1995-96	3879.99	968.00	4848,70	3686.59	920.48	4607.07	4466.91
1996-97	1790.00	446.79	2236.79	1639.10	409.28	2048.38	2163.98
1997-98	2000.00	499.21	2499.21	1940.70	536.24	2476.94	2431.79
1998-99	2078.44	518.58	2597.02	1235.64	308.42	1544.06	905.65
(Up to Sept' 98)							
Total	16499.55	4118.51	20618.06	15229.32	3700.99	18930.31	

Source : Developmental Schemes for Rural Women, First Report of Committee on Empowerment of Women, 1998-99, Lok Sabha Secretariat, New Delhi, March, 1999

Under the JRY, the share of women in the employment generated so far under this scheme was about 25 percent during the period 1989-90 to 1993-94. During 1996-97, 558.51 lakh mandays were generated for women out of a total of 4,288.58 mandays generated during this period. This fell to 1,116.71 lakh mandays representing 28.7 percent of total employment in 1997-98.[25]

The Committee on Empowerment of Women in its report on Development Schemes for Rural Women expressed concern over the fact that in several states including Andhra Pradesh, Himachal Pradesh, Kerala, Maharashtra, Meghalaya, Punjab, Sikkim, Tamil Nadu and Pondicherry, the average wages per manday paid to female unskilled workers was less than what was paid to the male unskilled workers.[26]

2. Employment Assurance Scheme

The Employment Assurance Scheme (EAS) was initiated in 1993 to provide gainful employment during the lean agricultural season, in manual work, to all male and female adults in rural areas. EAS also caters to the creation of economic infrastructure and community assets for promoting employment and development. The EAS target group consists of poor rural needy persons who desire work. The scheme gives the assurance of providing 100 days of employment to all men and women over 18 years and below 60 years. A maximum of 2 adults per family are provided employment under this scheme. The expenditure under EAS is shared between the centre and states on 80:20 basis. The scheme is being implemented in all the 5448 rural blocks of the country.

Under the EAS also a special provision has been made for women and 67 lakh mandays of work were generated for them during the year 1993-94 which was 13.5 percent of the total 494.74 mandays generated. In 1994-95, 313.37 lakh mandays out of a total of 1,191.29 lakh mandays or 26.3 percent of the mandays generated went to women. This figure rose to 30.94 percent women beneficiaries before February 1997.[27]

II. Self Employment Programmes

The Government of India has initiated a large number of self-employment programmes. In order to increase earning potential, skill-based self-employment programmes are important. Apart from this, women's preference for supplementary employment near their homes is another argument for promoting self-employment programmes. NSS surveys have also highlighted the importance of self-employment programmes for women. The surveys have revealed that a large number of women who reported not being available for 'work' under normal circumstances, were available for certain types of work, if such work was made available at their household premises.[28]

Integrated Rural Development Programme

Integrated Rural Development Programme (IRDP), one of the largest programmes for self-employment, was launched in all the blocks of the country in 1980 to enable the identified poor rural families to cross the poverty line through the acquisition of credit-based productive assets, which would provide self-employment on a sustainable basis. Assistance is given in the form of subsidy by the government and credit advances by financial institutions such as commercial banks, cooperative and regional rural banks for income generating activities in the primary, secondary and tertiary sectors of the rural economy. The programme is being implemented as a centrally-sponsored scheme, funded on a 50:50 basis by Centre and States.

The Department of Rural Employment and Poverty Alleviation of the Ministry of Rural Areas and Employment implements the programme. The target group of the programme consists of small and marginal farmers, agricultural labourers and rural artisans having annual income below Rs. 11,000 per annum defined as the poverty line during the Eighth Plan. It is stipulated under the programme that at least 50 percent of the target group should be from scheduled castes and scheduled tribes categories. In order to ensure better participation of women in the development process, it has been stipulated that at least 40 percent of the beneficiaries should be women, with priority given to women-headed households. More than 4.40 crore rural families have been assisted under the IRDP since 1980-81.[29]

Identification of families below poverty line is done through a household census undertaken at the beginning of the plan period. Selection of beneficiaries is done in Gram Sabha meetings in the presence of all those residing in the village. Bank officials and government officials are also present in these meetings. The implementing agency for the IRDP is the District Rural Development Agency at the district level.

Table 4 shows that that the stipulated target of at least 40 percent of the beneficiaries being women has not been met in any of the last five years. The best performance was 34.33 percent in 1997-98. The element of subsidy disbursed to the women beneficiary is also proportionally placed at around 31 per cent on an average during the last five years. Similarly, the quantum of credit disbursed to the women is also around 31 percent on an average during the last five years. Thus the non-achievement of the norm of 40 percent beneficiaries being women has had its effects on other facets as well.

The Department of Rural Employment and Poverty Alleviation has argued that women have been unable to reap the benefits of IRDP because women are predominantly engaged in agriculture and other allied activities which do not have viable bankability. Rejecting this argument as non-factual, the Report on Developmental Schemes for Rural Women submitted by the Committee on Empowerment of Women has highlighted that most rural women involved in agriculture sector are landless who would be happy to start any other income-generating/asset creating activity at the very first opportunity.

The process of identification of beneficiaries also suffers from avoidable infirmities. As per the guidelines of IRDP, selection of beneficiaries is the mandate of the Gram Sabha, with officials acting as facilitators and service providers. In practice, however, the Committee on Empowerment of Women, citing the Fourth Concurrent Evaluation of IRDP in 1992-93, has arrived at the conclusion that the officials of the state machinery continue to rule the roost. As many as 40 percent of the beneficiaries under the IRDP have been selected by state government officials, with the Gram Sabha accounting for about 53 percent. The non-involvement of Gram Sabha defeats the very concept of grass-root planning and the purpose of democratisation of the planning process. According to the Committee, the non-involvement of Gram Sabha in the selection process affects women more adversely as unlike their male counterparts they cannot as freely approach official channels. The Committee has, therefore, recommended that the Department should work out measures to make it mandatory that the selection of beneficiaries should be done by Gram Sabha only.

The 4th round of the concurrent evaluation done in 1992-93 has also revealed that there is poor linkage of IRDP with other schemes like Training of Rural Youth for Self-Employment (TRYSEM) and Development of Women and Children in Rural Areas (DWCRA). Only 2.09 percent of the families assisted under IRDP are reported to have been assisted under DWCRA and another 3.02 percent of the beneficiaries reported being trained under TRYSEM. It is this absence of backward and forward linkages of the IRDP, which is responsible for a lot of shortcomings in its implementation. Despite the general acceptance of the objectives and the organisational apparatus built to translate into reality, IRDP has not achieved the desired results, especially for rural women.

Table 4: Progress of Women Beneficiaries Under I.R.D.P. during 1993-94 to 1997-98

Year	*Total Families Assisted*	*Total Women Assisted*	*%age of Women to Total Families Assisted*	*Subsidy Disbursed (Rs. Crore)*			*Credit Disbursed (Rs. Crore)*		
				Total	*Women*	*% of Women to Total*	*Total*	*Women*	*% of Women to Total*
1993-94	25.39	8.54	33.64	800.82	250.14	31.24	1408.44	426.2	30.26
1994-95	22.15	7.51	33.71	818.3	256.29	31.32	1450.58	448.38	30.91
1995-96	20.89	6.99	33.43	870.2	271.01	31.14	1701.33	532.26	31.28
1996-97	19.24	6.44	33.47	905.94	278.73	30.77	1969.16	605.86	30.77
1997-98	17.07	5.86	34.33	863.11	269.62	31.24	1996.64	620.11	31.06
Total	104.74	35.34	33.74	4258.37	1325.79	31.13	8526.15	2632.81	30.88

Source : Developmental Schemes for Rural Women, First Report of Committee on Empowerment of Women; 1998-99, Lok Sabha Secretariat, New Delhi, March, 1999

Development of Women and Children in Rural Areas (DWCRA)

DWCRA, a sub-scheme of the IRDP, was introduced on a pilot basis in 50 districts but has now been extended to all the districts of the country. It was felt that the flow of financial assistance to women as a group had been marginal under the IRDP. Therefore, a separate scheme was launched. The objective of the scheme is to provide self-employment opportunities to women living below the poverty line in rural areas in order to improve their social and economic status. Through such social and economic empowerment, the programme seeks to bring about an improvement in the quality of life of women and children.

A distinguishing feature of DWCRA is that it is based on organising women into groups of 10-15 women each as against 'family as a unit of assistance' under IRDP. Each groups is given a lump sum grant of Rs. 25,000 as 'revolving fund,' which is shared by the Central Government and State Government, so that groups can start viable income generating activities to augment the income earning capacity of the group members. Till 1995, UNICEF also provided support to the fund. Table 5 shows that the financial performance of DWCRA has been sliding down during the last three years. While the outlay has remained constant all these years at Rs. 65 crore, the expenditure has gone down from Rs. 63.65 crore in 1995-96 to Rs. 59.96 crore in 1996-97 and further to Rs. 41.45 crore in 1997-98. This shortfall is due to several reasons:

1. The non-release of funds by the Department as some states may not have released matching shares against Central assistance.
2. Non-utilisation of 60 percent of the funds by District Rural Development Agency
3. Non-finalisation of audit reports for previous years.

Holding up of the funds of such an important scheme, according to the Committee on Empowerment of Women, exhibits an utter lack of coordination between the Department and the state governments.

While the scheme has achieved some success in states like Andhra Pradesh and Kerala, its overall performance is far from satisfactory. Several evaluation studies have revealed various shortcomings that have contributed to a not so impressive performance of DWCRA. These include inadequate staff, inadequate backward and forward linkages, inadequate training and marketing facilities, difficulties in forming groups and untimely release of funds.

Table 4: Outlay and Expenditure for DWCRA

Rs. Crores

Year	*Outlay*	*Expenditure*
1993-94	21.00	23.65
1994-95	21.00	31.00
1995-96	65.00	63.65
1996-97	65.00	56.96
1997-98	65.00	41.45

Source : Developmental Schemes for Rural Women, First Report of Committee on Empowerment of Women, 1998-99, Lok Sabha Secretariat, New Delhi, March, 1999

A study of DWCRA conducted in Thrissur district in 1997 revealed that only 15 percent of the total sample beneficiaries derived marked improvement in their household income and thereby crossed the poverty line. In terms of improvement in the asset position, only 15 percent experienced a positive change. No improvement was seen in the housing conditions of the beneficiaries. One of the most crucial problems faced by many of the units is marketing. The quality of the product does not receive the attention it deserves in many of the units. Some of the DWCRA products sold in the markets are of substandard quality and hence fail to command demand on a substantial basis.[30]

Based on regional and micro-studies, the problems of DWCRA can be summarized as follows: (1) DWCRA has mainly focussed on the economic activities and other components of the programme, namely child care, reduction in the drudgery of women's work, adult education and overall organisation of the women, have received inadequate inattention. (2) Though a number of groups have been formed under DWCRA, only some of them have started economic activities, and only few of them have been able to implement the scheme successfully (for instance, out of 112 groups formed in Junagadh district of Gujarat, only 35 groups could initiate economic activities and merely 3-4 groups are earning profits). (3) The group philosophy could not be implemented well, as either the groups organiser dominated or the voluntary agency did not train the group from this point of view. (4) Mukhya Sevikas and Gram Sevikas were not capable of understanding and implementing the spirit of the programme. They also lacked capabilities to provide adequate support to economic activities. (5) Marketing is one of the weakest points of the programme. Many groups find it difficult to face the competitive markets for their products. (6) Most DWCRA groups take up traditional economic activities and do not go in for non-traditional new activities.[31]

Despite the problems mentioned above, the DWCRA model seems to be the best one among all state interventions for increasing women's employment because it aims at empowering the rural poor women through economic means. It seeks to encourage collective action in the form of group, which are known to work better than individual efforts. One important aspect of DWCRA model is that that by encouraging the habit of thrift and credit, it aims at making poor women self-reliant. SEWA's (Self-Employed Women's Association) implementation of DWCRA with some modifications and flexibility has been successful. The women of Andhra Pradesh have shown also how the group approach is useful for raising women's employment and empowering them. Many lessons can be learnt from the DWCRA in this state.

Training of Rural Youth for Self-Employment (TRYSEM)

TRYSEM, a supporting component of the IRDP, was started in August 1979 with a view to facilitating development of IRDP activities away from the primary sector to the secondary and tertiary sectors through the acquisition and upgradation of skills. It aims at providing technical and entrepreneurial skills to rural youth from families below the poverty line to enable them to take up income generating activities. Technical skills are imparted to rural youth in the age group of 18-35 from families below the poverty line to enable them to take up self-employment and to an extent wage employment in any of the economic sectors. The minimum age is relaxed to 16 years for inmates of orphanages. The upper age limit of 35 years is relaxed to 45 years in case of women, freed bonded labourers, freed convicts, persons displaced by large development programmes and cured leprosy patients. A minimum of 50 percent of the youth trained should belong to

Scheduled Castes and Scheduled Tribes and 3 percent should be physically handicapped persons. The coverage of women under this programme is fixed at 40 percent.

Table 6 shows that annual allocations under TRYSEM have remained static at Rs. 90.50 crore from 1995 and the annual releases have gradually declined from Rs. 75 crore in 1995-96 to Rs. 37.08 crore in 1998-99. Similarly, Table 7 shows that the number of youths trained has also fallen from Rs. 30.16 lakh in 1995-96 to 24.64 lakh in 1997-98. Even the targets (number of youth to be trained) has been gradually downscaled from 30.40 lakh to 28.84 lakh in 1998-99.

Table 6 : Physical and Financial Performance of TRYSEM

Year	*Allocation*	*Releases*	*Expenditure*
1993-94	11123.87	8944.67	5501.54
1994-95	8916.50	7403.25	6846.21
1995-96	9050.00	7500.57	9882.60
1996-97	9050.00	7011.25	10027.01
1997-98	9050.00	6555.86	7910.43
1998-99	9000.00	370S.78	1435.72
Up to Sept'98			
Total	56190.37	41124.38	41603.51

Source : Developmental Schemes for Rural Women, First Report of Committee on Empowerment of Women, 1998-99, Lok Sabha Secretariat, New Delhi, March, 1999

Table 7 : Physical Targets and Achievements of TRYSEM

In Millions

Year	*Target No. of Youth to be Trained*	*No. of Youth Trained*	*No. of Women Trained*	*%age*
1993-94	3.500	3.038	1.539	50.7
1994-95	3.184	2.818	1.378	48.9
1995-96	3.540	3.016	1.299	43.1
1996-97	2.901	3.643	1.955	53.7
1997-98	3.041	2.464	1.273	51.7
1998-99	2.884	0.563	0.264	46.9
Upto Sept. 98				
Total	19.050	15.542	7.708	49.6

Source : Developmental Schemes for Rural Women, First Report of Committee on Empowerment of Women, 1998-99, Lok Sabha Secretariat, New Delhi, March, 1999

A 'Quick Evaluation' of TRYSEM was conducted in 1993 with the help of 16 research institutes and 61 districts of 10 states. The 'Quick Evaluation' Report identified the following areas of concern:[32]

1. Of the total beneficiaries who got training under TRYSEM, roughly 47.19 percent were unemployed after training.
2. A large percentage of beneficiaries, 68.18 percent, felt that the duration of the training was inadequate.
3. Majority of the beneficiaries, that is, 66.52 percent expressed lack of funds as the main reason for not taking up self-employment independently after the training.
4. A major proportion of TRYSEM trainees, that is, 53.57 percent, did not apply for loan under IRDP. Of the total beneficiaries who applied for loan under IRDP, only about 50 percent were given assistance.
5. A large number of beneficiaries, that is 62.91 percent, felt no improvement in their socio-economic conditions as a result of TRYSEM training.
6. 'Area Skill Surveys' were not carried out in 92 percent of the districts to assess the potential skill requirements.

These shortcomings indicate serious lapses in the planning and implementation of this important programme. TRYSEM could have provided the most appropriate backward linkage to both IRDP and DWCRA as their training and grooming ground. The Committee on the Empowerment of Women noticed during their visits to rural areas that these shortcomings still persist. The Government does not seem to have taken corrective remedial measures regarding the areas of concern pointed out by evaluation team way back in 1993. Inspite of the government having made it incumbent on the DRDAs and training institutions to complete all formalities for sanction of loans applications to the banks during the training period itself things are yet to improve. The delays in processing of their loan cases is the biggest disincentive for the trainees. This is more so in the case of women trainees. The problem of mismatch of skills still persists., as is borne out by the large number of complaints received by the Committee during the course of their interaction with TRYSEM trainees in Maharashtra, Gujarat, Rajasthan and Karnataka.

Programmes Launched Exclusively for Women

There are some specific programmes for the advancement and empowerment of women, which focus on income generating activities, support services and awareness generation. Some of these programmes are discussed below:

Rashtriya Mahila Kosh

The National Credit Fund for Women or the RMK was constituted as a independent registered society by the Department of Women and Child Development in Ministry of Human Resource Development in 1992 with a corpus fund of 31 crores. It's main objective was to provide micro-credit to poor women for income-generation activities for asset creation in the informal sector through the intermediation of the NGOs. In addition, the RMK has also supported the formation of women's thrift and credit societies popularly known as Self Help Groups.

Since its inception, RMK has so far, sanctioned credit worth Rs. 107.73 crore, benefiting 4.2 lakh women through 992 NGOs and disbursed Rs. 82.38 crore up to February 2002.[33] Loans recovery has exceeded 90 percent in the all the years, showing the credit worthiness of even the poorest women. Though the programme is a step in the right direction, the Committee on Empowerment of Women in its First Report has identified some areas of concern: (1) The multi-tier system of RMK assisting Resource NGOs; the Resource NGOs in turn training smaller NGOs; the subsequent formation of Self Help Groups; and finally the assistance reaching the borrower has complicated the delivery process. (2) Interest rates as high as 18.75 p. a can be charged from borrowers by the Self Help Groups who get credit from the Kosh. (3) NGOs have a miniscule presence in rural areas, which means that the RMK is more of an urban phenomenon.

The Committee has recommended a thorough review of RMK by the government from all angles to evaluate its performance to determine its linkages with other existing schemes and programmes to ensure that it is not duplicating the work of other agencies.

Swayamsiddha

The erstwhile programmes of Indira Mahila Yojana (IMY) and Mahila Samriddhi Yojana (MSY) were recast as Swayamsiddha in 2001 to empower women through awareness generation, achievement of economic strength through micro-level income-generating activities and convergence of various services such as literacy, health, rural development etc. It also aims at organising women into Self Help Groups to form a strong institutional base. Out of the Ninth Plan Outlay of Rs. 165 crore, no expenditure was incurred during the first 3 years of the Plan as the scheme was being recast. The expenditure during 2000-01 and 2001-02 was Rs. 8.95 crore to expand the existing 238 blocks in 1999-2000 to 650 blocks in 2001-02 to form 53,100 SHGs covering 9.3 lakh women beneficiaries. Since the scheme has been only recently recast, a study and evaluation of the erstwhile schemes is also undertaken below.

The IMY was launched in August 1995 in 200 ICFS blocks. It sought to provide a holistic strategy for women's empowerment through the group dynamics. The objectives of the schemes were: (1) convergence of the development schemes of all the on-going sectoral programmes. (2) awareness generation among the women from rural areas and urban slums. (3) to help women achieve economic strength through micro-level income generating activities.

IMY was based on the idea of the strength of the Self Help Groups. The development of Indira Mahila Kendras (IMKs) at the anganwadi level and also recognising other groups under the adult literacy programmes and integrating them or associating them with the IMKs at the Anganwadi level would provide the grassroots level organisations for women for various interactions. More than 40,000 groups had been formed under the scheme till December 1999.

MSY was introduced in 1993 to inculcate the habit of savings amongst rural women. The scheme aimed to give credit to women in order to empower them economically. An evaluation of this scheme was conducted by the Planning Commission in 1996. The evaluation report shows that 68 percent of the depositors did not make a second deposit and most of the people who withdrew money from it used it for personal expenses or household expenditure. The scheme has not built up credit self-reliance because the money deposited in the accounts has not been used for creating further income-generating opportunities for women. The scheme was also faultily conceived without consulting NGO credit infrastructure for women in the form of thrift and credit groups, or the National Credit Fund for Women. The scheme was recast and merged with the IMY on the advice of the Planning Commission in 1999.[34]

Support for Training and Employment Programme for Women

This scheme was launched in 1987 to provide skills and knowledge to poor and assetless women for enhancing their employment opportunities, including self-employment and development of entrepreneurial skills. The Support for Training and Employment Programme For Women (STEP) seeks to provide skills in areas such as agriculture, animal husbandry, dairying, fisheries, handlooms, handicrafts, khadi and village industries, sericulture, forestry and wasteland development. Women beneficiaries are organised into groups or cooperatives.

Since the inception of the programme, about 6.1 lakh women have been covered under 133 projects. So far, women in the dairy sector have received the maximum support, followed by handlooms, handicrafts, sericulture and poultry. About 8000 women's dairy cooperatives with more than 4 lakh members have been organised throughout the country mainly through the initiative of State Cooperative Milk Federations.[35]

STEP is one of the most successful government-sponsored programmes for women. An evaluation of the programme was conducted in 1995 by the Planning Commission. It was found that 83.34 percent of beneficiaries in the sample reported a rise in their social status within their families and 81.65 percent reported a rise in their social status outside their family as a result of the programme.[36]

As far as provision of backward and forward linkages is concerned, 50.34 percent beneficiaries in the sample received assistance for raw materials, out of which over 90 percent were satisfied with the assistance given, according to the evaluation report of the Planning Commission. No assistance in processing raw materials was given in the states of Himachal Pradesh, Kerala,

Bihar and Tamil Nadu. As far as marketing is concerned, 53.51 percent reported they had received assistance for this and 92.46 percent of those women were satisfied with the marketing facilities. In the states of Himachal Pradesh, Kerala and Tamil Nadu, no assistance was provided for marketing.

Access to credit was given only to 22.96 percent while the same percentage was provided with subsidies for taking up economic activities under various sectors. No special efforts have been made to provide credit facilities to the beneficiaries of this programme. Out of the total beneficiaries, 6.24 percent had also received benefits under the IRDP. Only 2.5 percent were covered under the MSY.

The Planning Commission Evaluation Report indicated that the programme was not very successful in providing support services to the employed women. No linkages for health check-ups and educational facilities were reported from the four projects falling in the states of Bihar, Kerala, Tamil Nadu and Uttar Pradesh. The linkage with mobile creches was established only in the states of Gujarat, Rajasthan and West Bengal. The progress in achieving a higher percentage of literacy was not very successful. After the projects were completed, 42.46 percent of the women in the sample were found illiterate. The utilisation of educational services increased only by 2.54 percent and literacy ratios increased by 14 percent.

Setting up of Employment-cum Income Generation-cum-Production Units (NORAD)

The Norwegian Agency for International Development (NORAD) assisted a programme for training and self-reliance through income generation for women in non-traditional areas. The programme was started in the country in 1982-83. Some of the areas are electronics, watch assembling, computer programming, garment making, secretarial practices, community health work, embroidery, weaving etc. Financial assistance is given to grantee organisations like Women's Development Corporations, autonomous bodies and voluntary organisations for hiring of training-cum production sheds, training costs and stipend to the trainees.

At present, the share of the Norwegian government constitutes about 33 percent of the total outlay. Since the programme was started, 1477 projects benefiting 2.28 lakh women have been approved.[37]

Provision of Support Services

The provision of support services for working women is a crucial ingredient in extending employment opportunities for women. The Central Social Welfare Board (CSWB) implements two schemes: (1) Working Women's Hostels Scheme was introduced in 1972 in order to provide accommodation to women who are working away from their homes. The Board provides assistance to voluntary organisations for running the hostels. Since its inception, 881 hostels have been funded throughout the country, giving accommodation to 62,308 girls till 2002.[38] The scheme has worked well but is concentrated in urban areas. It needs to be extended to rural areas and also expanded in the urban areas. (2) The CSWB funds the creation of creches in rural and urban areas for children of mothers from lower income group families who are working or ailing. Since its inception it has managed to fund only 12470 creches. The National Creche Fund, set up with a corpus of Rs. 20 crore, has so far managed to fund an additional number of 2455 creches. About 293 working women's hostels have creches attached to them, which can take up to 7668 children.[39]

A National Maternity Benefit Scheme (NFBS) was launched in 1995 whereby pregnant women get Rs. 300 during the period of pregnancy for the first two child births. In August 1998, the amount of assistance was increased to Rs. 500. The total number of women assisted under this scheme till 1999 is 21,03877. Amongst the states, Andhra Pradesh utilised Rs. 588.78 lakh out of the Rs. 746.75 lakh released under the scheme in 1997-98. Bihar, Gujarat, Madhya Pradesh, Rajasthan, Maharashtra, Orissa, Tamil Nadu and West Bengal spent less than 50 percent of funds released to them. The main reason for the poor performance of the scheme, according to the report of the Empowerment Committee, is poor publicity of the scheme.

One of the main reason for poor performance of the developmental programmes is lack of awareness amongst the targetted groups about the schemes. There is a need to create awareness about the various schemes and programmes being implemented by the government. It is also necessary to have a more effective and comprehensive mechanism for monitoring the implementation of these schemes. There should also be better coordination not only between the Central and State Governments but also between the various Ministries and Departments of the Central Government and also with the field level implementing agencies. Both the Central Government and State Governments have launched a large number of development programmes. There is a need to converge a number of these schemes to avoid overlapping and to enhance their effectiveness.

The majority of women in India are employed in the agrarian sector, therefore, there is a need to draw up an employment strategy for women in this sector. While on the one hand, there is a need to ensure that women are given their legal rights to land, on the other hand, there is a need to upgrade women's skills in farming practices, particularly in non conventional and high-income level areas like horticulture and floriculture.

While the focus of development programmes should continue to be on rural women in agriculture and non-farm sectors, there is also a need to launch new employment generation and skill upgradation schemes for poor women in urban areas since the number of urban development schemes are not adequate. Since a majority of women work in the unorganised sector in low-skilled and low paying jobs, there is need to launch skill training schemes in this sector. Skill training schemes should not merely be confined to areas traditionally associated with women but should venture into non-traditional areas. Skill training programmes need to be more in tune with market conditions in order to maximise their benefits.

Development programmes need to be more flexible and imaginative for creating productive and sustainable employment for women. There is a need for greater involvement from institutions like the panchyats, voluntary organisations and the community at large to improve the performance of the development programmes.

NOTES AND REFERENCES

1. *Air India v. Nargesh Meerza* (1981) SC 1829.
2. Government of A.P v P. B. Vijaykumar, (1995) SC 1648.
3. Thrity D. Patel, "Women and Economic Empowerment: Judicial

Approach," *Journal of Institute of Human Rights*, Vol. II, No. 1, 10th December, 1999, p.44.
4. Government of A.P v P. B. Vijaykumar, *opcit.*
5. C. B. Muthamma v Union of India, (1979), SC, 1868
6. Bombay Labour Union v International Franchise, (1966), SC, 942.
7. Maya Devi v State of Maharashtra, (1986), SC, 743.
8. Neera Mathur v Life Insurance Corporation, (1992), SC, 392.
9. Thrity Patel, *op cit.*, p. 51.
10. *Ibid.*, p. 52
11. Air India v Nargesh Meerza, *op cit.*
12. Mackinon Mackenzie and Co. v Audrey D' Costa, 1987, SC, 469.
13. *Shramshakti,. Report of the National Commission on Self-Employed Women and Women in the Informal Sector* (New Delhi: Government of India, 1988) p. 108.
14. National Commission on Labour, *Report of the Group on Women Workers and Child Labour. Part I* (New Delhi: Government of India, 2001) p. 99, 102.
15. Ministry of Labour, *Annual Report. 2000-2001* (New Delhi: Government of India, 2001) p. 119.
16. Vishakha and others v State of Rajasthan, 1997, SC.
17. AEPC v A. K. Chopra, 1999, SC, 625.
18. Department of Women and Child Development, Ministry of Human Resource Development, *Responses to Questions on India's First Report on CEDAW* (New Delhi: Government of India, 2000), p. 10.
19. *Ibid.*, p. 11.
20. Aanchal Kapur, (ed.), *Women Workers' Rights in India: Issues and Strategies – A Reference Guide* (New Delhi: ILO, 1999) p. 229.
21. A.P. Verma, M. M. Rehman, Poonam S. Chauhan (eds.), *Women Labour in India. A Comprehensive Manual* (Noida: V.V Giri National Labour Institute, 1996) pp. 163-164.
22. Women Workers' Rights in India: Issues and Strategies – A Reference Guide, *op. cit.*, p.233.
23. *Ibid.*
24. Women Labour in India: A Comprehensive Manual, *op. cit.*, pp. 168-169.
25. Mira Seth, *Women and Development* (New Delhi: Sage Publications, 2000) p. 206.
26. Committee on Empowerment of Women, Development Schemes for Rural Women (New Delhi: Lok Sabha Secretariat, 1999)
27. Mira Seth, *op. cit.*, p. 206.
28. S. Mahendra Dev, "State Intervention in Women's Employment," in T. S. Papola and Alakh N. Sharma (eds.), *Gender and Employment in India* (New Delhi: Vikas Publishing house, 1999) pp. 390-391.
29. Department of Rural Employment and Poverty Alleviation, Ministry

of Rural areas and Employment, *Annual Report 1999-2000,* (New Delhi: Government of India, 2000) p. 11.

30. U.T. Damayanthi, Development of Women in Rural Areas: A study of DWCRA in Thrissur District, www.krpcds.org.
31. S.Mahendra Dev, *op. cit.*, pp. 396-397.
32. Main Findings of Quick Evaluation Report of TRYSEM June –August 1993, www.rural.nic.in.
33. Planning Commission, *Tenth Five Year Plan 2002-2007,* (New Delhi: Government of India, 2002), p. 226.
34. Programme Evaluation Organisation, Planning Commission, *Evaluation Report on Mahilla Samriddhi Yojana* (New Delhi: Government of India, 1996) pp. 11-12.
35. Tenth Five Year Plan 2002-07, op. *cit.*, p. 223.
36. Programme Evaluation Organisation, Planning Commission, *Evaluation Report on Support to Training and Employment Programme* (New Delhi: Government of India, 1995).
37. Department of Women and Child Development, Ministry of Human Resource Development, *Annual Report 1999-2000* (New Delhi: Government of India, 2000) p. 33.
38. Tenth Five Year plan 2002-07, *op. cit.*, p. 224
39. Mira Seth, *op. cit*, p. 218.

Chapter 6

Women Workers: Strategies for Empowerment

This study examines the role of CEDAW in protecting the rights of women and empowering them to lead their lives with dignity. The women's convention has been often described as a comprehensive bill of rights. It includes a wide range of rights—civil and political, economic, social and cultural rights. In assessing the record of the Indian Government in fulfilling its obligations under CEDAW, this study has confined itself to assessing the rights of women workers. The status of women workers in India and the role played by the Indian government in protecting and promoting their rights has been examined.

CEDAW was adopted to bring women's issues into the mainstream of the human rights movement. However, critics have pointed out that CEDAW has in fact contributed to the 'ghettoisation' of women's concerns. The CEDAW Committee, which is often viewed as a 'poor relation' of other UN treaty bodies, needs to step up efforts to increase collaboration with other treaty bodies. The greatest challenge before CEDAW lies in bringing gender issues in the mainstream of human rights agenda.

CEDAW has been criticised for excluding a number of key issues like violence against women, abortion, caste-based discrimination and new economic policies from its provisions. However, the convention's strength lies in the fact that it is worded in an abstract manner and can be interpreted widely. The CEDAW Committee, through its power of making general recommendations, has been adapting and updating the convention to new issues and new insights.

Perhaps the greatest weakness of the convention lies in the fact that it is the most highly reserved treaty in the United Nations human rights system. State Parties have filed many formal reservations to the convention, which are often incompatible with objectives of the convention. Many State Parties justify the reservations on traditional, religious or cultural grounds. While reservations made possible the ratification of CEDAW by virtually all countries because they can opt out of some of its requirements, they have also jeopardised the integral and effective application of the convention.

The CEDAW Committee monitors the implementation of the Convention by consideration of reports submitted by State Parties and issuing concluding comments. One of the main weaknesses of the enforcement procedure of CEDAW was the absence of a right of individual petition. In 1999, an Optional Protocol to CEDAW, giving individuals the right to petition, was adopted. It came into force in 2000. The Optional Protocol to CEDAW follows the model of other individual complaints procedure available under other international human rights treaties. Despite the low rate of ratification so far, the importance of the Optional Protocol cannot be undermined since it can help in expanding jurisprudence on women's rights at both international and national level.

Despite all the criticisms levelled against CEDAW, it is a step in the right direction. Though a majority of State Parties have exhibited an utter lack of political will in improving the status of women, the judiciaries and legislatures in some countries like Japan, Panama, Netherlands, Australia and Nepal have begun responding to the obligations contained in the convention. To enable CEDAW to live up to its potential, women's groups need to build awareness about the convention at the national and local level.

In India, women workers face discrimination at several levels. There is an underestimation of women's work in the existing data system. Data collection systems fail to capture women's contribution in the non-monetised sectors. As a result, women continue to be viewed as 'mere housewives' or 'supplementary earners.' Despite some improvement in the data collection system, the problem of under enumeration of women's work persists.

Though the work participation rates for women has shown better growth than males as per the Census 2001 data, WPR for women is still far behind the WPR for men. (25. 8 percent for women compared to 52 percent for men as per 2001 Census). The increase in female WPR is mainly due to increase in proportion of female rural marginal workers. While the census data shows a growth in WPR from 19.7 percent (1981) to 25.8 percent (2001), the NSS data shows a fall from 29.6 percent (1983) to 25.9 percent (1999-2000). The increase in WPR for women in the Census 2001 could be because of better capture of women's work.

However, WPR trends vary widely across various parameters. As per Census 2001 data, 61 percent of marginal workers were women. The WPR varies widely across States/UTs both for rural and urban persons. As per NSS WPR trends (55th Round), the ratio for rural female population varies from a high of 47.8 percent (Andhra Pradesh) to a low of 7.3 percent (Tripura). It is also observed that high rural female WPR need not necessarily imply a high urban female WPR, though in most cases both move in tandem vis a vis all India averages.

There is also a glaring divergence in male and female worker literacy levels. As per NSS 55th Round data, 58.9 percent of female workers are not literate, as against 27.8 percent of male workers. As per the NSS data, 73.9 percent of rural female workers are in the non-literate category. While the overall female non-literate ratio has decreased as compared to the NSS 50th Round data, the rate of decrease is much faster for male workers.

A majority of women workers are employed in the primary sector in the rural areas. Agriculture is the dominant employment sector for women (85.4 percent). In the urban areas, the proportion of women employed in the tertiary sector has increased to more than 50 percent. Manufacturing, trade, hotel and restaurant and services sectors are the main employers.

As per the 1991 Census data, 96 percent of women were employed in the unorganised sector, and this ratio was 90 percent for men. It is evident that the unorganised sector is the major provider of employment for women. The share of women in the organised sector was at a mere 14 percent in 1991, and this is estimated to have grown to 17.2 percent as per the Tenth Five Year Plan document. Though the ratio has increased, it still continues to be sharply lower as compared to the ratio for men. In the unorganised sector, the share of women in total employment at 30 percent is relatively higher than their share in the organised sector, predominantly due to their contribution in agriculture and related activities.

The gender-based discrimination in the labour market is also reflected in the male-female wage differentials. Women workers face gender-based wage discrimination across all industry divisions. At an aggregate level, women workers in India received 83 percent of the salary paid to men workers in 1987-88, and this ratio has declined to 79.8 percent in 1993-94 (NSS). This ratio is more weighted against the women workers at the lower end of the literacy spectrum; non literate women workers received 59 percent of the wages paid to non literate male workers in 1987-88, and this ratio declined to 57.8 percent in 1993-94.

Analysis along rural-urban parameters also shows a stark disparity. In 1987-88, rural women workers employed in agriculture were paid 73.05 percent of the wages paid to men workers in this category. The ratio was at 57.85 percent in the rural construction industry. Even in urban India the disparity in the non literate category across select occupational groups is stark, with women workers receiving 59 percent of wages paid to men workers in this category and this ratio was lower at 57.8 percent in 1993-94. Spinners/weavers in this segment were the worst affected receiving 48.6 percent of salary paid to men workers in this category in 1987-88, and this ratio was 51.9 percent in 1993-94.

A more covert form of gender-based disparity in wages occurs through division of labour. Women are generally concentrated in low-skilled, low paid jobs. In agriculture, for example, there is a very clear division of labour on the grounds of gender. Women almost exclusively perform operations like transplanting, weeding and harvesting, which are more back breaking and less paying. In other sectors also women are concentrated in low skilled and low paying jobs. Women in construction industry, for example, are only engaged in unskilled occupations.

The discrimination faced by women workers in the labour market is substantiated by the study conducted on women workers in the textile industry of Mumbai and Bhiwandi. The discrimination faced by women can be seen at two levels: low WPR and clear gender-based division of labour.

In the textile mills of Mumbai, women formed a quarter of the workforce in the 1850s. Subsequently this figure oscillated between one-fifth and one-third. In 1919, women constituted 20.3 percent of the work force. This proportion rose to 22.9 percent in

1930, but from that year onwards there was a steady decline. In 1947 they constituted 11.17 percent of the workforce, in 1955, 8.47 percent, in 1965, 3.83 percent, in 1975, 1.97 percent, in 1980, 1.6 percent and in 2001, a mere 1.1 percent.

There is also a very rigid division of labour on the basis of gender in Mumbai's mills. Women in the mills are primarily employed in the winding department, while a small proportion are also employed as sweepers. While women employed in the winding department are categorised as skilled workers, in comparison to other skilled work, their work fetches them the lowest wages. Moreover, even in the winding department women have never been employed as jobbers or supervisors. Women working in Mumbai's mills, who fall under the category of 'staff', are only employed as clerks, stenographers or testers. In none of the mills surveyed were women employed in any managerial or supervisory capacity.

The low WPR for women in the mills is primarily due to 2 reasons. The first and most important reason is the strict division of labour. Women workers in the mills are only employed in the winding department. Since the inception of the textile industry of Mumbai, women worked in only winding and reeling departments. In the beginning, the gender-based division of labour was necessary because women were not willing to work with men. Hence the winding and reeling departments were run exclusively by women. The reason why only 2 departments were run exclusively by women was because during this stage there were not sufficient women to run other departments on an exclusively women basis. Later, when women were willing to work alongside men in other departments, they were denied entry into other departments. This was because of growing stereotypes of viewing work done by women in the winding section as 'light' work and work done by men in other sections of the mills as 'heavy' or 'highly skilled' work and assuming that it was beyond the capacity of women.

The other reason behind the low WPR for women in the mills is the prohibition of women from working in the night shift. The operation of night shift has been a regular feature of the mills since the 1930s and the prohibition of women from working in the night shift had serious repercussions on their employment. The prohibition on employment of women in the night shift resulted in a one-sided breakdown of the traditional division of labour on the basis of gender. While women are rarely employed in any other department other than winding, men began to be recruited in the winding department to work in the second and third shift. Gradually they also began to work in the first shift of the winding department. As a result, male workers outnumber female workers in the winding department also. Thus, while men have taken over areas traditionally associated with women workers, women have not made any in roads in work associated with men workers.

Even in the unorganised powerloom sector of the textile industry, WPR for women is very low. It is estimated that women constitute a mere 4 percent of the workforce in the powerloom sector in Bhiwandi. Moreover, there is a clear division of labour on the basis of gender. Women workers in Bhiwandi work only in the mending-clipping section of the powerloom units. As a result of introduction of new machines, the quality of grey cloth produced has improved. Hence very little mending work is required. Women are now mainly engaged in clipping work, which in comparison to other skilled jobs is the lowest paying.

Women workers in the organised mill sector receive much higher wages in comparison to women workers in the unorgainsed powerloom sector. They also enjoy most of the social security benefits due to them. However, in the powerlooms of Bhiwandi, labour laws are openly flouted. Women work under highly exploitative conditions. They get none of the benefits due to them, such as weekly holiday, paid leave, gratuity, provident fund, maternity benefits and separate wash areas. But in both the organised and unorganised sectors of the textile industry, WPR for women is dismally low and there is a clear gender-based division of labour.

The Government of India has adopted constitutional, legislative and statutory measures for protecting the rights of women workers. Article 14 of the Constitution guarantees equality before law and equal protection of the law. Article 15 of the Indian Constitution prohibits discrimination on grounds of sex. Article 16 guarantees equality of opportunity to all citizens relating to employment or appointment to any office under the State. The Supreme Court has, in most cases, taken a progressive stand in interpreting the constitution while dealing with rights of women workers.

Since women workers are most vulnerable to exploitation, most labour laws contain provisions which address problems of women workers. In recent times, the prohibition of night work by women under the Factories Act, 1948, has aroused some controversy. The recent Chennai High Court verdict permitting women to be employed in night shifts has received mixed response. Though the prohibition of night work by women does restrict women's employment in industries where work is performed in shifts, the unilateral lifting of such a ban could open the doors for exploitation, particularly sexual exploitation. The government should permit night work only on a case to case basis.

The Equal Remuneration Act was passed in 1976 to provide for the payment of equal remuneration to men and women and to prevent discrimination against women on the grounds of sex in matters related to employment. The Act lays down that women must be paid equal wages for 'same work or work of similar nature.' However, there has been a tendency to categorise tasks generally done by women as being of a slightly inferior nature. The Shramshakti report has recommended that it would be advantageous if a group of activities in any occupation are broad-banded into one category so that the present situation can be remedied. The piece rate system has also been another method of paying lower wages to women without contravening the provisions of the Equal Remuneration Act since a large number of women workers are paid wages under the piece rate system. While the time rate system follows the Minimum Wages Act, there are no such regulations for the piece rate system. The National Commission on Labour has recommended that the Equal Remuneration Act must be amended to remove the incompatibility between the piece rate and time rated systems.

It has been almost 3 decades since the Equal Remuneration Act was adopted; yet the practice of paying lower wages to women for same or similar work is still widespread. One of the main problems facing the implementation of the Act is the lack of gender sensitivity amongst those who enforce the law. Moreover, the inspecting agencies are generally overburdened with the enforcement of general labour laws. Thus there is an urgent need for initiating a process of gender sensitisation of law enforces and also the creation of a separate inspecting agency to detect and identify unequal wages for same or similar type of work.

The Maternity Benefit Act, 1961 provides for special benefits to women workers for certain periods before and after childbirth. However, the Act has very limited coverage because it applies to only those establishments where more than 10 persons are employed. It does not apply to the unorganised sector where a majority of women workers are employed.

The National Commission on Labour has made some recommendations for the protection of rights of women workers. Since a majority of women work in the unorganised sector, it has called for the adoption of an 'umbrella' legislation for the unorganised sector. The special concerns of women should be addressed within this 'umbrella' legislation. The Commission has also recommended the adoption of statues in sectors where women work in large number – agriculture, home-based work and women working as domestic workers.

Women workers also need to be provided security against sexual harassment at the workplace. Section 509 of the IPC prohibits any word, gesture or act intended to insult the modesty of women. However, there is no act specifically prohibiting sexual harassment at the workplace. The Supreme Court has played an important role in laying down guidelines on what constitutes sexual harassment at the workplace (*Vishakha and others v. State of Rajasthan, AEPC v. A. K. Chopra*). In the absence of domestic law in this area, it relied upon CEDAW in providing guidelines in protecting the rights of women.

Though India has a large number of labour laws, they tend to ignore women's experiences and their outlook tends to be paternalistic. While the provisions of a number of these acts need to be amended in order to make them gender sensitive, the enforcement of these acts also needs to be stepped up, particularly in the unorganised sector.

Till the early 1970s, government policy on women was based on the belief that industrialisation and development would generate conditions for women to develop alongside. However, in the mid 70s there was a growing realisation that women as group had been adversely affected by the nature of the economic processes accompanying industrialisation. It was felt that the government would have to extend direct benefits to women as part of its poverty alleviation and employment generation programmes. The National Perspective Plan for Women 1988-2000 recognised the need to bring women's concerns into the mainstream.

Government programmes affecting women workers have been reviewed in this study under three categories: (1) Wage employment programmes (2) Self-employment programmes (3) Programmes exclusively for women. JRY and EAS fall under the first category. Under the JRY, 30 percent of employment opportunities are reserved for women. It has been reported that in several states the average wages per manday paid to female unskilled workers is less than what is paid to male unskilled workers. This is indeed a very disturbing feature of JRY since it is a government funded scheme and is expected to adhere to the Equal Remuneration Act. Another worrying trend is that the financial allocation for JRY has been gradually decreasing. Since the JRY is targetted towards people living below the poverty line, this will adversely affect the employment opportunities available to the poor under this scheme.

Some of the important self-employment programmes initiated by the government are the IRDP, DWCRA and TRYSEM. IRDP is one of the largest self-employment programme. It has been stipulated that at least 40 percent of the beneficiaries should be women, with priority given to women-headed households. It has been reported that the target of 40 percent of beneficiaries being women has not been met in any of the last 5 years. The best percentage was 34.33 percent in 1997-98. The process of identification of beneficiaries also flouts the guidelines laid down under the scheme. As per the guidelines, selection of beneficiaries is the mandate of the Gram Sabha. In practice, however, state government officials select 40 percent of the beneficiaries. The non-involvement of the Gram Sabha goes against the purpose of democratisation of the planning process and affects women more adversely because unlike their male counterparts they cannot freely approach official channels. The IRDP also has very poor linkages with other schemes like DWCRA and TRYSEM.

DWCRA, a sub-scheme of IRDP, was introduced because it was felt that the flow of financial assistance to women as a group had been marginal under the IRDP. It has been seen that though the outlay for DWCRA has remained constant, the expenditure has gone down due to non-release and non-utilisation of funds. Holding up the funds of such an important scheme shows the extent of government apathy. While the scheme has achieved some success in states like Andhra Pradesh and Kerala, its overall performance is far from satisfactory. The group philosophy, which is the underlying feature of the scheme, has not been implemented well. Marketing of the products produced by women under this scheme is one of the weakest points of the programme.

TRYSEM, a supporting component of IRDP, aims at providing technical and entrepreneurial skills to rural youth below the poverty line. The coverage of women under this programme is fixed at 40 percent. The annual allocations under TRYSEM have remained static and annual releases have gradually declined. It has also been reported that out of the total beneficiaries under TRYSEM, roughly 47 percent were unemployed even after receiving training. This shows a serious lapse in planning and implementation of the programme. The problem of mismatch of skills and delays in processing of loans for the trainees is a big disincentive, particularly in the case of women trainees.

The government has also launched several development programmes exclusively for women, for example, RMK, Swayamsiddha, STEP and NORAD. RMK, a micro credit programme, provides credit to poor women for income-generation activities. It is heartening to note that loan recovery has exceeded 90 percent in all the years, showing the credit worthiness of even the poorest women. Though RMK is a step in the right direction, the process of processing credit is very complicated and needs to be simplified. It is also felt that RMK is more of an urban phenomenon. STEP was launched to provide skills to poor women for enhancing their employment opportunities. However, the provision of backward and forward linkages like help in receiving raw materials, assistance in marketing of products and access to credit continues to be poor.

The performance of the development programmes launched by the government has been poor due to several reasons. One of the main reasons is the lack of effective planning and coordination not only between the central and state governments but also between various ministries and departments of the central government and also with field level implementing agencies.

The developmental programmes need to more flexible for providing sustainable employment to women. There is also a need for greater involvement of panchayats, voluntary organisations and the community at large in developmental tasks. The role played by NGOs like SEWA and Disha in organising women in their struggles and assisting them in the task of empowerment to enable them to lead their lives with dignity is commendable. The direction shown by these groups needs to be followed by others.

The process of liberalisation of the economy is likely to cause further displacement of women workers. Increasing mechanisation and introduction of new technologies have led to displacement of women workers in areas such as agriculture and construction industry. While well-educated women in urban areas may find new opportunities as a result of liberalisation, women from poor families and rural areas have fewer opportunities. Where new opportunities have been created, the work conditions are very exploitative; for example, marine food processing industry or electronic industry in export processing zones. Employers in these industries prefer young, unmarried women who perform monotonous, time-consuming tasks. They often do not receive the minimum wages also. The work performed by them is often treated by employers as'unskilled' work. The skills used by them are viewed not as technical skills but skills practiced by women at home. Moreover, in a number of industries employers are resorting to outsourcing work. Although this has increased work opportunities for women, the earnings are low and sometimes well below the minimum wage, without any social security benefits. There is an urgent need to undertake skill-upgradation programmes, in tune with market realities, to create employment opportunities for women in the new economic environment.

Annexure I

Convention on the Elimination of Discrimination against Women

The States Parties to the present Convention,

Noting that the Charter of the United Nations reaffirms faith in fundamental human rights, in the dignity and worth of the human person and in the equal rights of man and women,

Noting that the Universal Declaration of Human Rights affirms the principle of the inadmissibility of discrimination and proclaims that all human beings are born free and equal in dignity and rights and that everyone is entitled to all the rights and freedoms set forth therein, without distinction of any kind, including distinction based on sex,

Noting that the States Parties to the International Covenants on Human Rights have the obligation to ensure the equal right of men and women to enjoy all economic, social, cultural, civil and political rights,

Considering the international conventions concluded under the auspices of the United Nations and the specialized agencies promoting equality of rights of men and women,

Noting also the resolutions, declarations and recommendations adopted by the United Nations and the specialized agencies promoting equality of rights of men and women,

Concerned, however, that despite these various instruments extensive discrimination against women continues to exist,

Recalling that discrimination against women violates the principles of equality of rights and respect for human dignity, is an obstacle to the participation of women, on equal terms with men, in the political, social, economic and cultural life of their countries, hampers the growth of the prosperity of society and the family and makes more difficult the full development of the potentialities of women in the service of their countries and of humanity,

Concerned that in situations of poverty women have the least access to food, health, education, training and opportunities for employment and other needs,

Convinced that the establishment of the new international economic order based on equity and justice will contribute significantly towards the promotion of equality between men and women,

Emphasizing that the eradication of apartheid, of all forms of racism, racial discrimination, colonialism, neo-colonialism, aggression, foreign occupation and domination and interference in the internal affairs of States is essential to the full enjoyment of the rights of men and women,

Affirming that the strengthening of international peace and security, relaxation of international tension, mutual co-operation among all States irrespective of their social and economic systems, general and complete disarmament, and in particular nuclear disarmament under strict and effective international control, the affirmation of the principles of justice, equality and mutual benefit in relations among countries and the realization of the right of peoples under alien and colonial domination and foreign occupation to self-determination and independence, as well as respect for national sovereignty and territorial integrity, will promote social progress and development and as a consequence will contribute to the attainment of full equality between men and women,

Convinced that the full and complete development of a country, the welfare of the world and the cause of peace require the maximum participation of women on equal terms with men in all fields,

Bearing in mind the great contribution of women to the welfare of the family and to the development of society, so far not fully recognized, the social significance of maternity and the role of both parents in the family and in the upbringing of children, and aware that the role of women in procreation should not be a basis for discrimination but that the upbringing of children requires a sharing of responsibility between men and women and society as a whole,

Aware that a change in the traditional role of men as well as the role of women in society and in the family is needed to achieve full equality between men and women,

Determined to implement the principles set forth in the Declaration on the Elimination of Discrimination against Women and, for that purpose, to adopt the measures required for the elimination of such discrimination in all its forms and manifestations,

Have agreed on the following:

PART I

Article 1. For the purposes of the present Convention, the term "discrimination against women" shall mean any distinction, exclusion or restriction made on the basis of sex which has the effect or purpose of impairing or nullifying the recognition, enjoyment or exercise by women irrespective of their marital status, on a basis of equality of men and women, of human rights and fundamental freedoms in the political, economic, social, cultural, civil or any other field.

Article 2. States Parties condemn discrimination against women in all its forms, agree to pursue by all appropriate means and without delay a policy of eliminating discrimination against women and, to this end, undertake:

(a) To embody the principle of the equality of men and women in their national constitutions or other appropriate legislation if not yet incorporated therein and to ensure, through law and other appropriate means, the practical realization of this principle;

(b) To adopt appropriate legislative and other measures, including sanctions where appropriate, prohibiting all discrimination against women;

(c) To establish legal protection of the rights of women on an equal basis with men and to ensure through competent national tribunals and other public institutions the effective protection of women against any act of discrimination;

(d) To refrain from engaging in any act or practice of discrimination against women and to ensure that public authorities and institutions shall act in conformity with this obligation;

(e) To take all appropriate measures to eliminate discrimination against women by any person, organization or enterprise;
(f) To take all appropriate measures, including legislation, to modify or abolish existing laws, regulations, customs and practices which constitute discrimination against women;
(g) To repeal all national penal provisions which constitute discrimination against women.

Article 3. States Parties shall take in all fields, in particular in the political, social, economic and cultural fields, all appropriate measures, including legislation, to ensure the full development and advancement of women, for the purpose of guaranteeing them the exercise and enjoyment of human rights and fundamental freedoms on a basis of equality with men.

Article 4. 1. Adoption by States Parties of temporary special measures aimed at accelerating de facto equality between men and women shall not be considered discrimination as defined in the present Convention, but shall in no way entail as a consequence the maintenance of unequal or separate standards; these measures shall be discontinued when the objectives of equality of opportunity and treatment have been achieved.

2. Adoption by States Parties of special measures, including those measures contained in the present Convention, aimed at protecting maternity shall not be considered discriminatory.

Article 5. States Parties shall take all appropriate measures:
(a) To modify the social and cultural patterns of conduct of men and women, with a view to achieving the elimination of prejudices and customary and all other practices which are based on the idea of the inferiority or the superiority of either of the sexes or on stereotyped roles for men and women;
(b) To ensure that family education includes a proper understanding of maternity as a social function and the recognition of the common responsibility of men and women in the upbringing and development of their children, it being understood that the interest of the children is the primordial consideration in all cases.

Article 6. States Parties shall take all appropriate measures, including legislation, to suppress all forms of traffic in women and exploitation of prostitution of women.

PART II

Article 7. States Parties shall take all appropriate measures to eliminate discrimination against women in the political and public life of the country and, in particular, shall ensure to women, on equal terms with men, the right:

(a) To vote in all elections and public referenda and to be eligible for election to all publicly elected bodies;
(b) To participate in the formulation of government policy and the implementation thereof and to hold public office and perform all public functions at all levels of government;
(c) To participate in non-governmental organizations and associations concerned with the public and political life of the country.

Article 8. States Parties shall take all appropriate measures to ensure to women, on equal terms with men and without any discrimination, the opportunity to represent their Governments at the international level and to participate in the work of international organizations.

Article 9. 1. States Parties shall grant women equal rights with men to acquire, change or retain their nationality. They shall ensure in particular that neither marriage to an alien nor change of nationality by the husband during marriage shall automatically change the nationality of the wife, render her stateless or force upon her the nationality of the husband.

2. States Parties shall grant women equal rights with men with respect to the nationality of their children.

PART III

Article 10. States Parties shall take all appropriate measures to eliminate discrimination against women in order to ensure to them equal rights with men in the field of education and in particular to ensure, on a basis of equality of men and women:

(a) The same conditions for career and vocational guidance, for access to studies and for the achievement of diplomas in educational establishments of all categories in rural as well as in urban areas; this equality shall be ensured in preschool, general, technical, professional and higher technical education, as well as in all types of vocational training;

(b) Access to the same curricula, the same examinations, teaching staff with qualifications of the same standard and school premises and equipment of the same quality;

(c) The elimination of any stereotyped concept of the roles of men and women at all levels and in all forms of education by encouraging coeducation and other types of education which will help to achieve this aim and, in particular, by the revision of textbooks and school programmes and the adaptation of teaching methods;

(d) The same opportunities to benefit from scholarships and other study grants;

(e) The same opportunities for access to programmes of continuing education including adult and functional literacy programmes, particularly those aimed at reducing, at the earliest possible time, any gap in education existing between men and women;

(f) The reduction of female student drop-out rates and the organization of programmes for girls and women who have left school prematurely;

(g) The same opportunities to participate actively in sports and physical education;

(h) Access to specific educational information to help to ensure the health and well-being of families, including information and advice on family planning.

Article 11. 1. States Parties shall take all appropriate measures to eliminate discrimination against women in the field of employment in order to ensure, on a basis of equality of men and women, the same rights, in particular:

(a) The right to work as an inalienable right of all human beings;

(b) The right to the same employment opportunities, including the application of the same criteria for selection in matters of employment;

(c) The right to free choice of profession and employment, the right to promotion, job security and all benefits and conditions of service and the right to receive vocational training and retraining, including apprenticeships, advanced vocational training and recurrent training;

(d) The right to equal remuneration, including benefits, and to equal treatment in respect of work of equal value, as well as equality of treatment in the evaluation of the quality of work;

(e) The right to social security, particularly in cases of retirement, unemployment, sickness, invalidity and old age and other incapacity to work, as well as the right to paid leave;

(f) The right to protection of health and to safety in working conditions, including the safeguarding of the function of reproduction.

2. In order to prevent discrimination against women on the grounds of marriage or maternity and to ensure their effective right to work, States Parties shall take appropriate measures:

(a) To prohibit, subject to the imposition of sanctions, dismissal on the grounds of pregnancy or of maternity leave and discrimination in dismissals on the basis of marital status;

(b) To introduce maternity leave with pay or with comparable social benefits without loss of former employment, seniority or social allowances;

(c) To encourage the provision of the necessary supporting social services to enable parents to combine family obligations with work responsibilities and participation in public life, in particular through promoting the establishment and development of a network of child-care facilities;

(d) To provide special protection to women during pregnancy in types of work proved to be harmful to them.

3. Protective legislation relating to matters covered in this article shall be reviewed periodically in the light of scientific and technological knowledge and shall be revised, repealed or extended as necessary.

Article 12. 1. States Parties shall take all appropriate measures to eliminate discrimination against women in the field of health care in order to ensure, on a basis of equality of men and women, access to health care services, including those related to family planning.

2. Notwithstanding the provisions of paragraph 1 of this article, States Parties shall ensure to women appropriate services in connexion with pregnancy, confinement and the post-natal period, granting free services where necessary, as well as adequate nutrition during pregnancy and lactation.

Article 13. States Parties shall take all appropriate measures to eliminate discrimination against women in other areas of economic and social life in order to ensure, on a basis of equality of men and women, the same rights, in particular:

(a) The right to family benefits;
(b) The right to bank loans, mortgages and other forms of financial credit;
(c) The right to participate in recreational activities, sports and all aspects of cultural life.

Article 14. 1. States Parties shall take into account the particular problems faced by rural women and the significant roles which rural women play in the economic survival of their families, including their work in the non-monetized sectors of the economy, and shall take all appropriate measures to ensure the application of the provisions of this Convention to women in rural areas.

2. States Parties shall take all appropriate measures to eliminate discrimination against women in rural areas in order to ensure, on a basis of equality of men and women, that they participate in and benefit from rural development and, in particular, shall ensure to such women the right:

(a) To participate in the elaboration and implementation of development planning at all levels;
(b) To have access to adequate health care facilities, including information, counselling and services in family planning;
(c) To benefit directly from social security programmes;
(d) To obtain all types of training and education, formal and non-formal, including that relating to functional literacy,

as well as, inter alia, the benefit of all community and extension services, in order to increase their technical proficiency;

(e) To organize self-help groups and co-operatives in order to obtain equal access to economic opportunities through employment or self-employment;

(f) To participate in all community activities;

(g) To have access to agricultural credit and loans, marketing facilities, appropriate technology and equal treatment in land and agrarian reform as well as in land resettlement schemes;

(h) To enjoy adequate living conditions, particularly in relation to housing, sanitation, electricity and water supply, transport and communications.

PART IV

Article 15. 1. States Parties shall accord to women equality with men before the law.

2. States Parties shall accord to women, in civil matters, a legal capacity identical to that of men and the same opportunities to exercise that capacity. In particular, they shall give women equal rights to conclude contracts and to administer property and shall treat them equally in all stages of procedure in courts and tribunals.

3. States Parties agree that all contracts and all other private instruments of any kind with a legal effect which is directed at restricting the legal capacity of women shall be deemed null and void.

4. States Parties shall accord to men and women the same rights with regard to the law relating to the movement of persons and the freedom to choose their residence and domicile.

Article 16. 1. States Parties shall take all appropriate measures to eliminate discrimination against women in all matters relating to marriage and family relations and in particular shall ensure, on a basis of equality of men and women:

(a) The same right to enter into marriage;

(b) The same right freely to choose a spouse and to enter into marriage only with their free and full consent;

(c) The same rights and responsibilities during marriage and at its dissolution;

(d) The same rights and responsibilities as parents, irrespective of their marital status, in matters relating to their children; in all cases the interests of the children shall be paramount;

(e) The same rights to decide freely and responsibly on the number and spacing of their children and to have access to the information, education and means to enable them to exercise these rights;

(f) The same rights and responsibilities with regard to guardianship, wardship, trusteeship and adoption of children, or similar institutions where these concepts exist in national legislation; in all cases the interests of the children shall be paramount;

(g) The same personal rights as husband and wife, including the right to choose a family name, a profession and an occupation;

(h) The same rights for both spouses in respect of the ownership, acquisition, management, administration, enjoyment and disposition of property, whether free of charge or for a valuable consideration.

2. The betrothal and the marriage of a child shall have no legal effect, and all necessary action, including legislation, shall be taken to specify a minimum age for marriage and to make the registration of marriages in an official registry compulsory.

PART V

Article 17. 1. For the purpose of considering the progress made in the implementation of the present Convention, there shall be established a Committee on the Elimination of Discrimination against Women (hereinafter referred to as the Committee) consisting, at the time of entry into force of the Convention, of eighteen and, after ratification of or accession to the Convention by the thirty-fifth State Party, of twenty-three experts of high moral standing and competence in the field covered by the Convention. The experts shall be elected by States Parties from among their nationals and shall serve in their personal capacity, consideration being given to equitable geographical distribution and to the representation of the different forms of civilization as well as the principal legal systems.

2. The members of the Committee shall be elected by secret ballot from a list of persons nominated by States Parties. Each State Party may nominate one person from among its own nationals.

3. The initial election shall be held six months after the date of the entry into force of the present Convention. At least three months before the date of each election the Secretary-General of the United Nations shall address a letter to the States Parties inviting them to submit their nominations within two months. The Secretary-General shall prepare a list in alphabetical order of all persons thus nominated, indicating the States Parties which have nominated them, and shall submit it to the States Parties.

4. Elections of the members of the Committee shall be held at a meeting of States Parties convened by the Secretary-General at United Nations Headquarters. At that meeting, for which two thirds of the States Parties shall constitute a quorum, the persons elected to the Committee shall be those nominees who obtain the largest number of votes and an absolute majority of the votes of the representatives of States Parties present and voting.

5. The members of the Committee shall be elected for a term of four years. However, the terms of nine of the members elected at the first election shall expire at the end of two years; immediately after the first election the names of these nine members shall be chosen by lot by the Chairman of the Committee.

6. The election of the five additional members of the Committee shall be held in accordance with the provisions of paragraphs 2, 3 and 4 of this article, following the thirty-fifth ratification or accession. The terms of two of the additional members elected on this occasion shall expire at the end of two years, the names of these two members having been chosen by lot by the Chairman of the Committee.

7. For the filling of casual vacancies, the State Party whose expert has ceased to function as a member of the Committee shall appoint another expert from among its nationals, subject to the approval of the Committee.

8. The members of the Committee shall, with the approval of the General Assembly, receive emoluments from United Nations resources on such terms and conditions as the Assembly may decide, having regard to the importance of the Committee's responsibilities.

9. The Secretary-General of the United Nations shall provide the necessary staff and facilities for the effective performance of the functions of the Committee under the present Convention.

Article 18. 1. States Parties undertake to submit to the Secretary-General of the United Nations, for consideration by the Committee, a report on the legislative, judicial, administrative or other measures which they have adopted to give effect to he provisions of the present Convention and on the progress made in this respect:

(a) Within one year after the entry into force for the State concerned; and
(b) Thereafter at least every four years and further whenever the Committee so requests.

2. Reports may indicate factors and difficulties affecting the degree of fulfilment of obligations under the present Convention.

Article 19. 1. The Committee shall adopt its own rules of procedure.

2. The Committee shall elect its officers for a term of two years.

Article 20. 1. The Committee shall normally meet for a period of not more than two weeks annually in order to consider the reports submitted in accordance with article 18 of the present Convention.

2. The meetings of the Committee shall normally be held at United Nations Headquarters or at any other convenient place as determined by the Committee.

· *Article 21*. 1. The Committee shall, through the Economic and Social Council, report annually to the General Assembly of the United Nations on its activities and may make suggestions and general recommendations based on the examination of reports and information received from the States Parties. Such suggestions and general recommendations shall be included in the report of the Committee together with comments, if any, from States Parties.

2. The Secretary-General shall transmit the reports of the Committee to the Commission on the Status of Women for its information.

Article 22. The specialized agencies shall be entitled to be represented at the consideration of the implementation of such provisions of the present Convention as fall within the scope of their activities. The Committee may invite the specialized agencies to submit reports on the implementation of the Convention in areas falling within the scope of their activities.

PART VI

Article 23. Nothing in this Convention shall affect any provisions that are more conducive to the achievement of equality between men and women which may be contained:

(a) In the legislation of a State Party; or
(b) In any other international convention, treaty or agreement in force for that State.

Article 24. States Parties undertake to adopt all necessary measures at the national level aimed at achieving the full realization of the rights recognized in the present Convention.

Article 25. 1. The present Convention shall be open for signature by all States.

2. The Secretary-General of the United Nations is designated as the depositary of the present Convention.

3. The present Convention is subject to ratification. Instruments of ratification shall be deposited with the Secretary-General of the United Nations.

4. The present Convention shall be open to accession by all States. Accession shall be effected by the deposit of an instrument of accession with the Secretary-General of the United Nations.

Article 26. 1. A request for the revision of the present Convention may be made at any time by any State Party by means of a notification in writing addressed to the Secretary-General of the United Nations.

2. The General Assembly of the United Nations shall decide upon the steps, if any, to be taken in respect of such a request.

Article 27. 1. The present Convention shall enter into force on the thirtieth day after the date of deposit with the Secretary-General of the United Nations of the twentieth instrument of ratification or accession.

2. For each State ratifying the present Convention or acceding to it after the deposit of the twentieth instrument of ratification or accession, the Convention shall enter into force on the thirtieth day after the date of the deposit of its own instrument of ratification or accession.

Article 28. 1. The Secretary-General of the United Nations shall receive and circulate to all States the text of reservations made by States at the time of ratification or accession.

2. A reservation incompatible with the object and purpose of the present Convention shall not be permitted.

3. Reservations may be withdrawn at any time by notification to this effect addressed to the Secretary-General of the United Nations, who shall then inform all States thereof. Such notification shall take effect on the date on which it is received.

Article 29. 1. Any dispute between two or more States Parties concerning the interpretation or application of the present Convention which is not settled by negotiation shall, at the request of one of them, be submitted to arbitration. If within six months from the date of the request for arbitration the parties are unable to agree on the organization of the arbitration, any one of those parties may refer the dispute to the International Court of Justice by request in conformity with the Statute of the Court.

2. Each State Party may at the time of signature or ratification of this Convention or accession thereto declare that it does not consider itself bound by paragraph 1 of this article. The other States Parties shall not be bound by that paragraph with respect to any State Party which has made such a reservation.

3. Any State Party which has made a reservation in accordance with paragraph 2 of this article may at any time withdraw that reservation by notification to the Secretary-General of the United Nations.

Article 30. The present Convention, the Arabic, Chinese, English, French, Russian and Spanish texts of which are equally authentic, shall be deposited with the Secretary-General of the United Nations.

IN WITNESS WHEREOF the undersigned, duly authorized, have signed the present Convention.

Annexure II

State Parties to the Convention on the Elimination of Discrimination Against Women

As of March 2003, 171 countries—almost ninety percent of he members of the United Nations—are party to the Convention and an additional 3 have signed the treaty, binding themselves to do nothing in contravention of its terms.

97 Signatures/171 ratifications, accessions and successions (Latest State: Afghanistan, 5 March 2003)

a/ Accession;
b/ Declarations or reservations;
c/ Reservation subsequently withdrawn;
d/ Succession

State	*Date of signature*	*Date of receipt of the instrument of ratification, accession or succession*
Afghanistan	14-Aug-80	5 March 2003 a/
Albania		11 May 1994 a/
Algeria		22 May 1996 a/ b/
Andorra		15-Jan-97 a
Angola		17-Sep 1986 a/
Antigua and Barbuda		1 August 1989 a/
Argentina	17-Jul-80	15 July 1985 b/
Armenia		13-Sep 1993 a/

State	*Date of signature*	*Date of receipt of the instrument of ratification, accession or succession*
Australia	17-Jul-80	28 July 1983 b/
Austria	17-Jul-80	31 March 1982 b/
Azerbaijan		10 July 1995 a/
Bahamas		6-Oct-93 a/ b/
Bahrain		18 June 2002 a/
Bangladesh		6-Nov-84 a/ b/
Barbados	24-Jul-80	16-Oct-80
Belarus	17-Jul-80	4-Feb-81 c/
Belgium	17-Jul-80	10 July 1985 b/
Belize	7-Mar-90	16-May-90
Benin	11-Nov 1981	12-Mar-92
Bhutan	17-Jul-80	31-Aug-81
Bolivia	30-May-80	8-Jun-90
Bosnia & Herzegovina		1-Sep-93 d/
Botswana		13-Aug-96 a/
Brazil	31-Mar-81 b/	1-Feb-84 b/
Bulgaria	17-Jul-80	8-Feb-82 c/
Burkina Faso		14-Oct-87 a/
Burundi	17-Jul-80	8-Jan-92
Cambodia	17-Oct-80	15-Oct-92 a/
Cameroon	6-Jun-83	23-Aug-94 a/
Canada	17-Jul-80	10-Dec-81
Cape Verde		5-Dec-80 a/

State	*Date of signature*	*Date of receipt of the instrument of ratification, accession or succession*
Central African Republic		21 June 1991 a/
Chad		9 June 1995 a/
Chile	17-Jul-80	7-Dec-89 b/
China	17 July 1980 b/	4-Nov-80 b/
Colombia	17-Jul-80	19-Jan-82
Comoros		31-Oct-94 a/
Congo	29-Jul-80	26-Jul-82
Costa Rica	17-Jul-80	4-Apr-86
Cote d'Ivoire	17-Jul-80	18-Dec-95 a/
Croatia		9-Sep-92 d/
Cuba	6-Mar-80	17 July 1980 b/
Cyprus		23 July 1985 a/ b/
Czech Republic		22-Feb-93 c/ d/
Democratic People's Republic of Korea		27-Feb-01 a/
Democratic Republic of the Congo	17-Oct-86	16-Nov-86
Denmark	17-Jul-80	21-Apr-83
Djibouti		2-Dec-98 a/
Dominica	15-Sep 1980	15-Sep 1980
Dominican Republic	17-Jul-80	2-Sep-82
Ecuador	17-Jul-80	9-Nov-81
Egypt	16 July 1980 b/	18-Sep 1981 b/
El Salvador	14-Nov 1980 b/	19-Aug-81 b/

State	*Date of signature*	*Date of receipt of the instrument of ratification, accession or succession*
Equatorial Guinea		23-Oct-84 a/
Eritrea		5-Sep-95 a/
Estonia		21-Oct-91 a/
Ethiopia	8-Jul-80	10-Dec-81 b/
Fiji		28-Aug-95 a/ b/
Finland	17-Jul-80	4-Sep-86
France	17 July 1980 b/	14-Dec-83 b/ c/
Gabon	17-Jul-80	21-Jan-83
Gambia	29-Jul-80	16-Apr-93
Georgia		26-Oct-94 a/
Germany	17-Jul-80	10 July 1985 b/
Ghana	17-Jul-80	2-Jan-86
Greece	2-Mar-82	7-Jun-83
Grenada	17-Jul-80	30-Aug-90
Guatemala	8-Jun-81	12-Aug-82
Guinea	17-Jul-80	9-Aug-82
Guinea-Bissau	17-Jul-80	23-Aug-85
Guyana	17-Jul-80	17-Jul-80
Haiti	17-Jul-80	20-Jul-81
Honduras	11-Jun-80	3-Mar-83
Hungary	6-Jun-80	22-Dec-80 c/
Iceland	24-Jul-80	18-Jun-85
India	30 July 1980 b/	9 July 1993 b/
Indonesia	29-Jul-80	13-Sep 1984 b/
Iraq		13-Aug-86 a/ b/

State	*Date of signature*	*Date of receipt of the instrument of ratification, accession or succession*
Ireland		23-Dec-85 a/ b/ c/
Israel	17-Jul-80	3-Oct-91 b/
Italy	17 July 1980 b/	10-Jun-85
Jamaica	17-Jul-80	19-Oct-84 b/
Japan	17-Jul-80	25-Jun-85
Jordan	3-Dec-80 b/	1 July 1992 b/
Kazakhstan		26-Aug-98 a/
Kenya		9 March 1984 a/
Kuwait		2-Sep-94 a/ b/
Kyrgyzstan		10-Feb-97 a/
Lao Peoples Democratic Rep.	17-Jul-80	14-Aug-81
Latvia		14 April 1992 a/
Lebanon		21 April 1997 a/ b/
Lesotho	17-Jul-80	22-Aug-95 a/ b/
Liberia		17 July 1984 a/
Libyan A. Jamahiriya		16 May 1989 a/ b/
Liechtenstein		22-Dec-95 a/ b/
Lithuania		18-Jan-94 a/
Luxembourg	17-Jul-80	2-Feb-89 b/
Madagascar	17-Jul-80	17-Mar-89

State	*Date of signature*	*Date of receipt of the instrument of ratification, accession or succession*
Malawi		12 March 1987 a/ c/
Malaysia		5 July 1995 a/ b/
Maldives		1 July 1993 a/ b/
Mali	5-Feb-85	10-Sep 1985
Malta		8 March 1991 a/ b/
Mauritania		10 May 2001 a/
Mauritius		9 July 1984 a/ b/
Mexico	17 July 1980 b/	23-Mar-81
Mongolia	17-Jul-80	20 July 1981 c/
Morocco		21 June 1993 a/ b/
Mozambique		16 April 1997 a/
Myanmar		22 July 1997 a/ b/
Namibia		23-Nov-92 a/
Nepal	5-Feb-91	22-Apr-91
Netherlands	17-Jul-80	23 July 1991 b/
New Zealand	17-Jul-80	10-Jan-85 b/ c/
Nicaragua	17-Jul-80	27-Oct-81
Niger		8-Oct-99 a/
Nigeria	23-Apr-84	13-Jun-85
Norway	17-Jul-80	21-May-81
Pakistan		12 March 1996 a/ b/
Panama	26-Jun-80	29-Oct-81

State	*Date of signature*	*Date of receipt of the instrument of ratification, accession or succession*
Papua New Guinea		12-Jan-95 a/
Paraguay		6 April 1987 a/
Peru	23-Jul-81	13-Sep 1982
Philippines	15-Jul-80	5-Aug-81
Poland	29-May-80	30 July 1980 b/
Portugal	24-Apr-80	30-Jul-80
Republic of Korea	25 May 1983 b/	27-Dec-84 b/ c/
Republic of Moldova		1 July 1994 a/
Romania	4-Sep 1980 b/	7-Jan-82 b/
Russian Federation	17-Jul-80	23-Jan-81 c/
Rwanda	1-May-80	2-Mar-81
Saint Kitts and Nevis		25 April 1985 a/
Saint Lucia		8-Oct-82 a/
St. Vincent & the Grenadines		4 August 1981 a/
Samoa		25-Sep 1992 a/
Sao Tome and Principe	31-Oct-95	
Saudi Arabia	7-Sep 2000	7-Sep-00 b/
Senegal	29-Jul-80	5-Feb-85
Seychelles		5 May 1992 a/
Sierra Leone	21-Sep 1988	11-Nov-88
Singapore		5-Oct-95 a/ b/

State	*Date of signature*	*Date of receipt of the instrument of ratification, accession or succession*
Slovakia		28 May 1993 d/
Slovenia		6 July 1992 d/
Solomon Islands		6-May-02
South Africa	29-Jan-93	15-Dec-95 a/
Spain	17-Jul-80	5-Jan-84 b/
Sri Lanka	17-Jul-80	5-Oct-81
Suriname		1 March 1993 a/
Sweden	7-Mar-80	2-Jul-80
Switzerland	23-Jan-87	27 March 1997 a/ b/
Tajikistan		26-Oct-93 a/
Thailand		9 August 1985 a/ b/ c/
The former Yugoslav Republic of Macedonia		18-Jan-94 d/
Togo		26-Sep 1983 a/
Trinidad and Tobago	27 June 1985 b/	12-Jan-90 b/
Tunisia	24-Jul-80	20-Sep 1985 b/
Turkey		20-Dec-85 a/ b/
Turkmenistan		1 May 1997 a/
Tuvalu		6-Oct-99 a/
Uganda	30-Jul-80	22-Jul-85
Ukraine	17-Jul-80	12 March 1981 c/
UK & Northern Ireland	22-Jul-81	7 April 1986 b/

State	*Date of signature*	*Date of receipt of the instrument of ratification, accession or succession*
United Republic of Tanzania	17-Jul-80	20-Aug-85
United States of America	17-Jul-80	
Uruguay	30-Mar-81	9-Oct-81
Uzbekistan		19 July 1995 a/
Vanuatu		8-Sep-95 a/
Venezuela	17-Jul-80	2 May 1983 b/
Viet Nam	29-Jul-80	17-Feb-82 b/
Yemen /		30 May 1984 a/ b/
Yugoslavia		12 March 2001 d/
Zambia	17-Jul-80	21-Jun-85
Zimbabwe		13 May 1991 a/

STATES THAT BECAME PARTIES IN 2002

Solomon Islands	6 May 2002
Bahrain	18 June 2002

STATES THAT BECAME PARTIES IN 2001

Democratic People's Republic of Korea	27 February 2001
Mauritania	10 May 2001

STATES THAT BECAME PARTIES IN 2000

Saudi Arabia	7 September 2000

Annexure III

Optional Protocol to the Convention on The Elimination of Discrimination against Women

UNITED NATIONS
General Assembly

15 October 1999

Fifty-fourth session
Agenda Item 109

RESOLUTION ADOPTED BY THE GENERAL ASSEMBLY
[*without reference to a Main Committee (A/54/L.4)*]
54/4. Optional Protocol to the Convention on the Elimination of All Forms of

Discrimination against Women

The General Assembly, Reaffirming the Vienna Declaration and Programme of Action1 and the Beijing Declaration 2 and Platform for Action,3

Recalling that the Beijing Platform for Action, pursuant to the Vienna Declaration and Programme of Action, supported the process initiated by the Commission on the Status of Women with a view to elaborating a draft optional protocol to the Convention on the Elimination of All Forms of Discrimination against Women4 that could enter into force as soon as possible on a right-to-petition procedure,

Noting that the Beijing Platform for Action also called on all States that have not yet ratified or acceded to the Convention to do so as soon as possible so that universal ratification of the

Convention can be achieved by the year 2000,

1. *Adopts and opens for signature, ratification and accession* the Optional Protocol to the Convention, the text of which is annexed to the present resolution;
2. *Calls upon* all States that have signed, ratified or acceded to the Convention to sign and ratify or to accede to the Protocol as soon as possible;
3. *Stresses* that States parties to the Protocol should undertake to respect the rights and procedures provided by the Protocol and cooperate with the Committee on the Elimination of Discrimination against Women at all stages of its proceedings under the Protocol;
4. *Stresses* also that in the fulfilment of its mandate as well as its functions under the Protocol, the Committee should continue to be guided by the principles of non-selectivity, impartiality and objectivity;
5. *Requests* the Committee to hold meetings to exercise its functions under the Protocol after its entry into force, in addition to its meetings held under article 20 of the convention; the duration of such meetings shall be determined and, if necessary, reviewed by a meeting of the States parties to the Protocol, subject to the approval of the General Assembly;
6. *Requests* the Secretary-General to provide the staff and facilities necessary for the effective performance of the functions of the Committee under the Protocol after its entry into force;
7. *Also requests* the Secretary-General to include information on the status of the Protocol in her or his regular reports submitted to the General Assembly on the status of the Convention.

28th plenary meeting
6 October 1999

OPTIONAL PROTOCOL TO THE CONVENTION ON THE ELIMINATION OF ALL FORMS OF DISCRIMINATION AGAINST WOMEN

The States Parties to the present Protocol,

Noting that the Charter of the United Nations reaffirms faith in fundamental human rights, in the dignity and worth of the human person and in the equal rights of men and women,

Also noting that the Universal Declaration of Human Rights5 proclaims that all human beings are born free and equal in dignity and rights and that everyone is entitled to all the rights and freedoms set forth therein, without distinction of any kind, including distinction based on sex,

Recalling that the International Covenants on Human Rights6 and other international human rights instruments prohibit discrimination on the basis of sex,

Also recalling the Convention on the Elimination of All Forms of Discrimination against Women ("the Convention"), in which the States Parties thereto condemn discrimination against women in all its forms and agree to pursue by all appropriate means and without delay a policy of eliminating discrimination against women,

Reaffirming their determination to ensure the full and equal enjoyment by women of all human rights and fundamental freedoms and to take effective action to prevent violations of these rights and freedoms,

Have agreed as follows:

Article 1

A State Party to the present Protocol ("State Party") recognizes the competence of the Committee on the Elimination of Discrimination against Women ("the Committee") to receive and consider communications submitted in accordance with article 2.

Article 2

Communications may be submitted by or on behalf of individuals or groups of individuals, under the jurisdiction of a State Party, claiming to be victims of a violation of any of the rights set forth in the Convention by that State Party. Where a communication is submitted on behalf of individuals or groups of individuals, this shall be with their consent unless the author can justify acting on their behalf without such consent.

Article 3

Communications shall be in writing and shall not be anonymous. No communication shall be received by the Committee if it concerns a State Party to the Convention that is not a party to the present Protocol.

Article 4

1. The Committee shall not consider a communication unless it has ascertained that all available domestic remedies have been exhausted unless the application of such remedies is unreasonably prolonged or unlikely to bring effective relief.
2. The Committee shall declare a communication inadmissible where:
   (*a*) The same matter has already been examined by the Committee or has been or is being examined under another procedure of international investigation or settlement;
   (*b*) It is incompatible with the provisions of the Convention;
   (*c*) It is manifestly ill-founded or not sufficiently substantiated;
   (*d*) It is an abuse of the right to submit a communication;
   (*e*) The facts that are the subject of the communication occurred prior to the entry into force of the present Protocol for the State Party concerned unless those facts continued after that date.

Article 5

1. At any time after the receipt of a communication and before a determination on the merits has been reached, the Committee may transmit to the State Party concerned

for its urgent consideration a request that the State Party take such interim measures as may be necessary to avoid possible irreparable damage to the victim or victims of the alleged violation.

2. Where the Committee exercises its discretion under paragraph 1 of the present article, this does not imply a determination on admissibility or on the merits of the communication.

Article 6

1. Unless the Committee considers a communication inadmissible without reference to the State Party concerned, and provided that the individual or individuals consent to the disclosure of their identity to that State Party, the Committee shall bring any communication submitted to it under the present Protocol confidentially to the attention of the State Party concerned.
2. Within six months, the receiving State Party shall submit to the Committee written explanations or statements clarifying the matter and the remedy, if any, that may have been provided by that State Party.

Article 7

1. The Committee shall consider communications received under the present Protocol in the light of all information made available to it by or on behalf of individuals or groups of individuals and by the State Party concerned, provided that this information is transmitted to the parties concerned.
2. The Committee shall hold closed meetings when examining communications under the present Protocol.
3. After examining a communication, the Committee shall transmit its views on the communication, together with its recommendations, if any, to the parties concerned.
4. The State Party shall give due consideration to the views of the Committee, together with its recommendations, if any, and shall submit to the Committee, within six

months, a written response, including information on any action taken in the light of the views and recommendations of the Committee.

5. The Committee may invite the State Party to submit further information about any measures the State Party has taken in response to its views or recommendations, if any, including as deemed appropriate by the Committee, in the State Party's subsequent reports under article 18 of the Convention.

Article 8

1. If the Committee receives reliable information indicating grave or systematic violations by a State Party of rights set forth in the Convention, the Committee shall invite that State Party to cooperate in the examination of the information and to this end to submit observations with regard to the information concerned.
2. Taking into account any observations that may have been submitted by the State Party concerned as well as any other reliable information available to it, the Committee may designate one or more of its members to conduct an inquiry and to report urgently to the Committee. Where warranted and with the consent of the State Party, the inquiry may include a visit to its territory.
3. After examining the findings of such an inquiry, the Committee shall transmit these findings to the State Party concerned together with any comments and recommendations.
4. The State Party concerned shall, within six months of receiving the findings, comments and recommendations transmitted by the Committee, submit its observations to the Committee.
5. Such an inquiry shall be conducted confidentially and the cooperation of the State Party shall be sought at all stages of the proceedings.

Article 9

1. The Committee may invite the State Party concerned to include in its report under article 18 of the Convention

details of any measures taken in response to an inquiry conducted under article 8 of the present Protocol.

2. The Committee may, if necessary, after the end of the period of six months referred to in article 8.4, invite the State Party concerned to inform it of the measures taken in response to such an inquiry.

Article 10

1. Each State Party may, at the time of signature or ratification of the present Protocol or accession thereto, declare that it does not recognize the competence of the Committee provided for in articles 8 and 9.
2. Any State Party having made a declaration in accordance with paragraph 1 of the present article may, at any time, withdraw this declaration by notification to the Secretary-General.

Article 11

A State Party shall take all appropriate steps to ensure that individuals under its jurisdiction are not subjected to ill treatment or intimidation as a consequence of communicating with the Committee pursuant to the present Protocol.

Article 12

The Committee shall include in its annual report under article 21 of the Convention a summary of its activities under the present Protocol.

Article 13

Each State Party undertakes to make widely known and to give publicity to the Convention and the present Protocol and to facilitate access to information about the views and recommendations of the Committee, in particular, on matters involving that State Party.

Article 14

The Committee shall develop its own rules of procedure to be followed when exercising the functions conferred on it by the present Protocol.

Article 15

1. The present Protocol shall be open for signature by any State that has signed, ratified or acceded to the Convention.
2. The present Protocol shall be subject to ratification by any State that has ratified or acceded to the Convention. Instruments of ratification shall be deposited with the Secretary-General of the United Nations.
3. The present Protocol shall be open to accession by any State that has ratified or acceded to the Convention.
4. Accession shall be effected by the deposit of an instrument of accession with the Secretary-General of the United Nations.

Article 16

1. The present Protocol shall enter into force three months after the date of the deposit with the Secretary-General of the United Nations of the tenth instrument of ratification or accession.
2. For each State ratifying the present Protocol or acceding to it after its entry into force, the present Protocol shall enter into force three months after the date of the deposit of its own instrument of ratification or accession.

Article 17

No reservations to the present Protocol shall be permitted.

Article 18

1. Any State Party may propose an amendment to the present Protocol and file it with the Secretary-General

of the United Nations. The Secretary-General shall thereupon communicate any proposed amendments to the States Parties with a request that they notify her or him whether they favour a conference of States Parties for the purpose of considering and voting on the proposal. In the event that at least one third of the States Parties favour such a conference, the Secretary-General shall convene the conference under the auspices of the United Nations. Any amendment adopted by a majority of the States Parties present and voting at the conference shall be submitted to the General Assembly of the United Nations for approval.

2. Amendments shall come into force when they have been approved by the General Assembly of the United Nations and accepted by a two-thirds majority of the States Parties to the present Protocol in accordance with their respective constitutional processes.
3. When amendments come into force, they shall be binding on those States Parties that have accepted them, other States Parties still being bound by the provisions of the present Protocol and any earlier amendments that they have accepted.

Article 19

1. Any State Party may denounce the present Protocol at any time by written notification addressed to the Secretary-General of the United Nations. Denunciation shall take effect six months after the date of receipt of the notification by the Secretary-General.
2. Denunciation shall be without prejudice to the continued application of the provisions of the present Protocol to any communication submitted under article 2 or any inquiry initiated under article 8 before the effective date of denunciation.

Article 20

The Secretary-General of the United Nations shall inform all States of:

(*a*) Signatures, ratifications and accessions under the present Protocol;

(*b*) The date of entry into force of the present Protocol and of any amendment under article 18;

(*c*) Any denunciation under article 19.

Article 21

1. The present Protocol, of which the Arabic, Chinese, English, French, Russian and Spanish texts are equally authentic, shall be deposited in the archives of the United Nations.
2. The Secretary-General of the United Nations shall transmit certified copies of the present Protocol to all States referred to in article 25 of the Convention.

Annexure IV

Ratifications and Signatories to the Optional Protocol to the Convention on the Elimination of Discrimination Against Women

Signatories: 75
Parties: 49
as of 12 January 2003

Participant	*Signature*	*Ratification, Accession (a)*
Andorra	9-Jul-01	14-Oct-02
Argentina	28-Feb-00	
Austria	10-Dec-99	6-Sep-00
Azerbaijan	6-Jun-00	1-Jun-01
Bangladesh	6-Sep-00	6-Sep-00
Belarus	29-Apr-02	
Belgium	10-Dec-99	
Belize		9-Dec-02 (a)
Bolivia	10-Dec-99	27-Sep-00
Bosnia and Herzegovina	7-Sep-00	4-Sep-02
Brazil	13-Mar-01	28-Jun-02
Bulgaria	6-Jun-00	
Burkina Faso	16-Nov-01	
Burundi	13-Nov-01	
Cambodia	11-Nov-01	
Canada		18-Oct-02 (a)
Chile	10-Dec-99	
Colombia	10-Dec-99	

Participant	*Signature*	*Ratification, Accession (a)*
Costa Rica	10-Dec-99	20-Sep-01
Croatia	5-Jun-00	7-Mar-01
Cuba	17-Mar-00	
Cyprus	8-Feb-01	26-Apr-02
Czech Republic	10-Dec-99	26-Feb-01
Denmark	10-Dec-99	31-May-00
Dominican Republic	14-Mar-00	10-Aug-01
Ecuador	10-Dec-99	5-Feb-02
El Salvador	4-Apr-01	
Finland	10-Dec-99	29-Dec-00
France	10-Dec-99	9-Jun-00
Georgia		30-Jul-02
Germany	10-Dec-99	15-Jan-02
Ghana	24-Feb-00	
Greece	10-Dec-99	24-Jan-02
Guatemala	7-Sep-00	9-May-02
Guinea-Bissau	12-Sep-00	
Hungary		22-Dec-00
Iceland	10-Dec-99	6-Mar-01
Indonesia	28-Feb-00	
Ireland	7-Sep-00	7-Sep-00
Italy	10-Dec-99	22-Sep-00
Kazakhstan	6-Sep-00	24-Aug-01
Kyrgyzstan		22-Jul-02
Lesotho	6-Sep-00	
Liechtenstein	10-Dec-99	24-Oct-01
Lithuania	8-Sep-00	
Luxembourg	10-Dec-99	
Madagascar	7-Sep-00	
Malawi	7-Sep-00	
Mali		5-Dec-00 (a)
Mauritius	11-Nov-01	
Mexico	10-Dec-99	15-Mar-02
Mongolia	7-Sep-00	28-Mar-02

Participant	*Signature*	*Ratification, Accession (a)*
Namibia	19-May-00	26-May-00
Nepal	18-Dec-01	
Netherlands	10-Dec-99	22-May-02
New Zealand	7-Sep-00	7-Sep-00
Nigeria	8-Sep-00	
Norway	10-Dec-99	5-Mar-02
Panama	9-Jun-00	9-May-01
Paraguay	28-Dec-99	14-May-01
Peru	22-Dec-00	9-Apr-01
Philippines	21-Mar-00	
Portugal	16-Feb-00	26-Apr-02
Romania	6-Sep-00	
Russian Federation	8-May-01	
Sao Tome and Principe	6-Sep-00	
Senegal	10-Dec-99	26-May-00
Seychelles	22-Jul-02	
Sierra Leone	8-Sep-00	
Slovakia	5-Jun-00	17-Nov-00
Slovenia	10-Dec-99	
Solomon Islands		6-May-02
Spain	14-Mar-00	6-Jul-01
Sri Lanka		15-Oct-02 (a)
Sweden	10-Dec-99	
Tajikistan	7-Sep-00	
Thailand	14-Jun-00	14-Jun-00
The former Yugoslav Republic of Macedonia	3-Apr-00	
Turkey	8-Sep-00	29-Oct-02
Ukraine	7-Sep-00	
Uruguay	9-May-00	26-Jul-01
Venezuela	17-Mar-00	13-May-02

Annexure V

Equal Remuneration Act, 1976

[Act No. 25 of Year 1976]

An Act to provide for the payment of equal remuneration to men and women workers and for the prevention of discrimination, on the ground of sex, against women in the matter of employment and for matters connected therewith or incidental thereto.

Be it enacted by Parliament in the Twenty-seventh Year of the Republic of India as follows:

CHAPTER I
PRELIMINARY

1. Short title, extent and commencement—(1) This Act may be called the Equal Remuneration Act, 1976.

(2) It extends to the whole of India.

(3) It shall come into force on such date, not being later than three years from the passing of this Act, as the Central Government may, by notification, appoint and different dates may be appointed for different establishments or employments.

2. Definitions—In this Act, unless the context otherwise requires-

(a) "appropriate government" means:

(i) in relation to any employment carried on by or under the authority of the central Government or a railway administration, or in relation to a banking company, a mine, oil-field or major port or any corporation established by or under a Central Act, the Central Government, and

(ii) in relation to any other employment, the State Government;

(b) "commencement of this Act" means, in relation to an

establishment or employment, the date on which this Act comes into force in respect of that establishment or employment;

(c) "employer" has the meaning assigned to it in clause (f) of section 2 of the Payment of Gratuity Act, 1972 (39 of 1972);

(d) "man" and "woman" means male and female human beings, respectively, of any age;

(e) "notification" means a notification published in the Official Gazette;

(f) "prescribed" means prescribed by rules made under this Act;

(g) "remuneration" means the basic wage or salary, and any additional emoluments whatsoever payable, either in cash or in kind, to a person employed in respect of employment or work done in such employment, if the terms of the contract of employment, express or implied, were fulfilled;

(h) "same work or work of a similar nature" means work in respect of which the skill, effort and responsibility required are the same, when performed under similar working conditions, by a man or a woman and the differences, if any, between the skill, effort and responsibility required of a man and those required to a woman are not of practical importance in relation to the terms and conditions of employment;

(i) "worker" means a worker in any establishment or employment in respect of which this Act has come into force;

(j) words and expressions used in this Act and not defined but defined in the Industrial Disputes Act, 1947 (14 of 1947), shall have the meanings respectively assigned to them in that Act.

3. Act to have overriding effect—The provisions of this Act shall have effect notwithstanding anything inconsistent therewith contained in any other law or in the terms of any award, agreement or contract of service, whether made before or after the commencement of this Act, or in any instrument having effect under any law for the time being in force.

CHAPTER II
PAYMENT OF REMUNERATION OF EQUAL RATES TO MEN AND WOMEN WORKERS AND OTHER MATTERS

4. Duty of employer to pay equal remuneration to men and women workers for same work or work of a similar nature—(1) No employer shall pay to any worker, employed by him in an establishment or employment, remuneration, whether payable in cash or in kind, at rates less favourable than those at which remuneration is paid by him to the workers of the opposite sex in such establishment or employment for performing the same work or work of a similar nature.

(2) No employer shall, for the purpose of complying with the provisions of sub-section (1), reduce the rate of remuneration of any worker.

(3) Where, in an establishment on employment, the rates of remuneration payable before the commencement of this Act for men and women workers for the same work or work of a similar nature are different only on the ground of sex, then the higher (in cases where there are only two rates), or, as the case may be, the highest (in cases where there are more than two rates) of such rates shall be the rate at which remuneration shall be payable, on and from such commencement, to such men and women workers.

PROVIDED that nothing in this sub-section shall be deemed to entitle a worker to the revision of the rate of remuneration payable to him or her with reference to the service rendered by him or her before the commencement of this Act.

5. No discrimination to be made while recruiting men and women workers—On and from the commencement of this Act, no employer shall, while making recruitment for the same work or work of a similar nature, [1][or in any condition of service subsequent to recruitment such as promotions, training or transfer,] make any discrimination against women except where the employment of women in such work is prohibited or restricted by or under any law for the time being in force:

PROVIDED that the provisions of this section shall not affect any priority or reservation for scheduled castes or scheduled tribes, ex-servicemen, retrenched employees or any other class or category of persons in the matter of recruitment to the posts in an establishment or employment.

6. Advisory committee—(1) For the purpose of providing increasing employment opportunities for women, the appropriate government shall constitute one or more advisory committees to advise it with regard to the extent to which women may be employed in such establishments or employments as the Central Government may, by notification, specify in this behalf.

(2) Every advisory committee shall consist of not less than ten persons, to be nominated by the appropriate government, of which one-half shall be women.

(3) In tendering its advice, the advisory committee shall have regard to the number of women employed in the concerned establishment or employment, the nature of work, hours of work, suitability of women for employment, as the case may be, the need for providing increasing employment opportunities for women, including part-time employment and such other relevant factors as the committee may think fit.

(4) The advisory committee shall regulate its own procedure.

(5) The appropriate government may, after considering the advice tendered to it by the advisory committee and after giving to the persons concerned in the establishment or employment an opportunity to make representations, issue such directions in respect of employment of women workers, as the appropriate government may think fit.

7. Power of appropriate government to appoint authorities for hearing and deciding claims and complaints—(1) The appropriate government may, by notification, appoint such officers, not below the rank of a labour officer, as it thinks fit to be the authorities for the purpose of hearing and deciding—

(a) complaints with regard to the contravention of any provision of this Act;

(b) claims arising out of non-payment of wages at equal rates to men and women workers for the same work or work of a similar nature;

and may, by the same or subsequent notification, define the local limits within which each such authority shall exercise its jurisdiction.

(2) Every complaint or claim referred to in sub-section (1) shall be made in such manner as may be prescribed.

(3) If any question arises as to whether two or more works are

of the same nature or of a similar nature, it shall be decided by the authority appointed under sub-section (1).

(4) Where a complaint or claim is made to the authority appointed under sub-section (1) it may, after giving the applicant and the employer an opportunity of being heard, and after such inquiry as it may consider necessary, direct—

(i) in the case of a claim arising out of non-payment of wages at equal rates to men and women workers for the same work or work of a similar nature, that payment be made to the worker of the amount by which the wages payable to him exceed the amount actually paid;

(ii) in the case of complaint, that adequate steps be taken by the employer so as to ensure that there is no contravention of any provision of this Act.

(5) Every authority appointed under sub-section (1) shall have all the powers of a Civil Court under the Code of Civil Procedure, 1908 (5 of 1908), for the purpose of taking evidence and of enforcing the attendance of witnesses and compelling the production of documents, and every such authority shall be deemed to be a civil court for all the purposes of section 195 and Chapter XXVI of the Code of Criminal Procedure, 1973 (2 of 1974).

(6) Any employer or worker aggrieved by any order may be an authority appointed under sub-section (1), on a complaint or claim may, within thirty days from the date of the order, prefer an appeal to such authority as the appropriate government may,

by notification, specify in this behalf, and that authority may, after hearing the appeal, conform, modify or reverse the order appealed against and no further appèal shall lie against the order made by such authority.

(7) The authority referred to in sub-section (6) may, if it is satisfied that the appellant was prevented by sufficient cause from preferring the appeal within the period specified in sub-section (6), allow the appeal to be preferred within a further period of thirty days not thereafter.

(8) The provisions of sub-section (1) of section 33C of the Industrial Disputes Act, 1947 (14 of 1947), shall apply for the recovery of monies due from an employer arising out of the decision of an authority appointed under this section.

CHAPTER III
MISCELLANEOUS

8. Duty of employers to maintain registers—On and from the commencement of this Act, every employer shall maintain such registers and other documents in relation to the workers employed by him as may be prescribed.

9. Inspectors—(1) The appropriate government may, by notification, appoint such persons as it may think fit to be inspectors for the purpose of making an investigation as to whether the provisions of this Act, or the rules made thereunder, are being complied with by employers, and may define the local limits within which an inspector may make such investigation.

(2) Every inspector shall be deemed to be a public servant within the meaning of section 21 of the Indian Penal Code (45 of 1860).

(3) An inspector may, at any place within the local limits of his jurisdiction—

(a) enter, at any reasonable time with such assistance as he thinks fit, any building, factory, premises or vessel;

(b) require any employer to produce any register, muster-roll or other documents relating to the employment of workers, and examine such documents;

(c) take, on the spot or otherwise, the evidence of any person for the purpose of ascertaining whether the provisions of this Act are being, or have been, complied with;

(d) examine the employer, his agent or servant or any other person found in charge of the establishment or any premises connected therewith or any person whom the inspector has reasonable cause to believe to be, or to have been a worker in the establishment;

(e) make copies, or take extracts from, any register or other document maintained in relation to the establishment under this Act.

(4) Any person required by an inspector to produce any register or other document or to give any information shall comply with such requisition.

10. Penalties—(1) If after the commencement of this Act, any employer, being required by or under the Act, so to do—

(a) omits or fails to maintain any register or other document in relation to workers employed by him, or

(b) omits or fails to produce any register, muster-roll or other document relating to the employment of workers, or

(c) omits or refuses to give any evidence or prevents his agent, servant, or any other person in charge of the establishment, or any worker, from giving evidence, or

(d) omits or refuses to give any information,

he shall be punishable [with simple imprisonment for a term which may extend to one month or with fine which may extend to ten thousand rupees or with both].

(2) If, after the commencement of this Act, any employer-

(a) makes any recruitment in contravention of the provisions of this Act, or

(b) makes any payment of remuneration at unequal rates to men and women workers, for the same work or work of a similar nature, or

(a) makes any discrimination between men and women workers in contravention of the provisions of this Act, or

(d) omits or fails to carry out any direction made by the appropriate government under sub-section (5) of section 6,

he shall be punishable 2[with fine which shall not be less than ten thousand rupees but which may extend to twenty thousand rupees or with imprisonment for a term which shall be not less than three months but which may extend to one year or with both

for the first offence, and with imprisonment which may extend to two years for the second and subsequent offences].

(3) If any person being required so to do, omits or refuses to produce to an inspector any register or other document or to give any information, he shall be punishable with fine which may extend to five hundred rupees.

11. Offences by companies—(1) Where an offence under this Act has been committed by a company, every person who, at the time the offence was committed, was in charge of, and was responsible to, the company for the conduct of the business of the company, as well as the company, shall be deemed to be guilty of the offence and shall be liable to be proceeded against and punished accordingly:

PROVIDED that nothing contained in this sub-section shall render any such person liable to any punishment, if he proves that the offence was committed without his knowledge or that he had exercised all due diligence to prevent the commission of such offence.

(2) Notwithstanding anything contained in sub-section (1), where any offence under this Act has been committed by a company and it is proved that the offence has been committed with the consent or connivance of, or is attributable to any

neglect on the part of any director, manager, secretary or other officer of the company, such director, manager, secretary or other office shall be deemed to be guilty of that offence and shall be liable to be proceeded against and punished accordingly.

Explanation—For the purposes of this section:

(a) "company" means any body corporate and includes a firm or other association of individuals; and

(b) "director", in relation to a firm, means a partner in the firm.

12. Cognizance and trial of offences—(1) No court inferior to that of a Metropolitan Magistrate or Judicial Magistrate of first class shall try any offence punishable under this Act.

(2) No court shall take cognizance of an offence punishable under this Act except upon-

(a) its own knowledge or upon a complaint made by the appropriate government or an officer authorised by it in this behalf, or

(b) a complaint made by the person aggrieved by the offence or by any recognised welfare institution or organisation.

Explanation—For the purposes of this sub-section "recognised welfare institution or organisation" means a social welfare institution or organisation recognised in this behalf by the Central or State Government.

13. Power to make rules—(1) The Central Government may, by notification, make rules for carrying out the provisions of this Act.

(2) In particular, and without prejudice to the generality of the foregoing power, such rules may provide for all or any of the following matters, namely:-

(a) the manner in which complaint or claim referred to in sub-section (1) of section 7 shall be made;

(b) registers and other documents which an employer is required under section 8 to maintain in relation to the workers employed by him;

(c) any other matter which is required to be, or may be, prescribed.

(3) Every rule made by the Central Government under this Act shall be laid, as soon as may be after it is made, before each House of Parliament while it is in session, for a total period of thirty days which may be comprised in one session or in two or more successive sessions, and if, before the expiry of the session immediately following the session or the successive sessions aforesaid, both Houses agree in making any modification in the rule or both Houses agree that the rule should not be made, the rule shall thereafter have effect only in such modified form or be of no effect, as the case may be; so, however, that any such modification or annulment shall be without prejudice to the validity of anything previously done under that rule.

14. Power of Central Government to give directions—The Central Government may give directions to a State Government as to the carrying into execution of this Act in the State.

15. Act not to apply in certain special cases—Nothing in this Act shall apply—

(a) to cases affecting the terms and conditions of a woman's employment in complying with the requirements of any law giving special treatment to women, or

(b) to any special treatment accorded to women in connection with—

(i) the birth or expected birth of a child, or

(ii) the terms and conditions relating to retirement, marriage or death or to any provision made in connection with the retirement, marriage or death.

16. Power to make declaration—Where the appropriate government is, on a consideration of all the circumstances of the case, satisfied that the differences in regard to the remuneration, or a particular species of remuneration, of men and women workers in any establishment, or employment is based on a factor other than sex, it may, by notification, make a declaration to that effect, and any act of the employer attributable to such a difference shall not be deemed to be contravention of any provision of this Act.

17. Power to remove difficulties—If any difficulty arises in giving effect to the provisions of this Act, the Central Government may, by notification, make any order, not inconsistent with the provisions of this Act, which appears to it to be necessary for the purpose of removing the difficulty:

PROVIDED that every such order shall, as soon as may be after it is made, be laid before each House of Parliament.

18. Repeal and saving—(1) The Equal Remuneration Ordinance, 1975 (12 of 1975), is hereby repealed.

(2) Notwithstanding such repeal, anything done or any action taken under the Ordinance, so repealed (including any notification, nomination, appointment, order or direction made thereunder) shall be deemed to have been done or taken under the corresponding provisions of this Act, as if this Act were in force when such thing was done or action was taken.

Bibliography

Primary Sources

Government Reports, United Nations Publications

Committee on the Elimination of Discrimination Against Women, *Consideration of Reports Submitted by State Parties Under Article 18 of the Convention on the Elimination of All Forms of Discrimination Against Women. Initial Report of India* (New York: United Nations, 1999).

Committee on Elimination of Discrimination Against Women, *Status of Submission of Reports by State Parties under Article 18 of the Convention* (New York: United Nations, 2002).

Committee on Empowerment of Women, *Development Schemes For Rural Women*, (New Delhi: Lok Sabha Secretariat, 1999).

Department of Women and Child Development, Ministry of Human Resource Development, *Annual Report 2000-01* (New Delhi: Government of India, 2001).

Department of Women and Child Development, Ministry of Human Resource Development, *Responses to Questions on India's First Report on CEDAW* (New York, Government of India, 2000).

Division for the Advancement of Women, *World Survey on the Role of Women in Development. Globalisation, Gender and Work* (New York: United Nations, 1999).

General Assembly, *Report of the Committee on the Elimination of Discrimination against Women. 24th Session* (New York: United Nations, 2001).

General Assembly, *Report of the Committee on the Elimination of Discrimination against Women. 25th Session* (New York: United Nations, 2001).

General Assembly, *Report of the Committee on the Elimination of Discrimination against Women. 26th Session* (New York: United Nations, 2002).

General Assembly, *Report of the Committee on the Elimination of Discrimination Against Women. 27th Session* (New York: United Nations, 2002).

General Assembly, *Report of the Committee on the Elimination of Discrimination against Women. Exceptional Session* (New York: United Nations, 2002).

Kapur, Aanchal, *Women Workers Rights' in India: Issues and Strategies – A Reference Guide* (New Delhi: ILO, 1999).

Labour *Bureau,* Ministry of Labour, *Socio-Economic Conditions of Women Workers in Selected Agarbathi Units in Selected States* (Chandigarh/Shimla: Government of India, 1998).

Labour Bureau, Ministry of Labour, *Socio-Economic Conditions of Women Workers in Selected Beedi Units in India* (Chandigarh/Shimla: Government of India, 1996).

Labour Bureau, Ministry of Labour, *Socio-Economic Conditions of Women Workers in Building and Construction Industry* (Chandigarh/Shimla: Government of India, 1990).

Labour Bureau, Ministry of Labour, *Socio-Economic Conditions of Women Workers in Selected Cashewnut Processing Units in Selected States* (Chandigarh/Shimla: Government of India, 1998).

Labour Bureau, Ministry of Labour, *Socio-Economic Conditions of Women Workers in Selected Handloom and Khadi Units in Bihar* (Chandigarh/Shimla: Government of India, 1995).

Labour Bureau, Ministry of Labour, *Statistical Profile on Women Labour (Fourth Issue)*, (Chandigarh/Shimla: Government of India, 1993).

Ministry of Labour, *Annual Report 2001-02* (New Delhi: Government of India, 2002).

Ministry of Textiles, *Annual Report 2001-02* (New Delhi: Government of India, 2002).

National Commission on the Self-Employed Women and Women in the Informal Sector, *Shramshakti* (New Delhi: Government of India, 1988).

National Commission on Labour, *Report of the Group on Women Workers and Child Labour, Part I,* (New Delhi: National Commission of Labour, 2001).

Planning Commission, *Tenth Five Year Plan 2002-07,* (New Delhi: Government of India, 2002).

UN Secretariat, *Ways and Means of Expediting the Work of the Committee* (New York: CEDAW, 2001).

Secondary Sources

Books and Reports

Alston, Philip, (ed.), *The United Nations and Human Rights. A Critical Appraisal* (Oxford: Clarendon Press, 1992).

Alston, Philip and Crawford, James, (eds.), *The Future of Human Rights Treaty Monitoring* (Cambridge: Cambridge University Press, 2000).

Anker, Richard and Hein, Catherine, (eds.), *Sex Inequalities in Urban Employment in the Third World* (London: Macmillan Press, 1986).

Arputhamurthy, Savitri, *Women, Work and Discrimination* (New Delhi: Ashish Publishing, 1990).

Banerjee, Anita and Sen, Raj Kumar, *Women and Economic Development* (New Delhi: Deep and Deep Publications, 2000).

Banerjee, Nirmala, *Indian Women in a Changing Industrial Scenario*, (New Delhi: Sage Publications, 1991).

Batra, S. L., *Employment for Women. A Study of Export Oriented Garment Industry* (New Delhi: Har Anand Publication, 1996).

Baud, I. S. A., *Forms of Production and Women's Labour. Gender Aspects of Industrialisation in India and Mexico* (New Delhi: Sage Publications, 1992).

Brettell B. Caroline and Sargent F. Carolyn, *Gender. In Cross Cultural Perspective* (New Jersey: Princeton Hall, 1993).

Bhadra, Mita, *Women Workers of Tea Plantations in India* (New Delhi: Heritage Publishers, 1992).

Byrnes, Andrew, Connors, Jane and Bik, Lum, (eds.), *Advancing the Human Rights of Women: Using International Human Rights Standards in Domestic Litigation* (Hong Kong: Commonwealth Secretariat, 1996).

Campbell, Tom and Goldberg, David, *Human Rights. From Rhetoric to Reality* (Oxford: Basil Blackwell Ltd., 1986).

Chandra, Susmita, *Women and Economic Development. A Case Study of Uttar Pradesh* (Delhi: B. R. Publishing, 2001).

Clark W. Alice, (ed.), *Gender and Political Economy. Explorations of South Asian Systems* (New Delhi: Oxford University Press, 1993).

Dunne, Tim and Wheeler J. Nicholas, (eds.), *Human Rights in Global Politics* (Cambridge: Cambridge University Press, 1999).

Everett, Jana and Savara, Mira, *Women and Organisation in the Informal Sector* (New Delhi: Himalaya Publishing, 1994).

Gandhi, Nandita and Shah, Nandita, *The Issues at Stake. Theory and Practice in the Contemporary Women's Movement in India* (New Delhi: Kali for Women, 1991).

Gopalan, Sarla, *Women and Employment in India* (New Delhi: Har Anand Publications, 1995).

Gothoskar, Sujata (ed.), *Struggles of Women at Work* (New Delhi: Vikas Publishing House, 1992).

Indian National Textile Workers' Federation and Ambedkar Institute for Labour Studies, *Socio-Economic Study of Powerloom Workers in the Bhiwandi Centre* (Mumbai: Unpublished, 1986).

Jackson, Stevi and Scott, Sue (eds.), *Gender. A Sociological Reader* (London: Routledge, 2002).

Jain, Shobhita and Reddock, Rhoda, (eds.), *Women Plantation Workers. International Experiences* (New York: Oxford, 1998).

Jose, A.V. (ed.). *Limited Options. Women Workers in Rural India* (Geneva: ILO, 1989).

Joseph, Cherian and Prasad K. V. Eswara, *Women, Work and Inequality. The Reality of Gender* (New Delhi: National Labour Institute, 1995).

Kalbagh, Chetna, (ed.), *Women and Development* (New Delhi: Discovery Publishing, 1991).

Kalpagam, U., *Labour and Gender. Survival in Urban India* (New Delhi: Sage Publications, 1994).

Kaushik, Susheela, *Women's Oppression. Patterns and Perspectives* (New Delhi: Vikas Publishing, 1985).

Klemp, Ludgera and Reddies, Bernd, *Women Textile Workers Demand Justice. On the Situation of Textile and Garment Industry in the Countries of the South* (Duseldorf: Freidrich Ebert Foundation, 1992).

Krishnaraj, Maithreyi and Deshmukh P. Joy, *Gender in Economics. Theory and Practice* (New Delhi: Ajanta Publications, 1993).

Lorber, Judith, *Paradoxes of Gender* (New Haven: Yale University Press, 1994).

Maharashtra Institute of Labour Studies, *Survey of Socio-Economic Conditions of Powerloom Workers of Bhiwandi* (Mumbai: Unpublished, 1997).

Mathur, R. N., *Quality of Working Life of Women Construction Workers* (New Delhi: Commonwealth Publishers, 1989).

Mc Phedran, Marilou, Bazili, Susan and others, (eds.), *The First CEDAW Impact Study* (Toronto: Centre for Feminist Research and International Women's Right Project, 2000).

Mies, Maria, Benhold, Veronika and Werlhof, von Thomsen, *Women: The Last Colony* (New Delhi: Kali for Women, 1988).

Murthy, K. Ranjana, (ed.), *Building Women's Capacities. Interventions in Gender Transformation* (New Delhi: Sage Publications, 2001).

Papola, T.S. and Sharma N. Alakh, *Gender and Employment in India* (New Delhi: Vikas Publishing House, 1999).

Parikh J. Indira, Garg, K. Pulin and Menon, Indu, *Women Weavers* (New Delhi: Oxford and IBH Publishing, 1991).

Peters, Julie and Wolper, Andrea (eds.), *Women's Rights. International Feminist Perspectives* (London: Routledge, 1995).

Punia, R. K., (ed.), *Women in Agriculture* (New Delhi: Northern Book Centre, 1991).

Ramegowda, A., *Gender Inequality* (Jaipur: Rawat Publications, 1997).

Rosemeyer, Sunanda Sagar *Women's Rights: Search for Identity* (New Delhi: Dominant Publishers, 2000).

Sanmugasundaran, Yashodha, *Women Employment in India* (Madras: Institute for Advanced Studies and Research, 1993).

Savara, Mira, Changing Trends in Women's Employment – A Case Study of the Textile Industry (New Delhi: Himalaya Publishing, 1986).

Seth, Mira, Women and Development (New Delhi: Sage Publications, 2000).

Sharma, N. Alakh and Sinha, Seema, *Women and Work. Changing Scenario in India* (New Delhi: Indian Institute of Labour Economics, 1992).

Tomasevski, Katarina, *Women and Human Rights* (London: Zed Books, 1993).

Tripathy, S. N., (ed.), *Unorganised Women Labour in India* (New Delhi: Discovery Publications, 1996).

Unni, Jeemol, *Women's Participation in Indian Agriculture* (New Delhi: Oxford and IBH Publishing, 1992).

Vaid, K. N., Wagh, R. Suman, Women in Construction (Mumbai: National Institute of Construction Management and Research, 1999).

Varandani, Gursharan, *Child Labour and Women Workers* (New Delhi: Ashish Publishing, 1994).

Verma, A. P, Rehman, M. M. and Chauhan, S. Poonam, *Women Labour in India. A Comprehensive Manual* (Noida: National Labour Institute, 1996).

Articles

Ahmed, S., "Changing Gender Roles in Irrigation Management. Sadguru's Lift Irrigation Cooperatives", *Economic and Political Weekly*, Vol. XXXIV, No. 51, December 18, 1999.

Ahooja-Patel, Krishna, "Gender Equality in the Third Millenium", *Mainstream*, Vol. XXXVII, No. 17, April 17, 1999.

Anker, Richard, "Theories of Occupational Segregation by Sex: An Overview", *International Labour Review*, Vol. 136, No. 3, 1997.

Apodaca, Clair, "Measuring Women's Economic and Social Rights

Achievement", *Human Rights Quarterly*, Vol. 29, No. 1, January 1998.

Banerjee, Nirmala, "How Real is the Bogey of Feminization", *The Indian Journal of Labour Economics*, Vol. 40, No. 3, Jan.-March 1997.

Banerjee, Nirmala, "Women in the Emerging Labour Market", *The Indian Journal of Labour Economics*, Vol. 42, No. 4, October-December 1999.

Beteille, Andre, "Empowerment", *Economic and Political Weekly*, Vol. XXXIV, No. 10–11, March 6, 1999.

Bhat, K. Sham and Nirmala, V., "Genderwise Determinants of Higher Occupational Scales in Service Sector", *The Indian Journal of Labour Economics*, Vol. 43, No. 4, October-December 2000.

Bhowmik, K. Sharit and More, Nitin, "Coping With Urban Poverty. Ex-Textile Mill Workers in Central Mumbai", *Economic and Political Weekly*, Vol. XXXVI, No. 52, December-January 2001.

Chopra, Ravi and Ghosh, Deepa, "Work Patterns of Rural Women in Central Himalayas", *Economic and Political Weekly*, Vol. XXXV, No. 52-53, December 30, 2000.

Deshpande, Sudha and Deshpande K. Lalit,"Gender-Based Discrimination in the Urban Labour Market in India", *The Indian Journal of Labour Economics*, Vol. 40, No. 3, January-March 1997.

Dutta, Indira, "Women Employment in Tertiary Sector: Quantity vs. Quality", *The Indian Journal of Labour Economics*, Vol. 43, No. 4, October-December 2000.

Elder, Sara, and Johnson, Jeffrey Lawrence, "Sex-Specific Labour Market Indicators: What They Show", *International Labour Review*, Vol. 138, No. 4, 1999.

Fellmeth, Xavier Aaron, "Feminism and International Law: Theory, Methodology and Substantive Reform", *Human Rights Quarterly*, Vol. 22, No. 3, August 2000.

Fraser, Avonne, "Becoming Human: The Origins and Development of Women's Human Rights", *Human Rights Quarterly*, Vol. 21, No. 4, November 1999.

Gallagher, Anne, "Ending the Marginalization: Strategies for Incorporating Women into the United Nations Human Rights System", *Human Rights Quarterly*, Vol. 19, No.2, May 1997.

Hapke, M. Holly, "Development Gender and Household, Survival in a Kerala Fishery", *Economic and Political Weekly*, Vol. XXXVI, No. 42, November 3, 2001.

Jeyaranjan, J. and Swaminathan, Padmini, "Resilience of Gender Inequities. Women and Employment in Chennai, Economic and Political Weekly, Vol. XXXIV, No. 16, April, 1999.

Kanan, Ramya and Kumar, N. Ravi, "More Travails for Women Feared", *The Hindu*, December 26, 2000.

Krishnaraj, Maithreyi, "How Gender Figures in Economic Theorising and Philosophy", *Economic and Political Weekly*, Vol. XXXVI, No. 17, April 28, 2001.

Kundu, Amitabh, "Trends and Patterns of Female Employment in India. A Case of Organised Informalisation", *The Indian Journal of Labour Economics*, Vol. 40, No. 3, January-March 1997.

Lahiri-Dutt, Kuntala, "From Gin Girls to Scavengers. Women in the Raniganj Collieries", *Economic and Political Weekly*, Vol. XXXVI, No. 44, November 3, 2001.

Lakdawala, M. H., "Bhiwandi. Gloom Town", *Islamic Voice*, Vol. 15-04, No. 172, April 2001.

Lalitha, N., "Women in the Unorganised Manufacturing Sector in India: A Sectoral Analysis", *The Indian Journal of Labour Economics*, Vol. 42, No. 4, October-December 1999.

Lucy, T.V., "Empowerment of Women for Sustainable Development", *Social Action*, Vol. 45, No. 2, April-June 1995.

Mitra, Arup and Mukhopadhyay "Female Labour Absorption in Construction Sector", *Economic and Political Weekly*, Vol. XXIV, No. 10, March 11, 1989.

O' Hare, Ursula, "Realizing Human Rights for Women", *Human Rights Quarterly*, Vol. 21, No.2, May 1999.

Padma, K., "Changing Crop Pattern and Employment Condition of Women Workers: A Case Study", *The Indian Journal of Labour Economics*, Vol. 42, No. 4, October-December 1999.

Patel, D. Thrity, "Women and Economic Empowerment: Judicial Approach", *Journal of Institute of Human Rights*, Vol. II, No. 1, December 1999.

Madhavan, S. and Shroff, Sangeeta, "Education, Employment and Earnings for Scientific and Technical Workforce in India: Gender Issues", *The Indian Journal of Labour Economics*, Vol. 43, No. 1, January-March 2000.

Menon-Sen, Kalyani and Prabhu, Seeta, "The Budget: A quick Look through a 'Gender Lens' ", *Economic and Political Weekly*, Vol. XXXVI, No. 14 and 15, April 14, 2001.

Misra, V. N, "Role of Female Labour Force Participation in Rural Poverty and Non-Farm Employment: Indian Experience", *The Indian Journal of Labour Economics*, Vol. 43, No. 2, April-June 2000.

Mukhopadhyay, Swapna, "Rural Works Programme and Female Casual Labour: How Far is the Goal of Guaranteed Employment", *Social Action*, Vol. 40, Issue 2, April-June 1990.

Nigam, Nonita, "Women in Household Industry: Emerging Trends and Issues", *Social Change*, Vol. 22, No. 2, June 1992.

Nirmala, V. and Bhat, K. Sham, "Female Work Participation in the Emerging Labour Market in India," *The Indian Journal of Labour Economics*, Vol. 42, No. 4, October-December 1999.

Pritchard, Sarah, "The Jurisprudence of Human Rights: Some Critical Thought and Developments in Practice", *Australian Journal of Human Rights*, Vol. 2, No. 1, 1995.

Rajuladevi, A. K., "Profiles in Poverty. Female Landless Agricultural Labour Households", *Economic and Political Weekly*, Vol. XXXV, No. 6, February 5, 2000.

Robinson, Derek, "Differences in Occupational Earnings by Sex", *International Labour Review*, Vol. 137, No. 1, 1998.

Rothboeck, Sandra and Acharya, Sarthi, "Gender-Based Segregation in the Indian Labour Market", *The Indian Journal of Labour Economics*, Vol. 42, No. 4, October-December 1999.

Rustagi, Preet, "Women Employment in the Unorganised Sector: Some Issues", *Social Action*, Vol. 40, Issue 1, April-June 1997.

Sharan, Ramesh and Dayal, Harishwar, "Deprivation of Female Farm Labourers in Jharkhand Region of Bihar", *Social Change*, Vol. 23, No. 4, 1993.

Sudarshan, Ratna and Kaur, Rupinder, "The Tobacco Industry and Women's Employment: Old Concerns and New Imperatives", *Indian Journal of Labour Economics*, Vol. 42, No. 4, October-December 1999.

Terrell, Katherine, "Female-Male Earnings Differentials and Occupational Structure," *International Labour Review*, Vol. 131, No. 4-5, 1992.

Thakur, Atanu, "A Post Modernist Enquiry Into Women's Workforce Participation", *The Indian Journal of Labour Economics*, Vol. 42, No. 4, October-December 1999.

Unni, Jeemol, "Women Workers in Agriculture: Some Recent Trends", *The Indian Journal of Labour Economic*, Vol. 40, No. 3, January-March 1997.

Unni, Jeemol, "Gender and Informality in Labour Market in South Asia", *Economic and Political Weekly*, Vol. XXXVI, No. 26, June 30, 2001.

Unni, Jeemol and Rani, Uma, "Informal Sector: Women in the Emerging Labour Market", *The Indian Journal of Labour Economics*, Vol. 42, No. 4, October-December 1999.